THE BRUNEVAL RAID

Flashpoint of the Radar War

GEORGE MILLAR
THE BRUNEVAL RAID

Flashpoint of the Radar War

With a Foreword by Admiral of the Fleet
The Earl Mountbatten of Burma

Doubleday & Company, Inc., Garden City, New York, 1975

PHOTO CREDITS:

Photographs 1, 2, 6, 8, 11, 14–17 courtesy of the Imperial War Museum.
Photograph 3 courtesy of A. P. Rowe.
Photograph 4 courtesy of Alfred Price.
Photograph 5 courtesy of R. V. Jones.
Photograph 9 courtesy of U. S. Air Force.
Photographs 7, 12, 13 courtesy of C. W. H. Cox.

Maps drawn by Maureen Verity.

940.54
M

Library of Congress Cataloging in Publication Data

Millar, George Reid.
    The Bruneval raid.

    Bibliography
    Includes index.
    1. World War, 1939-1945—Great Britain. 2. Radar. 3. Great Britain. Tele-
communications Research Establishment.   I. Title.
D810.R33M54   1975   940.54'21
ISBN 0-385-09542-2
Library of Congress Catalog Card Number: 74-3697

To Georges Molle,
Mayor of Vieilley

CONTENTS

AUTHOR'S NOTE AND ACKNOWLEDGMENTS

We happened to have the honor to be the very first British soldiers, Rifleman Jones, Rifleman Skinner, and Second Lieutenant Millar, whom Rommel's advance guard brushed up against (some brush!) when the German general made his final spectacular advance on Egypt. After a few ups and downs and whirligigs we were netted by those excellent troops, and I spent the following twenty months in the bag.

Accordingly, I heard and knew nothing of the Bruneval Raid until one day in 1970, hunting another fox in the rich literary coverts of the Air Historical Branch, Ministry of Defence, London, coverts then keepered by the celebrated L. A. Jackets, I stumbled upon the raid and finally changed foxes. First, therefore, I should like to thank Mr. Jackets and his staff for their initial and continuing help, and Group Captain E. B. Haslam, who now runs the Branch.

Following an initial and invigorating research success (every conscientious writer knows how such matters proceed) I ran into a period of patchy scent and awkward terrain. But then I had, at a time of near despair, the bright notion of writing to Earl Mountbatten of Burma, and suddenly hounds gave tongue, and we were off again at a steady hunting canter over a good bit of the vale. During this second hunt I had important assistance from Rear-Admiral P. N. Buckley, head of the Naval Historical Branch, and his staff, who were even able to turn up apposite German documents.

It seems to me that the general public, even the general reader, if the latter may be presumed to exist, little understands what a powerhouse of knowledge and interest is preserved in our service and civilian archives or begins to appreciate the enthusiastic work of the archivists, who are the finest in a world where competition is keen. In this context I must thank Miss Rose Coombs, Librarian of the Imperial War Museum, and her staff. Miss Coombs was one of those intrepid WAAFs who manned the radar scanners, and she survived a direct, long-distance attack (they watched it coming straight for them, all the way from France) on her mobile station. I also thank those two inspiring places and their very sympathetic staffs, the British Museum Reading Room and the London Library. A special word of thanks to the Rev. L. W. G. Hudson and to Tom Delmer for their expert advice.

I soon perceived that existing accounts of the Bruneval Raid contained discrepancies and vulgarities. These arose from wartime circumstance. Propaganda is a distorter. The first accounts were, quite understandably, expanded by newspapermen and then emasculated by censorship. To reconstruct in some measure, I decided to hunt down every survivor. The bloody action of the 2nd Battalion The Parachute Regiment in Tunisia, when encircling Germans three times demanded surrender and three times the battalion, led by John Frost, shot and carved its way out, and then the carnage of Arnhem, had sadly depleted the ranks and numbed the memories. But the raiders had been in their twenties in 1942, and survivors there are. Some remembered. And Frost and C. W. H. Cox had written down their impressions soon after the raid. Frost's account runs to twenty foolscap pages, and Cox's is little shorter.

Let me say then how grateful I am to Jock Company and to those who flew it and flew with it on the job, and how much I admire them for that and their subsequent operations in the war. I must especially thank for their help and their excellent company Major-General J. D. Frost, who now farms in Hampshire; John Ross, a lawyer in Dundee, who remembers with a clear mind and who had the prescience to keep intact his copy of Operational Orders; Charles Cox, whom I found running his prosperous wireless and television business in Wisbech, and as bright, cheerful, and efficient as even an East Anglian can be; Dennis Vernon, still an engineer but now very much in civvy street and prospering without any fuss or bother in peace as in war; and "Private Newman," no more like a private soldier now than then, but the most fascinating of companions; and all the others I met.

Here I should point out that nearly all the characters in this book—scientists, soldiers, sailors, and airmen—were decorated for unselfish service to their country. It seemed to me that so many acronyms had to be included—such as TRE and SOE, not to mention RAF—that I simply could not include decorations. Will the holders please understand?

Lord Mountbatten opened a second door for me. Rémy is a personal friend of his. And Rémy as a subject is any writer's dream. Before I began to work on this book I had read all his published work except *Bruneval, coup de croc.* I here express my deepest gratitude to Colonel Gilbert Renault and to those who worked with him; and most directly to the many who died for us, like Pol, boldly before the muzzles of enemy rifles, or like Bob, in agony and in loneliness.

Of course the Bruneval Raid made me ask, "Why?" Previously I had no conception that both Germany and England discovered radar at about the same time, and that they used it initially in different ways; and that this usage had such a vastly important effect on the outcome of the war. I prefer not to embarrass by naming them the scientists and workers of TRE (I live in Dorset, quite near Worth Matravers) whom I have consulted. Let me thank publicly only A. P. Rowe, whose modesty and apparent mildness might be thought to conceal his great services to us all. Derek Wood and Derek Dempster, in their fascinating study of the Battle of Britain, say this of Rowe (p. 138): "In August, 1938, Watson-Watt was promoted to the Air Ministry as Director of Communications, and A. P. Rowe took his place as Superintendent at Bawdsey. Although not professing to be an electronics expert, Rowe was a first class organizer with an unusual flair for analyzing problems and finding the right people to answer them."

I feel that while I was enjoying the war with a gun in my

hand, those scientists were winning the war, an unshouted victory. Apart from Rowe, I will express my gratitude only to one scientist individually, and to him really belongs the central point of meaning of the book. Professor R. V. Jones has the Chair of Natural Philosophy at Aberdeen University. He is today an intensely virile and active person. He remains (as I feel he should) something of a mystery. He will probably think that I have overdramatized his secret role in those vital and terrible episodes from our past.

Needless to say, *none* of the views expressed in these pages should or can be attributed to anyone but myself. Perhaps some of the more controversial passages concern the late Sidney Cotton. Soon after the war I met him and he told me some of his story; and he fascinated me. I wish there were more Australians like him in my country. And I wish Cotton were alive to read Chapters 13 and 14.

I would particularly like to thank the brilliant Wood and Dempster partnership, Ronald Clark, and Alfred Price (a regular RAF officer). The latter's remarkable study of the radar war is particularly worth reading for its evocation of the last terrible stages, as seen through both German and British eyes.

I am most grateful to the Controller of H.M. Stationery Office for permission to quote a letter; to Mrs. Thelma Cotton, Ralph Barker, and Messrs. Chatto & Windus for the numerous passages from *Aviator Extraordinary* in the two chapters about Sidney Cotton; to Constance Babington Smith and A. D. Peters for extracts from *Evidence in Camera*; to A. P. Rowe for long extracts from *One Story of Radar*; and to Rémy for his carte blanche authority to raid the riches of his own literary production.

Finally I express my gratitude to Major G. Norton, Curator, and Colour Sergeant T. Fitch, Custodian, of the Airborne Forces Museum at Aldershot.

GEORGE MILLAR
Sydling Court
Dorset 1973

On the night of February 27/28, 1942, we in Combined Operations pulled off a small but completely successful raid under the noses of the Germans. In the current climate of depression this was hailed as a counterblow which proved that the British still had their tails up. And so we had.

It was the first successful raid using parachute troops, who were dropped by the RAF on the cliff top at Bruneval to the north of Le Havre. They seized all the vital elements of a radar station and brought them safely back across a beach held by commando-trained soldiers to our assault landing craft, which were escorted by the Royal Navy and the Free French Navy.

We had excellent intelligence, not only from aerial photographs taken by the RAF, but also from the French Resistance network under their doughty chief known as Rémy, who has himself written an excellent account of the raid in a book published in France.

Not long ago, out of the blue, I received a letter from General Kurt Student, who had been watching the German version of the television series *My Life and Times*. He wrote: "I was particularly impressed by the suggestion you made at the beginning of 1942 as Chief of Combined Operations, namely to take the Bruneval Station in a 'coup de main' from the air. This was a grand plan, just to my liking as the creator of the German paratroopers. . . . The successful execution by Major Frost sent a great shock through Hitler's headquarters."

This raid had two quite separate consequences; primarily its importance to the war was to enable our scientists to evaluate a certain German radar set, and secondly, its effect on morale was out of all proportion to the size of the raid. I feel, therefore, that it is high time that a book about Bruneval should be published in English, and I congratulate George Millar.

He has written a fascinating account, ranging over the whole preliminaries and explaining the real importance of the Bruneval Raid, to which I am delighted to write this Foreword. It also gives me a further opportunity to pay a tribute to the brilliant planners and to the gallant men who made such a success of the raid.

Mountbatten of Burma
A.F.

ABBREVIATIONS

ABDA, American/British Defence Association

AEAF, Allied Expeditionary Air Forces

AI, air interception (airborne radar)

AOC, Aircraft Operating Company ("Lemnos" Hemming)

ASV, air-to-surface vessel (radar)

BCRA(M), Bureau Central de Renseignements et d'Action (Militaire)

CAS, Chief of Air Staff

CH, Chain Home (radar)

CHL, Chain Home Low (radar)

CID, Committee of Imperial Defence

CND, Confrérie Notre-Dame

DEM, Détection Électromagnétique

Do, Dornier (bomber)

D/T, Dezimeter Telegraphie (radar)

DTN, Defence Teleprinter Network

DZ, dropping zone

FMG, Funk Messgerät (radar)

FUP, forming-up point

GCI, ground-controlled interception (radar)

GEC, General Electric Company

GEMA, German radar company

GFP, Geheime Feldpolizei

GPO, General Post Office

He, Heinkel (bomber)

HE, high explosive (bombs)

HF/DF, high-frequency direction finding

H_2S, centimetric radar bombing aid

IF, radar intermediate frequency (unit)

IFF, identification friend from foe (radar)

JG, *jagdgeschwader* (fighter wing)

Ju, Junker (bomber or fighter)

KG, *kampfgruppe* (squadron)

KGr, *Kampfgruppe* (independent squadron)

LCA, assault landing craft

Me, Messerschmitt (fighter)

MGB, motor gunboat

NID, Naval Intelligence (Department)

OKL, Supreme Command, Luftwaffe

PDU, Photographic Development Unit

POW, prisoner of war

PRU, Photographic Reconnaissance Unit

PTS, Parachute Training Squadron

RAE, Royal Aircraft Establishment (Farnborough)

RDF, Radio Direction Finding (radar)

RE, Royal Engineers

R/T, radio telephony

RX, reception (radar)
SD, Sicherheitsdienst
SOE, Special Operations Executive
TRE, Telecommunications Research Establishment
TX, transmitter (radar)
VHF, very high frequency
VHF/DF, very high frequency direction finding
WAAF, Women's Auxiliary Air Force

THE BRUNEVAL RAID

Flashpoint of the Radar War

On January 21, 1942, Lord Louis Mountbatten, the newly appointed naval commodore leading Combined Operations, submitted to the three British Chiefs of Staff a proposal to raid a cliff site on the German-occupied French coast between Le Havre and Étretat.

Admiral of the Fleet Sir Dudley Pound, Air Marshal Reginald Henry Portal, and General Sir Alan Brooke discussed the proposal with an understandable lack of enthusiasm. They were informed that Prime Minister Winston Churchill favored the raid, having been interested in it by his scientific *éminence grise* Professor Frederick Alexander Lindemann of Oxford University, recently raised to the peerage as Lord Cherwell.[1] Behind Cherwell was Dr. Reginald Victor Jones on the Air Staff.

The object of the raid appeared to be a long-term one that might benefit the Air Force. Portal was friendly to the proposal, Pound was negative, and Brooke, as so often happened, took the middle ground, trying to assess unemotionally the possibilities and advantages of success.

At best, it would be the smallest of successes in an ocean of calamity. . . .

The combined strength of the Wehrmacht and the Luftwaffe had knocked out Poland, Denmark, Norway, France, and the Low Countries, but the Royal Air Force had successfully held off the Luftwaffe until a twentieth-century repeat of the Norman Conquest seemed too much of a gamble to the Germans, and Hitler had decided to starve Britain out. The French Bay of Biscay harbors had been turned into submarine bases. And now, in January 1942, Admiral Karl

Doenitz had five Atlantic U-boats operating for every one he had had only eighteen months previously. The graph of their sinkings showed an impressive rise. It had reached four hundred thousand tons a month and would go much higher with the entry of the United States into the war.

But the three British Chiefs of Staff knew of a secret ray of hope. It was said with confidence that at Worth Matravers, on the chalk downs of the Dorset coast, the scientists of the Telecommunications Research Establishment (TRE) had developed a gadget which, once installed in the aircraft of Coastal Command, would spell the death of the U-boats.

Apart from the U-boats, the war at sea contained another major headache, that of the capital ships. Although the Germans had lost the *Graf Spee*—scuttled in the shallows of the River Plate—and the *Bismarck*—which had performed according to the book, taking H.M.S. *Hood* down with it—they had commissioned *Tirpitz*. Brand new, and said to be the world's most potent warship, *Tirpitz* threatened to break out at any moment from her North Sea base and wreak havoc on Allied shipping. Meanwhile, at the western end of the Channel, three formidable German ships, the battle cruisers *Scharnhorst* and *Gneisenau* and the cruiser *Prinz Eugen* were embayed in Brest. With such potential marauders on either flank, the Royal Navy had to keep a powerful counterforce on standby at Scapa Flow in the Orkneys. Britain was getting desperately short of marine tonnage. The antisubmarine invention at Worth Matravers would have to be damned good, and its introduction to Coastal Command must not be long delayed. . . .

The technical reason for the raid proposed by Mountbatten was top secret. British scientific intelligence had recently discovered that radar, which had been regarded as a British trump card and which had played a major part in the victory of the Battle of Britain, was understood and employed by the enemy. Much of Britain's war production and effort was being channeled into Bomber Command, whose increasingly heavy attacks on Germany were meeting an effective defense.

Losses at this time were averaging four heavy bombers out of every hundred sent over German or German-occupied territory. In the light of the most recent assessments, these losses were attributable to a disquieting factor—German radar.

With the help of the Photographic Reconnaissance Unit (PRU), that exclusive high-speed Spitfire unit of the RAF, Dr. Jones and his assistants had quickly come to an understanding of what a layman might describe as the long-range, non-precision German radar unit, the "Freya." They had the Freya taped. They could locate it, listen to it, decode with ease its messages sent back to German guns and fighters, and at any moment, if they wanted to, they could jam it, neutralize it or, better still, feed it false information.

But they also knew of the existence of another German radar unit, one with a shorter range but more precision; a unit that it was feared could clamp on to a Lancaster or Stirling bomber and, holding it in its narrow, invisible beam, set the killers—German night fighters—on to it. This unit was small and presumably easy to manufacture in quantity. It was taking the most precious of British lives—RAF lives. Many such units had been located at long range by "smeller" reconnaissance Wellingtons of the RAF. Now at last, thanks to a brilliant bit of photographic work by a Spitfire pilot, one of those infernal machines (apparently it was shaped like a saucer standing on its rim and resembled an enlarged electric bowl heater) had been located in a vulnerable site on the Channel coastline of France. It was on a cliff top immediately north of the small village of Bruneval, some twelve miles north of Le Havre. Dr. Jones and the scientists of TRE urgently wanted the vitals of that German radar unit so that they could devise some means of neutralizing it.

Mountbatten, on behalf of Combined Operations, stated that the vitals could be snatched. He asked only for minimal forces: one company of the Parachute Regiment; one section of airborne Royal Engineers; a couple of radar mechanics from the RAF establishment; a squadron of Whitley bombers to take the parachutists to their objective; and suitable light naval forces to bring them back to England.

Bruneval, the three Chiefs of Staff saw, was in a ravine that ended in a cliff-encircled beach guarded by concrete pillboxes. An evacuation of a small force by sea in perfect weather seemed feasible. The PRU coverage was excellent, and local intelligence was being sought through De Gaulle's agents, who were confident that they could get it.

No time was lost in approving the Bruneval project. Contact was made immediately, through the leader of the airborne forces, Major-General F. A. M. Browning,[2] with the 2nd Parachute Battalion, which was in process of forming at Hardwick Hall, near Chesterfield, in the Midlands.

I

In January 1942, Major John Frost, a regular soldier commissioned in the Cameronians with a conventional background (father a brigadier in the Indian Army; educated at Wellington and Sandhurst; a shooter and a foxhunter), was adjutant of the 2nd Parachute Battalion when his commanding officer, shortly after that January meeting of the Chiefs of Staff, was ordered to send one company down to Salisbury Plain, in Wiltshire.

"C" Company, the most efficient at Hardwick Hall, was known as Jock Company, being made up almost entirely from Scots regiments. But at that time it was led by an Englishman from an English regiment. Frost was told that if he could, within the space of a week, complete his parachute jumps to the statutory number (he had so far only done two, and had got water on the knee as a result) he, as a Cameronian, might change places with the Englishman Major Philip Teichman. Meanwhile, Teichman was sent with the advance party to the Plain, on the understanding that if Frost, through accident or bad weather, failed to complete his jumps within the week Teichman would keep the command, which he badly wanted.

So did Frost. He had just passed his thirtieth birthday. He was tall, healthy, highly strung, with a secretive look to him. When he arrived at Ringway, the efficient and well-informed parachute training center near Manchester run by the Royal Air Force, he saw that the staff took a special interest in him. He even heard them talking about "the last time," a reference, he was sure, to the only previous British operation with parachutists. A band of them led by "Tag"

Pritchard of the Royal Welch Fusiliers had been dropped to destroy an aqueduct in southern Italy. Not a single parachutist had returned. They were said to be languishing in prison camp in Italy.[1]

Fog, strong winds, and a shortage of aircraft at Ringway made Frost's qualifying jumps a matter of luck. He completed them within hours of the time limit, hurried back to Hardwick Hall, took command of "C" Company, and entrained for Salisbury Plain. Teichman was anything but pleased to see him, and he said so. Both had become parachutists to find action, and Frost, perfectly understanding the other's anger, felt that it was a bad start.

Frost's company had been assigned quarters in part of Tilshead Camp. The camp was run by the Glider Pilots' Regiment, which was forming and expanding there. Frost thought Tilshead a miserable hole, and he was not cheered by the news that Major-General F. A. M. Browning, who commanded the 1 Airborne Division from his headquarters at Syrancote House, near Tilshead, intended to inspect "C" Company the following day. "Boy" Browning had been a disciplinarian adjutant at Sandhurst, and he could be relied on to notice every deficiency in turn-out and conduct. "Our men were a wild crew," he says.[2] "At that stage of the war clothing and equipment were scarce, and for a few months we had been concentrating on toughness and on weapon- and parachute-training. We'd had little time for drill, and still less for making ourselves look glamorous, or even clean. After a prolonged and uncomfortable railway journey, the Jocks had found time to work the dreadful Tilshead mud deep into the fabric of their uniforms. They looked horrible."

When Browning had inspected the company he led Frost aside. "Just let Peter Bromley-Martin know exactly what you need in the way of transport, stores, and equipment. And see here, Frost! Every man is to get a new uniform, for that is the filthiest company I ever saw in my life."

Later that same day Browning's liaison officer, Major Peter Bromley-Martin, Grenadier Guards, arrived in the company office. Bromley-Martin was something of a legend. Frost and his young officers had been looking forward to meeting him. His report on his first parachute jump, on February 4, 1941, was regarded as a classic. He had jumped fourth, following his friend H. O. Wright: "The next recollection I have," he wrote, "is of Major Wright with parachute open and canopy fully filled, some one hundred and fifty feet *above* me. My parachute, sir, had not then fully opened, and I had the gravest doubts as to whether it would function before it had been repacked. I was unable to devise a method of repacking it in the limited time at my disposal. As I was also unable to think of any satisfactory means of assisting the contraption to perform the functions which I had been led to suppose were automatic; in my submission I had no alternative but to fall earthwards at, I believe, the rate of thirty-two feet per second, accelerating to the maximum speed of one hundred and seventy-six feet per second. . . . This I did. . . . And having dropped a certain distance, my parachute suddenly opened, and I made a very light landing."[3]

Bromley-Martin told the officers that they had been brought south to stage an exercise judged to be vital for the future of the Airborne Division. Churchill was known to prefer the notion of sea-borne landings on the Axis perimeters, using commandos. He was going to take a lot of convincing as to the usefulness of parachutists. To influence the Prime Minister, "C" Company was to simulate a raid on an enemy headquarters in occupied territory. The demonstration would be on the Isle of Wight. The War Cabinet and Churchill would be present. Alton Priors, near Tilshead, would be their initial training ground for moving from the dropping zone (DZ) to their objective and from the objective to the imaginary coast. They would be issued with the most modern and most lethal weapons, and their comfort would be seen to. At a later stage in their training for the demonstration they would work with the distinguished RAF unit that would drop them, and with the Royal Navy landing craft that would evacuate them, once the simulated operation had been successfully completed. For the exercise, Bromley-Martin concluded, the company would be split into assault parties of differing sizes, each trained and equipped for a specific task. The tactics, in short, would be laid down by headquarters, a policy with which Frost violently disagreed, particularly for a night operation, and he said so. The atmosphere became hostile and Bromley-Martin departed.

Frost and his platoon commanders were furiously disappointed. They were tired. They were depressed by the mud and the rain and even by their hosts, the glider pilots. The staff officer's briefing had seemed a piece of unctuous nonsense.

Next morning Bromley-Martin reappeared in the company office and told Frost that he wanted a private interview. After emphasizing that Frost must maintain the "Prime Minister cover story" with his officers and his men and must ensure that they really believed it, Bromley-Martin went on to say that Frost would be taking his company over to France before the end of February. It was up to Frost to see that everything worked properly and that his men were in peak condition; otherwise there wouldn't be a hope of bringing them out alive. The raid, Bromley-Martin said, had a special objective which he was not yet at liberty to describe. And the enemy's dispositions were complex. Frost must accept the fact that, in order to secure the line of retreat, or rather withdrawal, and to give maximum protection to the men dismantling the objective, the plan of battle would be drawn up for him by headquarters. If he wanted to lead the raid he must fall in with those terms, even if privately he disagreed with them.

"Let's have a gin," Frost said, determined to accept, although he felt that he was being blackmailed.[4] Division's insistence on a rigid plan continued to worry him (and was to infuriate him during the raid).

"You'll have noted my use of the verb 'dismantle,'" the staff officer said. "That's why you've found under your orders here a section of the First Parachute Field Squadron, Royal Engineers. Under the present plan for the raid, which may of course be altered, four of your sappers will carry out an antitank role. The rest of them will be in your dismantling party."

"Sounds exciting," Frost said drily.

"Also in your dismantling party will be two RAF sergeants. Then, except for one man, Newman I believe they call him, your strength will be complete. . . . I don't think I should tell you about Newman yet. . . . I must say I find the whole thing fascinating."

"That's good," Frost said. He had the impression that Bromley-Martin was planning the raid, and he did not like that idea at all.

2

"Radar" is a reversible word brought to the war when the Americans, with their talent for new words, came in and helped to build on the framework developed by British scientists, research departments of the armed services, the radio industry, and the General Post Office (GPO).[1] "Radar" is an abbreviation of "radio direction and ranging." It is a good word and will be used here, although in the 1930s, when England and Germany independently discovered radar (each refusing to believe that the other might have it), they had their own cover names for it: Radio Direction Finding (RDF) in England, Dezimeter Telegraphie (D/T) in Germany.

What is scientific discovery? Occasionally it is an abrupt breakthrough; usually it grows like a tree, one research branch topping its predecessors until suddenly the tree is complete and powerful. Radar evolved from the experiments of the nineteenth-century German physicist Heinrich Hertz (1857–94). Hertz, who himself continued the work of the British physicists Michael Faraday (1791–1857) and James Clerk Maxwell (1831–79), may be said to have discovered and demonstrated the true nature of radio waves. He showed, for example, that the waves were reflected from metal sheets. But he could see no practical use for this momentous discovery. Three years after Hertz died another German, Professor Karl Ferdinand Braun (1850–1918), invented the Braun tube, which the Germans continued to call by that name and the English called the cathode-ray tube. (It is the cathode-ray tube that reproduces the image on a television screen.) In 1904 Professor Ambrose Fleming, working at University College, London, made the first true radio valve, the diode. That year, too, a young German, Christian Hülsmeyer, took out British Patent No. 13,170 for his invention, a "Hertzian Wave Projecting and Receiving Apparatus."[2] His patent comprised a radio transmitter and a receiver mounted side by side in a ship. He claimed that if the waves sent out by his transmitter encountered a metal body on the sea (presumably another ship), they would close an electrical contact in the receiver and ring a bell.

How much nearer to radar could one get than that? But Hülsmeyer's idea was unpopular at a time when the British Admiralty and its friends and rivals were thinking in terms of armor and gunnery. Three years later, in 1907, an American, Professor Lee De Forest, improved dramatically on Fleming's valve. In 1924 two Americans, Dr. Gregory Breit and Dr. Merle A. Tuve, evolved a technique for sending out a series of radio "shouts," or short pulses; and that same year, using their technique, Professor E. V. Appleton (later Sir Edward) in England was able to calculate the height (sixty miles) of the Heaviside layer, the layer of radio-reflective ionized gases surrounding the earth. Five years later, in 1929, Professor Hidetsugu Yagi published in Japan the results of his successful experiments with directional aerials which made it possible to send out radio signals in narrow beams.

So, by the 1930s, the scientific groundwork existed for the discovery of radar. (How many more such discoveries, one wonders, lie among the lumber in the attics of science, waiting for the kiss of recognition, of life—or for the breath of war?)

Dr. Rudolf Kuhnold, a sonar expert working with the German Navy, was independently engaged in research with radio waves (he had not heard of Hülsmeyer). In 1933, using new valves developed by Philips, the Dutch electrical firm, he set up an experimental transmitting-receiving apparatus on a balcony overlooking Kiel Harbor, aimed his dished aerials at a battleship five hundred meters away, and got satisfactory echoes in his receiver.[3]

A company, GEMA, was formed to develop Kuhnold's discovery and to sell it in the growing German market for work relating to armaments. In October 1934, demonstrating an improved version of his apparatus to Navy staff and engineer officers at Pelzerhaken, Kuhnold got strong echoes from a ship at a range of seven miles. GEMA was promptly given a research grant of seventy thousand reichmarks. Turning from continuous waves to pulses, Kuhnold by 1936 had increased the range of his naval set to twelve miles. This success was reported to Hitler and all German Chiefs of Staff.

In Germany the question posed by Dezimeter Telegraphie (it had been placed under the cover of the German Post Office) was this: how could it best be used in attack? Plainly it could be used for setting and ranging guns—first naval and later antiaircraft guns—and also, presumably, searchlights. GEMA proceeded to produce for the Navy the "Seetakt," a gun-laying ranger. The prototype was tried out at sea in 1937, and the pocket battleship *Graf Spee* was secretly fitted with Seetakt when in the summer of 1938 she did her publicized Spanish Civil War standing-patrol.

Meanwhile, in 1936, Dr. Kuhnold's GEMA company had also produced a promising early-warning radar called "Freya," with a rectangular aerial revolving around a vertical axis. It was semimobile, easy to man and to service, and its initial range on aircraft of thirty miles was soon increased to fifty and then to seventy-five miles. Once more GEMA did business, this time with the Luftwaffe.

That year GEMA faced a powerful commercial rival when the Telefunken manufacturing complex entered the field of D/T with something many years ahead of its time: the "Würzburg," which had a round dish aerial capable of following any fast-moving target (fast-moving, that is, by aircraft standards). It had a useful range of some twenty miles, was comparatively simple to handle, and had remarkable accuracy. It was an obvious complement in any defensive scheme to the wider-ranging but less accurate Freya. Further, it was a workhorse, tough and durable and mounted on four wheels that retracted when it went into action. It was therefore suited for forward duty with the Luftwaffe, working with the German 88-mm flak gun.

It was after seeing an early demonstration of the Würzburg in its antiaircraft role that Reichsmarschall Hermann Göring, deeply impressed by its phenomenal performance, dropped his celebrated brick by announcing that the Ruhr would never be bombed. Yet he took no steps to accelerate its production because it was defensive and the German philosophy of the moment was attack, strike, annihilate.

If the Würzburg suffered initially from neglect and consequent production difficulties, and if it never quite fulfilled its early promise as a gun-laying instrument, that was because few experts on either side in World War II understood that the flak gun was as clumsy a weapon as the bomber. But later, when the Würzburg worked in conjunction with the night fighter, it was to be a different story.

Germany, then, had made a good start in radar before the war. But Göring summed up the official attitude toward the new science when he remarked to his commander of Luftwaffe Signals, General Wolfgang Martini, "Radio aids contain boxes with coils; and I do not like boxes with coils."

In England radar may be said to have begun one summer morning in 1934. The only assistant in the office of the Directorate of Scientific Research at the Air Ministry had left London for Biggin Hill, in Kent, the central RAF base of the London defense perimeter, to see a sound locator working. His name was Albert Percival Rowe and he was twenty-six years old.

England's early-warning system then consisted of sound locators. That day at Biggin Hill the sound locator was nullified, not by simulated enemy action but by a Kentish milkman whistling as he drove his horse along an air base road which should have been declared out of bounds, the milk cans behind him jangling pleasantly. Rowe saw nothing pleasant in the scene. He hurried back to the Air Ministry and called for every document on early-warning systems for air defense. There were fifty-three files.[4] When he had gone through the lot and found not a workable idea in any of them, he wrote a letter to his chief, Harry Egerton Wimperis.

Wimperis in his turn wrote to Lord Londonderry, Secretary of State for Air, urging that a small committee be set up, including independent scientific members, to find a new method of air defense. Had not Lord Londonderry appointed that particular committee, England might be speaking German today. The men chosen were Wimperis, who had suggested it, with Dr. Rowe as secretary, and three distinguished scientists, Henry Tizard (later Sir Henry), Professor Archibald Vivian Hill, and Professor Patrick Maynard Stuart Blackett (later Lord Blackett).

Tizard was England's leading defense scientist. The son of a naval officer, he had served in World War I, first as a gunner, then in the Royal Flying Corps. He was an outstanding pilot, and before embarking on his scientific career he had served for a while with the RAF. As Rector of Imperial College of Science and Technology from 1929, he had constantly been the key man on various Air Force committees and was known for his habit of cutting through to the marrow of any problem.[5]

Hill, a physiologist, had initiated operational research (cooperation between scientist and fighting man) in World War I. Blackett had served in the Navy until 1918 and had gone then to the Cavendish Laboratory at Cambridge, where he worked with the mighty Baron Rutherford. As a physicist he was known widely outside his own country and he was to play a vital part in the sea war that lay ahead.

At its first meeting on January 28, 1935, the committee, known from its inception as the Tizard Committee, arrived quickly at a vital decision (both Wimperis and Tizard having already been investigating the problem). They asked Robert Watson-Watt (later Sir Robert), a sharp-tongued scientist with many admirers and not a few enemies, to give them a paper on the radio detection of aircraft.

Ten days before the first meeting of the Tizard Committee, Wimperis had asked Watson-Watt, who worked in the Radio Research Station at Ditton Park, near Slough, in Buckinghamshire, about the possibility of a death ray which would kill air crew at long range. That afternoon Watson-Watt talked about the death-ray notion (then a popular fancy) with his assistant A. F. Wilkins. The pair agreed that the death ray would take too much power and was a non-starter.

During a subsequent talk, casting about for some other means of solving the Tizard Committee's problem, they recalled a General Post Office report.[6] The GPO had been experimenting at Dollis Hill, just north of London, with very high frequency (VHF) radio, trying to find an economical means of communication between the Scottish mainland and the Hebrides. The engineers had commented on a "flutter" in their earphones each time an aircraft passed. Did this not mean, the two scientists pondered, that aircraft re-radiated radio waves? And if so, could not re-radiation be used for an early-warning system? Watson-Watt asked Wilkins to work out what power would be needed to get a detectable signal from an aircraft and Wilkins' calculations were favorable, suggesting that aircraft might be located at long range by means of radio waves or pulses.

On February 14 the Tizard Committee were handed Watson-Watt's paper, entitled *The Detection and Location of Aircraft by Radio Methods*. Each of the five perceived that a breakthrough had been made. Watson-Watt was engaged immediately in prolonged discussion which continued over luncheon. Next morning Wimperis, representing the Tizard Committee, asked Air Marshal Sir Hugh Dowding, then in charge of research and development, for £10,000 from public funds.

Dowding insisted on a practical experiment. Overnight Wilkins got his equipment together—an improvised receiver linked to a cathode-ray oscillograph—and stowed it in the Radio Research Station's trailer, which was hitched to a Morris car. Next day he and Dyer, the station's driver, drove north and parked the trailer near the old Cavalry School at Weedon in Northamptonshire. Here Wilkins was joined by Watson-Watt and Rowe. Together they would observe on the oscillograph an aircraft, from the Royal Aircraft Establishment (RAE) at Farnborough in Hampshire, which was going to fly through the BBC's short-wave transmissions emanating from the high masts at nearby Daventry.

Flight Lieutenant R. S. Blucke, a test pilot of the Farnborough Flight, was ordered to fly the demonstration in a twin-engined Heyford bomber. He thought it odd that he was briefed by a young civilian (Rowe). February 26 dawned clear, with a strong wind from the south. Blucke flew over Daventry at the required time and altitude, one thousand feet, fired a Very light signal, turned east, climbed to six thousand, turned at a stipulated mark, and flew back to Daventry at the Heyford's maximum of 130 knots. Over Daventry, bored with the whole thing, he again fired a Very and set course for home.[7]

Below in the trailer Watson-Watt, Wilkins, and Rowe watched the oscillograph, which showed the 50-meter beam from Daventry as a straight line. But when the Heyford lumbered into the beam the line was bent. An oscillation of over an inch was registered. Rowe went back to London to report. The next day the Treasury handed over the money.

Blucke imagined that he had been flying "some scatty BBC stunt." But his simple flight laid the foundation for the defense of a Britain whose initial Allies were to crumble before the power of the eagle.

3

On February 1, 1942, in the Chain Home (CH) radar station
at Hartland Point in North Devon, Sergeant C. W. H. Cox
was handed a railway pass to London and ordered to catch
the noon express out of Bideford. Cox, whose father was a
postman and whose mother was an actress, was a cinema pro-
jectionist and radio ham from Wisbech, Cambridgeshire. He
was a true East Anglian—quick, staunch, perky, humorous,
efficient, and patriotic. Before joining the RAF in 1940 he
had never been far from Wisbech. He had never been on a
ship or in an airplane. Now he was one of the best radar
mechanics in Britain.

In the morning he reported to Air Commodore V. H. Tait
(later Sir Victor) at the Air Ministry.

"You've volunteered for a dangerous job, Sergeant Cox."

"No sir."[1]

"What d'ye mean, no sir?"

"I never volunteered for anything, sir."

"There must be some mistake. I asked for volunteers from
among the comparatively few with exactly your qualifications.
. . . But now you're here, Sergeant, *will* you volunteer?"

"Exactly what would I be letting myself in for, sir?"

"I'm not at liberty to tell you. . . . I honestly think the
job offers a reasonable chance of survival. It's of great importance to the Royal Air Force. And if you're half the chap
I think you are, you'll jump at it."

"I volunteer, sir."

Cox was promoted to flight-sergeant and was given another railway pass, this time to Manchester. They also gave

him a chit. He was to report to the adjutant of No. 4 PTS at nearby Ringway.

Ringway mystified him. "Bus loads of soldiers kept entering and leaving. Some had queer pots of helmets on, rather like the Boys' Brigade." Finally he asked the RAF sergeant in the guard room, "What *is* this joint, Sarge?"

"Number four PTS, mate."

"What's PTS when it's at home?"

"Parachute Training Squadron."

"Let me out of here."

Twelve days later he was told that they would let him out next morning for Tilshead, on Salisbury Plain. That night he would make his last jump. He got into his harness once more and entered a balloon basket with an RAF sergeant-instructor. They rose silently to five hundred feet. The balloon tugged at its cable, making it grunt.

"Ready, son?"

"Sarge."

"Then let's have a good jump. . . . Chin up. Hands by your sides. Relax. Get ready . . . Go!"

He gauged his drop by a dark-purple line of trees, made a good rolling landing, and gathered up his chute. He doubted if he had ever felt better in all his life.

When he reached Tilshead, Major Frost and Captain John Ross, the second in command, gave him an initiatory week of physical training, route marching with full kit, unarmed combat, weapons training, knife fighting, barbed-wire scaling (one parachutist lay across the wire and the others, using his body as a springboard, ran over him), and night patrols. He rather liked his fellow sergeants in "C" Company: "If you could understand half what they said, they weren't a bad bunch."

Cox gathered from what he could understand that his new friends thought they were preparing for an exercise. He, of course, was in no doubt at all that he was destined, for the first time in his life, to make a short trip abroad. He was not surprised when Sergeant-Major Strachan told him that he would be working with the section of Royal Engineers (REs) under Lieutenant Dennis Vernon. Nor was he surprised when a mobile gun-laying radar on loan from the local Antiaircraft Command was parked inside the perimeter of the camp and he was told to explain to the REs exactly what it was and how it worked.

Vernon, then twenty-four, was a Londoner who had spent much of his time at Cambridge, first at the Leys School and then reading economics at Emmanuel. As a junior officer in the REs, believed by many to be the most impressive unit in the British Army, Vernon was outstanding. Cox saw this at once. It had been proposed that there should be two radar mechanics, but the second one had injured himself in his parachute training, and it was Cox who suggested to Air Commodore Tait that Lieutenant Vernon would be quite as capable of handling any radar as was he himself.

In the "exercise," Vernon was told, four of his sappers would be detached from the section in "an antitank role." The remaining six, together with himself and Flight-Sergeant Cox, would be "dismantling the objective." Was he familiar with the Leica camera, he was asked. (He was.) And had he taken photographs with an automatic flash, as fitted on the Leica. (He had.)

Immediately after their arrival at Tilshead, Frost had promoted Ross, who was commissioned in the Black Watch and now one of his platoon commanders, to be second in command and a temporary, acting, unpaid captain. Company Sergeant-Major Strachan was also Black Watch and, Frost noted, "the very best sort of senior NCO in the world." Between Strachan and Ross, "an imperturbable and extremely intelligent officer from Dundee," the administration of "C" Company went smoothly. Those were days of parsimonious supplies for the troops at home, but not, it seemed, for "C" Company. Ross put in a requisition one day for nine Bren guns; the following day eighteen brand new Brens arrived. Anything he asked for was immediately supplied—uniforms, boots, binoculars, compasses, pistols, flashlights, trucks. They got things, too, that he had not ordered—antitank mines, two portable mine detectors, and a new kind of submachine gun, the Sten. At first acquaintance it seemed an ideal weapon for close fighting—short, light, and handy, with magazines easy to change in the dark, and a high rate of fire on "automatic." But they soon found in training that it had been put together hastily and was not entirely reliable. Then they were given four No. 38 radio sets, one for each platoon and one for Company Headquarters, and two No. 18 sets "for contact with the Navy."[2]

None of the parachutists thought well of the No. 38 set. Frost says it was temperamental and difficult to keep from drifting. "If practice could have made the sets perfect, they would have worked for us. Most nights in the early stages of training at Tilshead we were prowling about the Plain. I fear we caused the Glider Pilot Regiment some headaches. We never knew when we might appear for meals, and they were horrified at the amount of food we consumed. The men worked well, and the NCOs, taking their cue from Strachan, were first class. We worked them all just as hard as we could, but whenever we had a night in camp I made sure that those who wanted relaxation got leave to Salisbury and that transport was laid on for them."

One day the Company, the REs, and Cox drove to Thruxton Aerodrome, thirty miles from Tilshead, to meet No. 51 Squadron, which had been detailed to provide their aerial transport; trap doors were being cut in the floors of their Whitley bombers. Commanding 51 Squadron was one of the exceptional characters produced by the RAF during the war, Wing-Commander Charles Pickard. Pickard, tall, fair-haired, and pipe-smoking, had already seen much action, and he was a celebrity with the public because as the pilot of *F for Freddie* he had played a leading part in a popular RAF film, *Target for Tonight*. The parachutists instantly liked him, as everybody did, whether he was hanging by his feet from a rafter in the Mess bar, proving that he could drink a pint of beer upside down, or whether he was landing a single-engine Lysander in a dark field in the Occupied Zone of France.

Immediately on their return to Tilshead from Thruxton, the sergeant-major brought before the company commander a small but handsome man dressed as a private soldier in the Pioneer Corps. He had been detailed to join "C" Company as German interpreter and came from Combined Operations headquarters via the 1st Division Headquarters at Syrancote House. Frost was instructed to put him on the Company list as "Private Newman." This, then, was the mysterious "Newman" whom Bromley-Martin had referred to as the man who would complete "C" Company's strength.

Not only did "Newman" speak perfect German, he *was* German. His father had come to England before the war as an enemy of the Nazis. Frost studied Newman carefully, noting his many good points—toughness, intelligence, humor. He also spoke perfect English, so there would be no need for any but himself, John Ross, and Sergeant-Major Strachan to know his real nationality. Obviously the fewer the better, in case he was captured.

Newman seemed to have been everywhere and to have done everything. He appeared to have lived in Paris (he spoke about his mother there), as well as in Berlin, Vienna, Budapest, New York, and London. His background was international, and Frost felt very uneasy about him. "The Germans then seemed invincible. Their armies knew no halting, and in spite of their recent reverses, or apparent reverses, in the snow in front of Moscow, they were truly formidable. . . . So many things could go wrong with our little party, and we had been taught to fear the enemy's Intelligence. With all the talk in England then and previously about the Fifth Column, I could not help thinking that the enemy probably knew all about us, and what we were training for. There was a distinctly eerie feel to having a Hun on the strength."[3]

The German's arrival brought the strength up to one hundred and twenty.

Next day "C" Company with its Royal Engineers, its RAF flight sergeant, and its German interpreter entrained for Scotland.

4

"One of the loveliest places on earth," was A. P. Rowe's description of Orford Ness, where the first radar research station was set up in 1935. "At Aldeburgh, in Suffolk, the River Ore flows to within a few yards of the sea and then, fortunately, turns south and flows for eleven miles, leaving an isthmus of singular beauty. It was known as 'The Island,' and those who first worked there on radar were 'The Islanders.'"[1]

Here Robert Watson-Watt, a volcano of assurance, led a small group. The preliminary towers were seventy feet high. Experiment led to improvement on improvement until in March 1936 their new 240-foot tower enabled them to locate an aircraft at a range of seventy-five miles; and thanks to Watson-Watt's new discoveries, the cathode-ray tube also informed them of the aircraft's bearing and its altitude.

But later in the spring of 1936 that idyllic "Island" had to be abandoned when a nearby RAF airfield objected to the height of the 240-foot radar tower. Furthermore, it had become clear that the experimental station now needed a more elaborate setting. Radar had become England's hope.

Bawdsey Manor, Sir Cuthbert Quilter's estate in Suffolk, twenty miles south of Orford Ness and also on the coast, attracted Wimperis and Rowe because of its extensive stables and outbuildings in a wooded area of 250 acres. One afternoon the pair picked up a rumor that Sir Cuthbert might be induced to sell, with the result that the Treasury bought Bawdsey for the nation and the scientists and their mechanics and tradesmen moved in. Rowe regretted the purity of Orford Ness but he relished Bawdsey's seclusion and style.

He liked the lawns, the sandy beach under the cliffs, and the motto above the front door which read PLÛTOT MOURIR QUE CHANGER.

By late spring Bawdsey's lattice steel towers soared above the dark cedars of Lebanon and Mediterranean pines and the experimental station became operational. It had been decided to make it both the nucleus of applied research on radar and the first early-warning station of the CH radar stations in the series now planned to encircle England. Just as at Orford Ness radar had become England's hope, so now at Bawdsey, with the birth of the CH, it had become her main defense.

Radar in England now began to feel its way through political shoals that might have wrecked it, for all its progress and its promise. There was opposition to it in the corridors of power. Lord Cherwell, Churchill's scientific adviser, who had independently urged some means of early warning, was initially lukewarm about the radar project because Henry Tizard was at the heart of it. Cherwell disliked his brilliant contemporary and had good reason to suspect that radar was not invulnerable.

In 1935 the Tizard Committee had brought radar to life in England. Soon, however, Ramsay MacDonald, the first Labour Prime Minister, formed another committee, a subcommittee of the Committee of Imperial Defence (CID). Its chairman was Sir Philip Cunliffe-Lister (shortly to be Lord Swinton), Secretary of State for Air. On June 7 of that same year MacDonald departed from 10 Downing Street and Stanley Baldwin moved in. That day Winston Churchill flayed the CID in the House of Commons for its "lethargy" and also wanted to know why Lord Cherwell had not been invited to sit on the Tizard Committee. Even out of office Churchill was a force. A month later his scientific adviser, though unliked, was invited to join the Tizard Committee and Churchill himself attended his first meeting as a member of the politically more powerful CID. Lord Swinton was a friend of radar, and the argument at the meeting was that radar must have priority even over fighter aircraft. Wimperis, another member of the Swinton Committee, watched Churchill as he sat back listening and scribbling on the pad before him, a half-smile on his mischievous features. When he slid his scribble across the table, Wimperis saw that he had written the first two lines of an eighth-century Greek hymn:

> Art thou weary, art thou languid,
> Art thou sore distrest?

Churchill had emended the seventh verse:

> Seeking, finding, following, keeping,
> Is he sure to bless?
> Angels, martyrs, prophets, virgins
> Answer . . .[2]

altering the bell-like and triumphant final "Yes!" of the hymn to his own dubious "M'yes." It was an apt summing up of his own and Cherwell's doubts about radar.

Although Churchill, well informed as he was, both in and out of office, and aware as he was of England's peril, was not hostile to radar, he often felt that it was monopolizing the country's resources at the expense of conventional rearmament. In scientific matters he trusted Cherwell, who certainly did nothing to dissuade Churchill from acting as a catalyst, from seeking to goad such bodies as the Tizard Committee into "that period when men cease to be satisfied with present performance and strive to surpass the possible."

Through the summer of 1936 Churchill and Cherwell were thought by many to be determined on disrupting the radar effort. On June 10 Churchill, in a Cherwell-inspired complaint to the CID, attacked the Tizard Committee (of which Cherwell was by now a member). Two days later Churchill and Cherwell supported Watson-Watt in his attempt to overturn the management. The inventor complained that progress was snaillike. Rather, he said, than trying to flog a dead horse (the Air Ministry), the development of radar should be entrusted to a new and specially formed organization. The Ministry was not pleased; it was officially felt that progress, far from being slow, had been sensational.

At the mid-July meeting of the Tizard Committee, Cherwell rejected the interim report, and Professors Hill and Blackett, deciding that they could no longer work with him, sent their resignations to Lord Swinton. On September 3 Swinton informed Cherwell that the Tizard Committee was dissolved; but the following month he reconstituted it, replacing Cherwell with Professor E. V. Appleton, whose contribution to the development of radar has been described earlier.

The wrangles here should not be regarded as prejudicial to any of the participants, including Cherwell, who was often to put England in his debt. During the prewar period of quarrels in and out of committee, much was achieved. It was, for example, in the name of the Tizard Committee that Cherwell drew attention to the work of Dr. R. V. Jones. At Oxford Jones, who was Skynner Senior Student in Astronomy at Balliol, worked in Cherwell's Oxford laboratory, the Clarendon. In 1934, when he was only twenty-three, Jones was retained by an inventor connected with the United States Navy who wished to interest the British Government in an infrared detection method for aircraft. As a result of Jones's work, it became possible, probably for the first time, for one aircraft to recognize another by infrared means. Although Tizard invited him to continue his infrared research at Imperial College, Jones was given the impression that the Committee wished to close down the work at Oxford because it was being carried out in Cherwell's laboratory. The Committee made sure, however, that Jones, even while he continued to work at Oxford, was made a member of the Air Ministry Staff.

Henry Tizard's unusual value lay in his talent for applying science to service practices. He thought as a scientist and also as the pilot he had been. (Cherwell also had been an outstanding pilot.) It was not enough, Tizard knew, for the RAF to have warning when hostile aircraft approached; its reactions to such attacks must be trained reactions. However successful the new British fighter designs—they were having their troubles—and however rapid their production— it remained disappointingly low—the system of airborne patrols must be changed. The new, much faster, more heavily armed fighters must sit on their home fields ready to spring at the intruders. They must be guided to within sight of the enemy by controllers who, watching the enemy and their own aircraft with radar, could bring the two together. This seems mere common sense today. In the summer of 1936, when Tizard was allowed to carry out some experiments at Biggin Hill, it was a pipe dream—and time was running out.

At Biggin Hill Wing-Commander E. O. Grenfell acted as host and worked with Tizard's small group. Tizard had asked Rowe to pick him a young scientific assistant. The choice was Dr. B. G. Dickins, then working at Farnborough, and they were joined by Squadron-Leader R. L. Ragg, also from Farnborough, and Flight-Lieutenant W. P. G. Pretty, a signals officer. They had three Hawker Harts to represent enemy bombers. Their fighters, three Gloster Gauntlet biplanes, waited at Biggin until ordered off and then were guided by radio to the interception. The trials showed that *if* a fifteen-minute warning was given, and *if* the controller was good and had first-rate radiotelephone (R/T) communication with the pilot, and *if* the fighter had a performance equal to or superior to that of the bomber, the system worked.

After a fortnight of interceptions Dickins suggested to Tizard that it would be better to have R/T contacts at one-minute, rather than five-minute, intervals. Tizard then got the Air Ministry's authority to tell his assistants that radar existed and that Bawdsey was making contact at a hundred miles and more.

When straightforward interceptions became easy, the "bombers" were ordered to jink, or change course. The defender's original course had to be altered in mid-flight, and the controller had to work fast. Here Tizard came in once more. He produced a "principle of equal angles": at any stage of the interception, a line could be drawn between fighter and bomber, which was the base of an isosceles triangle; the prolongation of the bomber's course was the second side of the triangle; and the course to be given the fighter made the third side. This formula became known in the RAF as the "Tizzy Angle."

In the course of one trial Grenfell, the controller, saw that a mistake had been made in the fighter courses. There was no time to work out a new Tizzy Angle. He therefore corrected by eye and the pilot made the kill. Tizard deduced from this that an experienced fighter controller would do much of his work almost by instinct.

The scope of the experiments was then widened, with more aircraft and more controllers. It was found that the best controllers could manage four interceptions simultaneously. At the end of almost a year the work carried out at Biggin Hill had changed the form of defensive air war. Now others would step forward to refine and expand the new law of the air that Tizard and his Biggin Hill group had made.[3]

"Pip-Squeak" was an Air Force gadget dating back to 1932. Air Marshal Dowding called in Watson-Watt and the Bawdsey scientists to develop it and to help improve the high-frequency direction-finding (HF/DF) that, following Tizard's experiments, was seen to be needed. Dowding asked for three HF/DF stations in each Fighter Command sector. The fighter pilot's "Where am I?" of the (good) old days was to be done away with. Ground must know exactly where he was and Ground would direct him either on to the enemy or home. It was, initially, an unpopular notion with the pilots. Pip-Squeak automatically switched on the high-frequency transmitter in the fighter for fourteen seconds in each minute of flight. The pilot had an override control on the device should he need his radio during the squeaking seconds. A clock with its face in four colored sectors was duplicated in the control room and the direction-finding stations. The clock told them which aircraft was pip-squeaking, and the position of each fighter was fixed each minute by plots from the three stations.

Simpler and perhaps more romantic, if only because it called for human endurance, was another most important part of air defence, the Observer Corps, which maintained a ground-based, round-the-clock watch on the entire British sky. It was a mass of superior volunteers hung on a skeleton of professionals. The Corps had operated in 1918, lapsed after the Armistice, and had begun to form again in 1924. It was first run by the police, and fortunately, when the Air Force took over from the police, it was kept as a civilian body. Germany's parallel organization, the Flugmeldedienst, was a less effective, uniformed service, which functioned in the later years of World War II; in Britain the harder the civilian Corps worked, the better it became. The map of the Observer Corps is an impressive sight, covered, apart from gaps in Cornwall, West Wales, and the West of Scotland, by the five-mile-radius circles of the section posts. There were some thirty posts to each center, and thirty-two centers, divided into five zones, were connected to Dowding's Fighter Command Headquarters at Bentley Priory, Stanmore, Middlesex. (In 1936 "Stuffy" Dowding had left the Research and Development job with the Air Council, to become Commander in Chief of the RAF Fighter Command.)

The Observer Corps was at full strength in 1938 when the Munich crisis came and Hitler, fortunately for Britain if not for Czechoslovakia, decided to buy more time with lies. At that time the General Post Office had all but finished the immense installation of direct lines from the posts to the command centers of the Corps. The GPO had been laying land lines for the RAF since the inception of radar, and in the year following Munich the mileage of the lines was doubled. In July 1938 the GPO began to set up its own apparatus, the Defence Teleprinter Network (DTN), a communications system that carried most of the important routine business during the Battle of Britain—requisitions, damage assessments, supplies, casualties, etc.

Finally, perhaps the crowning achievement evolving from the work of Tizard and his men was the early-warning defense that had been completed by the outbreak of war. Back in 1935 the Treasury had authorized the building of five radar stations between Bawdsey and South Foreland, on the coast near Dover, to cover the air approaches to London. This was the beginning of the Chain Home series and, as we have seen, it was at Bawdsey that the first CH station was established. Even this start was an enormous undertaking for a secret project: the work had to be channeled through public firms, contractors, steel factories, the radio and power industries, and the General Post Office. The twenty final CH stations had 350-foot lattice steel towers for the transmitters and 240-foot wooden towers for the receivers. They could range, fix, and read the altitude of aircraft 120 miles distant, and they could normally distinguish their own from hostile aircraft. Advance stations had 90-foot steel towers and mobile equipment. Intermediate stations had 240-foot towers and mobile or experimental equipment.

In addition, before the German air attacks began, thirty Chain Home Low (CHL) stations were operational. These were coastal defense radar sets with revolving aerials. They had been designed at Bawdsey and developed for the Royal Navy to locate and range hostile ships and submarines. The Air Force, however, saw the set as a possible answer to low-flying marauders. The radar floodlight effect, or "twilight," transmitted by the huge masts of CH did not descend to the surface of the sea, and it was possible to fly under it. It was felt that CHL would close that gap. The installations were rushed through under the leadership of a Cambridge don, Professor John Cockcroft. In addition to the CHL system, the Observer Corps gave "Low Raid Urgent" priority to low-flying aircraft.

If the British had failed in many respects to ready themselves for the fight against Nazi Germany that had become inevitable in the 1930s, they had done wonders with their aircraft early-warning system; they had been as thorough and as painstaking as they had been inventive. Its like existed in no other country. Invisible walls had been built round the United Kingdom, walls twelve miles high and one hundred and twenty miles thick. H. G. Wells himself could never have imagined such defenses. . . . And the gallant young men in their flying machines were there to hold the walls.

Oddly enough, although the United Kingdom's efforts and expenditures in making these installations were proportionally as great as Egypt's when the Pyramids were built, the Germans still knew nothing about British radar. Nothing at all.

5

In the beautiful little town of Inveraray on Loch Fyne, in the coastal fringe of Argyll, "C" Company and its appendages were swallowed up by the Royal Navy. They were accommodated aboard H.M.S. *Prins Albert* in the cold January weather of 1942.

Prins Albert had been built for the Belgian Government in 1937. At the outset of war the ship had been remodeled and was commissioned for special service in September 1941. Her 15,000-horsepower diesels gave her a maximum speed of twenty-two knots on a length of 370 feet, a beam of forty-six feet, and a draft of thirteen feet. She could carry eight assault landing craft (LCAs). Her armament consisted of two twelve-pounders, two two-pounders, and six Oerlikons (20-mm antiaircraft quick-firers), and she was manned by thirty-five officers and 161 enlisted men. "C" Company fitted into her guest accommodation most comfortably, for she could carry thirty-nine Army officers and three hundred other ranks. After the mud and huts and duckboards of Tilshead the ship seemed a floating hotel, spotless, hospitable, and with excellent food and drink.

"Even the subalterns had enough to eat," Frost says. "And there was no shortage of the civilized things in life. We were lucky with the weather, and all of us greatly enjoyed splashing about in the landing craft, even if it meant long hours and frequent wetting in the icy waters of Loch Fyne."[1]

LCAs were of Thornycroft design and were built in yacht yards. They were forty-one feet long, with a ten-foot beam and a draft of only two feet six inches. Powered by two Ford V8 engines, they were supposedly capable, on flat water, of ten knots. Each carried a crew of four, and a maximum of thirty-five fully-armed marines or soldiers. Although Frost had not yet been authorized to say a word to any of his officers or men about the purpose of their training and the cover story—that they were to do an exercise in order to convince the Prime Minister—was still maintained, it is doubtful if any of them failed to suspect that something more urgent lay ahead. So the wooden-hulled boats with the quirks of their gasoline engines endeared themselves to the soldiers. They represented perhaps the difference between glory dead and glory alive.

Operationally, though, Inveraray was one prolonged headache. The men were disconcerted to find that night embarkations off the rock-strewn beaches were extremely difficult and, if the weather suddenly turned foul, hazardous. And there was always that phenomenon, the tide. Whether it was flowing or ebbing, always it seemed to be wrong for what they wanted to do. Then, too, the naval crews seemed to have the greatest difficulty in finding the dark figures on the darker shores. They never appeared to be able to distinguish flashlight signals, and they often missed colored Very lights. All in all, there had not been a single successful night embarkation.

Frost was getting increasingly worried by the failures when he was asked in the Ward Room if he and his men could make themselves scarce the next morning during a visit by Admiral Lord Louis Mountbatten to inspect the ship. Frost and his men were accordingly busy with an exercise ashore when they heard the ship's whistle and saw the landing craft leaving her side. At the same time, messages came through on Company Headquarters' 38 set that the admiral urgently required their presence.

Mountbatten addressed all ranks of both services, plus Flight-Sergeant Cox. Until that moment the Navy had not known that its "guests" were parachutists or that what they were trying to do there was to be repeated in an action in which *Prins Albert* would take part. The admiral made it clear that a military exploit of small scale but of great significance depended upon absolute co-operation between the three services.

At Tilshead, "C" Company officers had been visited by a good many outsiders as well as by officers from the 1st Airborne Division. Politicians and scientists, soldiers and airmen, all had made much of them. Mountbatten struck them as being businesslike, matter-of-fact, and reserved. He saw Frost alone, after the meeting. Both were young men, the admiral unusually so for the responsibilities he carried. He asked Frost if he had any doubts or worries. Frost replied that he was unhappy about Private Newman.

Newman was at once sent for, and Mountbatten subjected him to what Frost admiringly considered to be a tremendous barrage in absolutely fluent German. Mountbatten stood him up in front of the desk and shouted at him. He answered quietly and smoothly. They shook hands, Newman was dismissed, and the admiral turned to Frost. "Take him along," he said. "You won't regret it for he's bound to be very useful. I judge him to be brave and intelligent. After all, he risks far more than you do, and of course he would never have been attached to you if he hadn't passed Security on every count." As for Newman, he remembers Lord Louis' interrogation on the ship as a pleasant and gentlemanly affair. He thought the admiral utterly charming.[2]

Next morning *Prins Albert* steamed down Loch Fyne and the parachutists caught a train from Gourock for Salisbury, bound for another dose of Tilshead Camp and hoping that the Glider Pilots' Regiment would be glad to see them. The ship steamed southwards, bound for Portsmouth.

As on their previous arrival at Tilshead, they were to meet General Browning the following morning, but this time they were to call on him by parachute. Frost subsequently confided his disgust to his diary:

"It's a bombing squadron with a fine operational record. But it has never dropped live parachutists. There was disorder and confusion and a mighty waste of time on the aerodrome—a shambles in fact. It was not until late in the day that we tumbled out on to a piece of brick-hard ground right in front of Syrancote House. By a miracle there was, thank God! no grief, not even a twisted ankle. The General said he was satisfied. More than I was. . . . Sergeant Grieve made the rest of us look slow, he's taught his Seaforths to deplane so amazingly quickly—yet another thing to get right. . . ."[3]

6

In the field of intelligence the British had long been skilled at calling an apple a turnip, a turnip a diamond, or (as in this case) a diamond a turnip. It was clearly impossible to hide twenty Chain Home stations with multiple 350-foot lattice steel towers, so they were passed off as radio stations. What kind of radio? A story was disseminated, and credited in both Germany and England, that the Royal Air Force was being strategically wrecked by a too-tight system of radio control from the ground. The Luftwaffe lost no opportunity of studying the RAF. The esprit de corps of the British service and its smartness, the practical neatness of its airfields, the officer training at Cranwell, the thoroughness of its ground engineers—all these were admired in Germany. But the Luftwaffe had had the new kinds of aircraft—heavy metal-winged bullets—before any other nation. It knew it was the best air force in the world. Its fighter pilots had enjoyed a taste of active service in the Spanish Civil War that had taught them much about tactics with the new type of aircraft. They noted with scorn that the RAF, which had not had the advantage of a Spanish try-out, was still clinging to the old-fashioned close-knit fighter formations that looked so attractive at air displays.

Throughout 1937 and 1938 England was overflown by unarmed Heinkel He 111s. Officially these aircraft were carrying out timetable and weather flights on behalf of Lufthansa, Germany's civil airline. In reality they were doing photoreconnaissance for the Target Data Unit Information Department of the German Air Ministry on Leipziger Strasse, Berlin. As a result, German bombers would be well docu-

mented when it came to briefings for the attack on England.
CH stations were photographed and described. It was noted
that the ancillary buildings were tucked in under the towers
and protected by sandbags and bomb-blast walls, and that
the towers themselves were enormously high. They would
make interesting strafe targets. The Stuka dive bombers
would enjoy them. But priority was given to pictures of naval
dockyards and of the bigger commercial ports—London, Bristol, Liverpool, Glasgow. Second on the list (showing the current German undervaluation of the Royal Air Force) were
RAF targets—all the airfields south of London and west to
Plymouth and Bristol, and the many big ones made or in the
making for the British bomber bases in East Anglia. A special section of the photographic coverage—and this was
particularly well presented and annotated—dealt with the
civilian factories that were now producing aircraft and aircraft
components and weapons.

General Wolfgang Martini, commanding Luftwaffe Signals, could not quite see the towers as part of a Dezimeter
Telegraphie-type radar system. Even so, he knew as a conscientious officer that something should be done about them.
Accordingly, he got agreement from the Air Staff for the employment of the huge dirigible *Graf Zeppelin* (LZ 130), sister
ship of the original *Graf*, as a flying radio laboratory. The
Graf's gondola was packed with high-frequency receivers, and
an aerial array was fixed below.[1]

General Martini was aboard when at the end of May 1939
the *Graf Zeppelin* unhooked from a Friedrichshafen mooring
and crossed the North Sea, making landfall at the mouth of
the Deben, just south of Bawdsey. At Canewdon, one of the
CH stations, and at Bawdsey (now withdrawn from the
Chain Home and merely a research radar station) the biggest
imaginable blip appeared on the radar screens and moved
majestically across them. The English tracking system, delighted to have such a jumbo practice run at the German
taxpayer's expense, followed the *Graf* mile by mile as it
thrummed its way north up the coast. The weather was thick,

and the airship reported its position to Frankfurt as off the Humber. At Fighter Command Headquarters in Bentley Priory this caused amusement, for the German navigator's reckoning was nine miles east of his true position; he was actually flying over England. The flight continued up the coast to the north of Scotland, then turned for home. It was a complete failure. All that Martini and his crew received for their pains was loud static. They thought the trouble might be caused by installation faults or by reflections from the skin of the airship.

A second run was made on August 2, 1939, in thick weather and high winds. The *Graf* cruised from Suffolk to the Orkneys and aroused a good deal of uneasiness, for she was sighted intermittently by coast guards and lighthouse keepers, yet this time there was no trace of her on the radar screens. Were the Germans, then, operating some form of jamming? We shall see later that when the occasion warranted, General Martini was a jamming artist, but it seems unlikely that he would have bothered to shield a simple scouting flight—for one thing, he did not yet know the CH frequencies.

The *Graf's* second flight was also abortive as a radio search. This made the Germans wonder if the British employed jamming to hide whatever those tall towers were transmitting.

One more *Messkorb* (measuring basket) flight was made by the *Graf*, but again no British transmissions were picked up.

Abwehr (meaning "defense") was originally the counter-espionage organization of the German Army. From 1921 the Abwehr, which had barely survived Germany's troubles after World War I, was steadily and carefully expanded, and its duties came to include offensive as well as defensive intelligence, in Germany and abroad. The service was deliberately decentralized. Its officers were chosen with care from the educated upper class. Its biggest secret station outside

Berlin was in the great seaport of Hamburg with its Anglo-
American and international connections.

The transmitting station was some distance from the receiving one. Highly trained operators manned the stations
on twenty-four-hour shifts. For communications and for detecting, filing, and decoding enemy transmissions, the radio
work of the Abwehr was of a high standard. The Abwehr
chief, Wilhelm Canaris, was an admiral. (He had ended his
long career in the Navy with the rank of captain). The son
of an industrialist, with some Italian blood in him, Canaris
was what the English call a gentleman. He was a reflective
man, in many ways a moralist, fiercely anti-Communist, a
leader who gave his men much scope and who expected and
obtained from them unlimited devotion.

In the fields of sabotage and fifth-column operations, particularly at the beginning of the war, the successes of the
Abwehr's "Brandenburg Commandos" were phenomenal. In
the more classical sides of its work, intelligence and espionage, it would appear to have succeeded wherever British
intelligence was weak—in France, the Low Countries, Spain
(Franco and Canaris were friends), Italy, Scandinavia (except for Sweden), all the Central European countries, the
Balkans, and the Middle East. It would appear to have failed
in the United Kingdom and the United States.

Those failures or partial failures are often blamed on the
hostile atmosphere in which the Abwehr had to work. For
as soon as the Nazis' own security service under Himmler,
the Sicherheitsdienst (SD), grew strong, it began to steal
power from the Abwehr, which it finally broke in pieces in
1944 by sending Canaris to a concentration camp where he
was executed. As one of the Abwehr's former officers, Paul
Leverkuehn, has written: "This political organisation (the
SD) had been one of the major factors in limiting the efficiency of the German Secret Service. . . . Once Canaris had
gone, the Abwehr soon began to disintegrate . . . while the
Nazi SD, using methods which to Canaris were anathema,

tried with only limited success to fulfil the functions of an Intelligence Service."[2]

As for the United Kingdom, opportunities for German espionage there were restricted (as compared with Europe), even in the 1930s. A strong mistrust of Germany existed following Britain's terrible losses in World War I, and this increased, for all the country's apparent torpor, as Hitler's power and evidence of his barbarity increased. The German governess or tutor had gone out of fashion, the German Hospital and centers of German trade in London were closely watched, and counterespionage both in Britain and in North America was much more intense than in other countries. The German ambassador in London, Joachim von Ribbentrop, was hostile to the Abwehr and insisted on running his own private intelligence service, which was penetrated by the British counterespionage. After the outbreak of war, and particularly in 1940, after Dunkirk, the United Kingdom bristled with arms, and its naturally suspicious and xenophobic inhabitants became more watchful than ever. The parachuting method for infiltrating agents, which the British used so successfully in Occupied Europe, was made nearly impossible for the Germans by the all-embracing watch of the British Observer Corps.

Abwehr cells in the United Kingdom must have existed, and some of them must have been able to communicate with Hamburg. But such cells cannot have got near the roots of British power or British secrets. Of this we can be sure: no German Intelligence source informed the German High Command of the remarkable extent to which the British had transformed their air defenses. The High Command suspected before the outset of war that the British possessed some crude form of D/T. Probably this suspicion arose from some report from Abwehr One TLw (Luftwaffentechnik) Section; but one of the Abwehr's increasing worries was that as political hostility to it grew, its reports tended to be ignored or disclaimed by politicomilitary figures like Reichsmarschall Göring.

Göring indeed now had his own Intelligence center, which had been formed by the amalgamation of the Target Information Department and the Foreign Air Forces Department, formerly two separate sections of the Air Ministry. Abteilung (Department) 5, the new amalgam, was commanded by Major Josef ("Beppo")[3] Schmid, a member of the Nazi Party and a protégé of the Air Chief of Staff, General Jeschonnek. Major Schmid apparently knew, as did many German bureaucrats and fighting men, that Hitler and Göring, though formidable, were avid for good news and readily angered by bad. Since obviously the Luftwaffe was vastly superior to any other air force, for a long time Major Schmid could conscientiously hand out only good news and forecast that the omens, too, were favorable. (The information issued by that department often had Wagnerian overtones.)

By the time Schmid took charge, the Germans already knew a great deal about the French Armée de l'Air; indeed, they knew more about French military and political weaknesses than did France's main ally, Britain. General Martini knew, for example, that Détection Électromagnétique (DEM), the French early-warning device, was quite useless. What Martini did not know was that the British were skeptical of DEM and offered to share their own radar system with their French ally.

On May 23, 1939, a French military mission to London was shown the subterranean filter room at Fighter Command Headquarters in Bentley Priory. The British radar machine had then been tested and retested, changed, and perfected. To say that the French officers were flabbergasted would be an understatement.

Early in June 1939 six French radio specialists, two of them from each service, came to England and went through the full radar course, including a study of manufacturing, installation, and maintenance. A scheme was promulgated in France to erect CH stations, but like so many other schemes at that time and earlier, nothing had come of it before the coming of the Germans. Even if Major Schmid had not been informed of that, he was able to read in up-to-date Intelligence reports of the irreparable damage done to France's strength by Léon Blum's Socialist government in 1936–37, when Air Minister Pierre Cot nationalized and all but wrecked a strong aircraft industry. Schmid could read, too, of the ineffectuality of an elderly French General Staff that commanded respect everywhere in the world save Germany and the Soviet Union. Russia, like Germany, was properly informed on all aspects of life, commerce, and armament in France, and should Russia be on Germany's side at the *beginning*, her agents could and would play a big part in the internal affairs of France.

Schmid was required to assess the air strengths of Poland, Russia, and Great Britain. The first two were comparatively easy. And he managed to get out a long report, *Studie Blau* (*Blue Study*), about the Royal Air Force and about British air defense and bomber strength. His sources were not numerous. Luftwaffe Generals Erhard Milch and Ernst Udet, for example, had made a successful official visit to England in 1937, when they had inspected RAF units and some of the air industry's factories and shadow factories. Both generals, but especially Milch, who was next in seniority to Göring, had been impressed. Milch had gone so far as to say that in time the Luftwaffe might find the RAF a hard nut to crack. (Göring was reported to be furious.) Otherwise, Schmid's sources were standard ones—air reconnaissance, the German air attaché's office in London, and the excellent English technical and semitechnical periodicals connected with aeronautics and the air industry. Throughout the Battle of Britain *Studie Blau* held its place as a German text book. *There was no mention in it of the new methods of warning, communication, and command that had been developed by the British.*

"Born of the spirit of the German airmen of the First World War," Göring, on September 1, 1939, began his Order of the Day heralding the German advance on Poland, "inspired by faith in our Führer and Commander in Chief, the Luftwaffe today is ready to carry out every command of our Führer with the speed of lightning and undreamed-of power." And Major Schmid's victory calculations were confirmed. The Luftwaffe smashed the Polish Air Force—four hundred aircraft—in two days, many of the Polish machines being caught by Stukas on the ground in the first twenty-four hours.

An unusually hard winter then precluded further German attacks. The Polish campaign had been systematically used and analyzed as an exercise as well as a conquest. The Germans now believed that they understood the tactics of a new form of war. One key to it, as in the Napoleonic and other wars, was good weather; but now the reason was different, since the main striking force was their air force. The spring weather forecasts, however, were entirely favorable. On April 9, 1940, German armor violated Danish neutrality at five in the morning, and by that evening Denmark was conquered, its Air Force strangled by sudden attack. Norway was a degree more complicated. The Luftwaffe was surprised to lose, in taking Norway, fifty-four bombers and thirty-five Junkers Ju 52 three-engined transports.

In May it was to be the turn of Belgium, Holland, and France. And it was a wonderful month of May. The sun that shone was a German sun. For France it pitilessly illuminated her unsuspected military decay. The German plan for attack was based on achieving complete air superiority in two days. This was done by Luftflotten 2 and 3, and both air fleets then turned to Army co-operation, the role for which they had been designed. The VIII Fliegerkorps' four hundred Stuka dive bombers performed as mobile artillery for the German armored thrust aimed at the Channel coast.

For the Royal Air Force the month from the beginning of the German attack in May to the end of the Dunkirk evacuation in June 1940 was the most painful of the whole war. Committed by the French Supreme Commander, General Maurice Gamelin, to a hurried advance into Belgium, the

RAF, like the British Expeditionary Force was caught in the worst of the chaos. The squadrons had no early-warning system. They were outclassed and outnumbered by a Luftwaffe acting "with the speed of lightning and undreamed-of power."

Fortunately for England, Hitler was nervous about using his armor at Dunkirk and gladly accepted Göring's assurances that the British evacuation could be extinguished from the air. Göring had 550 fighters in the area, most of them the formidable Messerschmitt Me 109s and he could deploy the bombers of the I, II, IV, and VIII Fliegerkorps. Even though hampered by the clouds of smoke that often shrouded Dunkirk, by the fierce ground fire of concentrated British troops, and by the hostile reaction of such ships as were armed, the Luftwaffe should have contained the evacuation. That they did not was a victory for the RAF, but neither the British nor the Germans regarded it as such. Air Marshal Dowding used his Spitfires for the first time over Dunkirk, but his fighters were operating outside their HF/DF and radar system. They had to mount old-fashioned defensive patrols, and they were still flying the tight prewar formations. British fighter losses were heavier than German. But the evacuation was completed.

In her greatest days, the Nazi conquerors claimed, England had never won a victory to compare with Germany's 1940 triumph. Paris had fallen. Hitler was there, in Paris. France, Belgium, and Holland were outstandingly rich and attractive countries. Nobody in Berlin gave exceptionally high priority or urgency to the planning of Operation Sealion, the invasion of England. But the Luftwaffe flowed like quicksilver into the Channel airfields of France—Luftflotten 2, 3, and 5 were to handle England.[4] But even in the Luftwaffe June was a month of détente, of triumph enjoyed. There was no realization that the hard work was only about to begin.

In May the Germans had captured at Boulogne a British

mobile radar set. Analysis of enemy military equipment was the responsibility of General Udet's Air Production Department, but General Martini's Signals Department was also asked to give an analysis. It was decided that the British set was crude and ill-made and that it worked on an impractical wavelength. In the same period Udet's department examined complete specimens of the Hurricane and Spitfire fighter planes captured on French airfields and declared them to be of poor quality and technically inferior to the Messerschmitt Me 109 and 110 fighters. The German analysts appeared to base this assessment on the lack of cannon armament (at that time) in the British machines, the lack of armor behind the pilot, and the fact that neither had fuel-injection engines. It was true that at high altitudes fuel injection gave the Me 109 an advantage, since it could go straight into a dive without risk of cutting out; but no consideration was given to the high rate of fire and the reliability of the eight Browning machine guns in the wings of each British fighter or to the handling qualities and the ability of both Hurricane and Spitfire to take punishment and keep fighting.

General Udet's findings were passed on to Major Schmid and were publicized. Radar, the Hurricane, the Spitfire, all dismissed as inferior! It was this kind of wrong thinking in German Intelligence that was to distract the Luftwaffe pilots during the Battle of Britain. As for the twin-engined Me 110, Göring's "destroyer," far from being superior to the Hurricane or Spitfire, it was all but helpless before them, and its failure, since it had a longer range than the redoubtable Me 109, was a severe blow to the Luftwaffe. Another failure of German Intelligence was at the French Air Ministry in Paris, where the vital lead into British radar secrets was totally missed. The French, contrary to their security promises to the British, had actually put out tenders with commercial contractors for the erection of CH-type stations on the Biscay coast.

By the end of June 1940 Göring had ordered the II and VIII Fliegerkorps to sweep the English Channel and obtain deep air supremacy. General Martini had come to the Channel coast with his Signals sections and some German radar had moved in. There were three Freya radar stations in northern France, and a Seetakt gun-laying ranger had been installed near Cape Gris-Nez to sharpen the gunnery attacks on British convoys negotiating the Straits of Dover.

Action in war where two strong combatants are involved is inclined to be self-stoking, and while Dowding jealously husbanded his fighters in the convoy battles, knowing quite well what the enemy was after and hating the high-flying Me 109 cover, Fighter Command was kept so busy that the British regarded July 10 as the beginning of the Battle of Britain.

Naturally enough, the Germans were overconfident. Major Beppo Schmid's optimism went right through the service. Victory over Britain might prove bloodier than it had over other conquered countries, but it was inevitable.

Then a discordant voice was raised. It was the voice of General Martini. Now that there was a great deal of air activity (even if the official Eagle Day, on which the all-out battle was to begin, had not yet been fixed), Luftwaffe Signals' monitors had had a surprise. On the twelve-meter band the ether pulsated with signals emanating from the tall towers of the CH stations—the radar twilight. And when the German squadrons flew northward across the water, Martini's men heard on the high frequencies the process of RAF fighter squadrons being talked into battle. It was evident, though how it came about was yet a mystery, that British officers sitting somewhere near London were actually "seeing" the Germans take off from runways lying well back in France. The British obviously thought they knew exactly where their own fighters were, even when they were airborne. The German monitoring staffs also heard the pilots answering the controllers and talking to their companions. And often the British leader would cry into his microphone, "Tally ho! . . . Heinkels with 109s . . . Tally ho!"

Martini and his staff knew they were hearing something important; that the British had developed an original form

of aerial defense. But the German High Command refused
to be ruffled. Worry made cowards. Boldness brought vic-
tories. Once more Major Schmid's Abteilung 5, in an appre-
ciation of the British defense issued to the three attacking
Luftflotten and the two Fliegerkorps, told the senior officers
what they wanted to hear. "Because the British fighters are
controlled from the ground by radiotelephone, their units
are tied to their respective ground stations and are therefore
restricted in mobility even if, as is likely, the ground stations
are sometimes mobile. It follows that the forming of a strong
fighter force at crucial points and at crucial times is unlikely. There will be confusion in the defense during mass
attacks . . ."

This facile and erroneous interpretation of the radar
twilight, the chatter, the pips, and the squeaks was to boom-
erang on Abteilung 5, particularly in conjunction with 5's
habit of publicizing exaggerated claims of British losses.[5]
What was taken to be "restrictive" control was in fact a control that gave the outnumbered British pilots some time to
rest on the ground and that could draw them rapidly from
a wide area to a narrow front. German pilots, continually
hearing and reading that hundreds of Spitfires and Hurricanes had been destroyed, grew exasperated as they continued to be met on nearly every sortie by more and yet
more Spitfires and Hurricanes.

And Martini's monitors came to loathe the all but incomprehensible phrase "Tally ho!"

Göring told his entourage, and Hitler, that all he needed
to finish off England with his Eagles was one week of such
glorious weather as they had enjoyed over France in May.
Any English farmer could have told him that August is one
of the most fickle months in the English calendar. In the end
he lost patience and named August 13 as his Eagle Day, the
official start of a fight that had been going on for more than a
month. The day before, the twelfth, was a dangerous day
for England.

Heavy and repeated German attacks across the Channel began at seven-thirty in the morning. At nine o'clock five British radar stations were bombed, and soon after fifteen Junkers Ju 88s skillfully lacerated Ventnor CH station on the Isle of Wight. Every building at Ventnor was damaged and on fire. While Dover, Pevensey (Sussex), and Rye (Sussex) CH stations suffered badly, the controls, ancillaries, and power lines at Ventnor were completely knocked out. Every other radar station was operational by nightfall, but Ventnor could not be resuscitated.

On Eagle Day the Germans, who did not realize how well they had done the day before, flew 1,485 sorties, and things went ill for them. Although Luftwaffe Supreme Command claimed seventy Hurricanes and Spitfires and eighteen Blenheim fighter-bombers destroyed, the true figures were thirteen RAF aircraft destroyed and forty-five German. Many of the forty-five were Stukas (Ju 87s), and from the radar viewpoint that was important. Until now the Stuka had been a war winner, but what happened in just five minutes on Eagle Day was typical of the battle as a whole: thirteen Spitfires of 609 Squadron saw a formation of Stukas heading for Middle Wallop aerodrome in Hampshire under a cover of Me 109s. The Messerschmitts were already involved with other British fighters. The Spitfires dived through them, bringing down one Me 109 and destroying *nine* Stukas.

August 15 was a field day for the Chain Home. Luftwaffe Supreme Command decided to attack on three fronts. Luftflotte 5 in Norway and Denmark sent bombers across the North Sea; the Chain Home picked them all up at full range, and squadron after squadron of fighters went up to destroy them. The Luftwaffe launched 1,786 sorties on August 15. Fighter Command on that day flew 974, lost thirty-four aircraft, and claimed 182 enemy bombers, but actually shot down seventy-five.

There were grim faces at Karinhall, where an irascible Göring had summoned his junior commanders to a conference. That day the Luftwaffe had lost every type of aircraft that was being used against England—Dornier Do 17; Heinkel He 59, 111, 115; Junkers Ju 87, 88; Messerschmitt Me 109, 110; and Arado 196. Göring, having called for a frank discussion, chose to blame his fighter pilots for failing to protect their bombers, particularly the Stukas, which he loved. He was infuriated by their reports that the Me 110 was no match for either British fighter and that at low altitudes the Hurricane was as good as, and the Spitfire possibly superior to, the Me 109. Another aspect of the British campaign enraged him: photographs showed that British forward airfields, previously reported "destroyed" or "obliterated," were still being used. Photographs also showed—and this was indeed alarming—that German daylight bombing under pressure was not precise and reliable, as it had been in the other campaigns when air supremacy had been instantly won. He turned to the question of losses. Too many Luftwaffe officers had died or had been shot down over England; from that day on there was to be a maximum of one officer in each aircrew. . . . He was asked if he stood by his directive that, in the night bombing of England the special squadron, Kampfgruppe 100, should be used. Yes, Göring answered, it must be used. It was pointed out that there was a lot of secret equipment in each He 111 of Kampfgruppe 100. Equipment! There had been too much talk about British equipment. Wars were won by men, not by equipment.

From England's point of view, indeed from any point of view, the most important of Göring's decisions at that important conference on August 15 concerned radar. "It is doubtful," he said, "if there is any sense in continuing the attacks on Dezimeter Telegraphie stations, since not one of those so far attacked has stopped transmitting." Yet, even as he spoke, engineers, contractors, electricians, scientists, RAF specialists, and GPO secret squads were toiling on the Isle of Wight, where Ventnor CH had been knocked out and was still off the air.

Even if Göring did think it a waste of time, the following day Ventnor was again dive bombed and was again

severely mauled. It was not until seven days later, when a
mobile station began to operate at Bembridge, that the
Ventnor gap in the CH system was plugged.

Luftflotten 2 and 3 attacked savagely across the Channel
on August 18. Poling CH station, on the serene Sussex Downs
behind Littlehampton, was lashed by Stukas. Ninety bombs
fell inside its perimeter. But no other radar stations were
attacked, and again Stukas were lost—twelve of them inside
ten hours. And the hitherto victorious angular two-seater,
with its vulture profile and screaming dive was removed from
the Battle of Britain. Six Stuka groups had been lined up for
the attack, but by the end of that crucial month, August,
they had all been withdrawn to be used on other fronts where
the opposition was less hot.

So the battle burned on and radar played its essential part,
until the attacker, always under pressure and ill-prepared
mentally to settle down and fight coolly against such resistance, made the final error of turning to attack London.

7

No battle has ever been so public as the Battle of Britain. The bombs, the bullets, the spent cases, the burning aircraft, the pilots, German and British, living and dead, fell among the British people. One doubts whether the Royal Air Force could have fought so well had it not had such constant and warm support from the whole population, from the other services, from the government, from factory and inn, field, hospital, and shop. It was the country's battle for survival; it was the people's affair.

Increasingly, as the daylight battle continued, the enemy droned and rumbled over by night. It is hard to be courageous at night, and the wail of the sirens, the harsh noise of the guns, the whistle and crump of bombs made it still harder. The people fought to get used to these hateful and unnatural things. Only a handful of them in high places knew that Britain had entered the war quite unready for such night attacks. A secret battle was being fought, and never made public, to protect the country from German night bombing of great potential menace.

In June 1940, just before the Battle of Britain began, Flight-Lieutenant H. E. Bufton was suddenly posted from his bomber squadron to the Experimental (Wireless and Electrical) Flight at Boscombe Down on Salisbury Plain.[1] He was an experienced instructor in the use of the German blind-approach Lorenz equipment which was common to both the RAF and the Luftwaffe. He knew he had been called to Boscombe for something special, but he felt he had come down in the world when he was assigned an Anson training aircraft into which had been fitted an American short-wave receiver of the type used by the Chicago Police. Nineteen days before the air attack on England began, Bufton learned the true nature of his assignment. He received a call from R. S. Blucke, now a squadron leader, who had once been his blind-approach instructor, telling him that he was to hunt for a beam—a beam sent over England from Germany.

He was to hunt for it on the 30- and 31.5-megacycle bands of his radio and geographically over the area between Huntingdon and Lincoln, in east-central England. When Bufton pointed out the limited range of the Anson he was told he might fly to Wyton, Huntingdonshire, refuel there, and take off in the late evening. If the beam existed, it was perhaps switched off through the daylight hours.

It was a lovely summer night, the shortest night of a fateful year for England and for Germany. Bufton's Anson climbed slowly—it was never an exciting aircraft—to between four and five thousand feet.

There Bufton and his companion, Corporal John Mackie, heard clear signals—dots on 31.5 megacycles.

He knew exactly what to look for. He brought the aircraft's nose to the north. The night sky was empty. No glimmer from the factories below, working through the night. . . . Still dots. . . . After a few minutes they crossed what he was looking for—a beam, or continuous note. Then, as he again expected, they were flying through a zone of dashes. The old Anson was no longer dull. . . . More dashes. . . . Then no signal. His job now was to plot the beam and if possible estimate its width. And up there he understood that he was charting what amounted to a secret road leading from Germany to the blacked-out multiple heart of industrial England. Beneath him were the machines and the skilled workers the Germans would seek to destroy.

He came down for fuel at Wyton, flew on immediately to Boscombe Down, and hurried to the telephone. He had orders to call Blucke, no matter what the hour. Blucke merely told him to get some sleep and to be at the Air Ministry in London early next morning. Then Squadron-Leader Blucke telephoned a man who spent his days at the Air Ministry but who slept in Richmond, Dr. R. V. Jones.

Jones, it will be recalled, had done important research in infrared methods for detecting aircraft, working in the Clarendon Laboratory at Oxford. Technically speaking, he had been attached to the Air Ministry Staff from 1936, and both Cherwell and Tizard were aware of his powers. He did a spell of duty in the Air Ministry from April to July 1938, and during that short period A. E. Woodward-Nutt, at that time Secretary of the vital Tizard Committee (he had succeeded Wimperis), noticed that Jones "continually got himself mixed up with Intelligence matters" and appeared to have a flair. Woodward-Nutt also had worked on research at the Air Defence Experimental Department, Farnborough, with Jones and knew him well. It was at his suggestion, strongly supported by Tizard, that Jones was brought back to the Air Ministry and allocated a small office, but no secretary, as "a scientist with a special interest in German weapons." His beginnings afford a contrast with the more comfortable and apparently more assured ones of Major Schmid in Berlin. Those who have studied the air war in any detail know that Jones's appointment was a crucial one, although at first it did not seem so to any but Jones himself. The terms of his employment were scarcely defined, and nine men out of ten would have failed to bring the new job to life.

Jones was the tenth man. He had been much influenced by his parents, who were deeply suspicious of German intentions after the 1914–18 war. "Also relevant," Jones says "were the views of my headmaster at Alleyn's School on the theory of forgiveness. He held that for a sinner to be forgiven, it was necessary that he should first repent. Since the Germans had never expressed repentance for the First World War, but only sorrow and dismay that they had lost it, they could not be forgiven for it. 'And mark my words,' he would say, 'as soon as they are ready, they'll be at it again.' So I was well alerted, even before going to Oxford."[2]

To all his research and his advice—"the test of a good Intelligence Service in war is not merely that you are right, but that you persuade your operational or research staff to take the right countermeasures"—Jones brought the logic and, even more important, the honesty of the scientist. Frequently he had to lay before the Air Ministry, the War Cabinet, and the defense scientists disagreeable evidence that they at first refused to credit. As he later wrote: "The path of truthful duty is not easy; there were several attempts to get me removed from my post because of my insistence on unpalatable facts being faced. I survived—but I might not have done so had the situation not been so serious."[3] And as his deductions and discoveries proved to be accurate, his power grew.

"My first Intelligence task in 1939," Jones says, "was to report on the 'secret weapon' which Hitler was alleged to have vaunted in an early war speech. After assessing the evidence and examining what he had actually said (rather than what he had been reported to have said), I concluded that he was not referring to a special weapon. I had just written my report (which was due to go to the Prime Minister, Mr. Chamberlain) but had not circulated it, when the news of the magnetic mine broke. A report from Naval Intelligence came in that a German naval officer had said this was indeed the 'secret weapon.' It was tempting to alter my report. But I decided that this one remark ought not to be equated in weight to all my previous analysis, and so I rejected it—as it turned out, correctly. . . . I have seen committees, even up to cabinet level, almost stampeded by isolated pieces of 'stop-press' information, and there is no doubt that timing is an important device in the art of the advocate. But it should be eschewed in analysis proper."[4]

Jones's next problem was the Oslo Report, as it has come to be called, whose provenance is still a well-kept secret.

"At times of alarm, such as followed the outbreak of war and Hitler's speech, informers crop up in large numbers," Jones told the Royal United Services Institution on February 19, 1947. "Much of this information is useless, but soon after Hitler's speech one casual source came up whose information was of remarkable interest. It happened this way. Our naval attaché in Oslo received an anonymous letter telling him that if we would like a report on German technical developments all we need do was to alter the preamble on our German news broadcast on a certain evening, so as to say, 'Hier ist London,' instead of whatever we usually said. We duly altered the preamble."

On November 4, 1939, the naval attaché in Oslo found on his desk a packet of documents in German purporting to describe the new weapons at the disposal of the Reich. The sender described himself as "a Friendly German scientist."

"He told us," Jones said, "that the Germans had two kinds of radar equipment, that large rockets were being developed, that there was an important experimental station at Peenemunde, and that rocket-propelled gliding bombs were being tried there. There was also other information—so much of it in fact that many of our people argued it must be a plant, because no one man could possibly have known of all the developments that the report described. But as the war progressed, and one development after another made its appearance, it was obvious that the report was largely correct; and in the few dull moments of the war I used to look up the Oslo Report to see what was coming along next."[5]

In December 1939 Jones drew up a report of his own. It suggested a drastic change in the structure of Intelligence, particularly scientific Intelligence. He wanted a single body, directed by a single man, which would advise all three services. "But the importance of scientific Intelligence was not yet appreciated. I failed to get an inter-service organization. I also failed to get any help at all, even a secretary." His effort to get a more logical framework having been rejected, he decided that "I would go on alone, to see whether I could prove my beliefs by practical demonstration. . . . The demonstration came even sooner than I had expected."

As 1940 began and what was popularly called the "phony war" continued, Jones came to believe that the Germans had a system using radio beams with which they hoped to bomb accurately at night. In his searches of German material he had come across the word "*Knickebein*" (meaning a "crooked leg"). The Germans were ridiculously informative with their code names. "*Knickebein*" did sound like a description of a beam or of its emitter. Making his interest known through the Directorate of Intelligence, he waited and watched until March, when a German reconnaissance aircraft, a Heinkel He 111 of KG (Kampfgruppe) 26, was shot down near Scapa Flow. The navigator's notes were soon with Jones. He read:

> NAVIGATION
> *Radio beacons working on Beacon Plan A.*
> *Additionally from 0600 Beacon Dunhen.*
> *Light beacon after dark.*
> *Radio beacon Knickebein from 0600 on 315.*

RAF interrogation of the comparatively few German airmen captured over British territory in those early days was both skillful and sensitive. Soon after Jones read the notes translated above, a German prisoner said that the beam sent out by a Knickebein was so exact that two of them could pinpoint a London target with an accuracy of less than a thousand meters. He said, further, that Knickebein in some ways "resembled X-Gerät" (obviously taking it for granted that the British were familiar with both).

When another He 111 of KG 26 was brought down, a diary was taken from the wreckage and flown to London. Jones read:

> *March 5: Two thirds of the Flight on leave. Afternoon training on Knickebein, collapsible boats, etc.*

Going back through the files, he found that a He 111 had force-landed near Edinburgh back in October 1939. He obtained the complete report on the examination of the aircraft by Farnborough experts, who had recorded that the Heinkel's Lorenz blind-landing set was many times more sensitive than its RAF equivalent. If German aircraft picked up Knickebein beams sent from Germany on their extra-sensitive Lorenz receivers, that would bear out Woodward-Nutt's theories at Farnborough. He had maintained that a radio transmission could be condensed into an exceptionally narrow, long-reaching beam.

Had Jones had the power in March 1940, he would have ordered up aircraft with listening sets to hunt for Knickebein beams. But he was new and junior. He must, as he said later, not bark until he knew his bark would be accepted as a danger signal. He would be patient, for he held two keys to the power chamber—both Tizard and Cherwell knew him and, he believed, liked him.

Cherwell sent for him on June 12. He wanted to know if Jones believed that the Germans had radar. Jones countered by suggesting the possibility that the Germans had radio-beam aids for their night bombers. Cherwell argued against it. He said that all known evidence showed that radio waves on the 30 megacycles frequency or thereabouts (Jones had cited the frequency mentioned in the captured notes and observed on the Edinburgh Heinkel's Lorenz receiver) traveled in straight lines through space rather than curving with the earth's surface. It would be impossible, therefore, for Knickebein beams to reach the Midlands let alone Scapa Flow.

But next day Jones called again on Cherwell. He had found an unpublished paper by Thomas Eckersley, a scientific adviser to the Marconi Company and a respected expert at the Air Ministry. From Eckersley's graphs, it seemed that radio beams from Germany could be received by aircraft over much of Britain. Cherwell, now won over to Jones's theory, sat down and wrote an "Urgent" memo to Churchill:

There seems to be reason to suppose that the Germans have some type of radio device with which they hope to find their targets. . . . It is vital to investigate and to discover what the wavelength is. If we knew this, we could devise a means to mislead them. . . . If they use a sharp beam this could be made ineffective. . . .

Churchill wrote across the bottom of Cherwell's memo, "This seems to be intriguing, and I hope you will have it thoroughly examined." He had it taken to the Secretary of State for Air, Sir Archibald Sinclair, who the next day, Friday, June 14, asked Air Marshal Sir Philip Joubert de la Ferté to form a committee of inquiry. The following day the committee met and did exactly what Jones would have done had he then had the authority. They put Squadron Leader Blucke (who in 1936 had done the first radar-proving flight in the Heyford bomber over Daventry) in charge of the flying side of the investigation. Three Ansons were to be fitted with suitable receivers and experienced Lorenz-trained pilots were to be chosen by Blucke. . . . As the committee sat, the German Army was marching into Paris.

By now, another captured German airman had, under interrogation, spoken of Knickebein and had confirmed that Knickebein beams were picked up on the adapted Lorenz receivers in German aircraft. And on Tuesday, June 18, papers from a German aircraft shot down weeks earlier in France were on Jones's desk. In them he found:

Long-range Radio Beacon =	VHF [very high frequency]
1st Knickebein	54°39'
	8°57'
2nd Knickebein	51°47'5"
	6° 6'

Transferring the Knickebein positions to the map of Germany, he found the first was at Bredstedt, in Schleswig-Holstein, and the second near Kleve, near the Dutch frontier in Rhein-Wesphalia. Scapa Flow's bearing from the Bredstedt position was 315°, so that tallied with the navigator's notes retrieved from the He 111 in March. The two Knicke-bein positions were sufficiently far apart to give reasonable cross-bearing of "fixes" on most important targets in Britain.

Next, Jones got the notes of a dead German radio operator. A minelaying Heinkel of KG 4 had been shot down. At the head of his list of German radio beacons, with their frequencies, the dead man had written "Knickebein, Kleve, 31.5." The RAF monitoring service confirmed that all the frequencies for the beacons were correct for the night concerned.

And finally, on the morning of June 20, a He 111 with twin Jumo 211 motors, a new type, was winged by a fighter over southeastern England. The radio operator landed by parachute. Before he was found, he tore his working notes into very small pieces which he was burying when his captors came upon him. An astute RAF Intelligence NCO saved every scrap of paper and by three the next morning these had been pasted together and were on their way to London. Jones read:

VHF	54°38'7"	North	Stollberg
Knicke	8°56'8"	East	
	51°	N	(30 mc/s)
	1°30'	Eqms	
Cleve	51°47'4"	N	
	6° 2'	E	
	55°	N	(31.5 mc/s)
	2°	Eqms	

This timely jigsaw confirmed for Jones the positions of two Knickebein stations. That the last positions were given more accurately than the earlier ones (the beam apparently *did* narrow) and that the modern city Kleve was spelled in them with the old-fashioned C was a better Intelligence confirmation than exact conformity would have been. The two other positions were out in the North Sea, possibly turning points.

Later that same morning, June 21, Jones returned to his office in the Air Ministry building and found a note asking him to report immediately at the Cabinet Room, 10 Downing Street. Suspecting that someone was playing a joke, he telephoned the Ministry's executive department. It was genuine! They had been hunting for him everywhere. Grabbing his papers, he tore round to Downing Street. He was appallingly late. The special meeting called by Mr. Churchill had been in process for half an hour. The door was opened for him and he hurried in, making his apologies to the Prime Minister.

Churchill sat at one side of the table, with Lord Cherwell on his left hand and Lord Beaverbrook, the owner of Express Newspapers and the new Minister of Aircraft Production, on his right. Facing the redoubtable trio were Sir Archibald Sinclair (Secretary of State for Air), Air Chief Marshal Sir Cyril Newall (Chief of Air Staff), Tizard (Newall's scientific adviser), Watson-Watt (now representing Communications at the Air Ministry), and Air Marshals Portal and Dowding (Commanders in Chief, Bomber and Fighter Commands). The meeting was obviously urgent and tense and seemed more so because the proceedings were secret. No secretary was present and no minutes were taken.

As Jones entered, Cherwell beckoned to him to sit among the gods at the emptier side of the table. But the young man hesitated. He would not take sides. Tizard was as much a friend as Cherwell was, and there was hostility in the air. He sat down alone, at the end of the table nearest the door.

An argument was continuing. . . . Did the beams exist or didn't they? Tizard was skeptical. The Prime Minister turned to look down the table. He asked Jones a technical question and Jones, feeling he could not sensibly answer it out of context, said, "Hadn't I better tell you the story from the beginning, sir?"

He laid before them the evidence from German aircraft

and aircrew given above and mentioned, as he had previously done to Cherwell alone, the deductions of Eckersley, the Marconi scientist. He convinced the meeting. And Churchill, marveling at the size and vitality of the speaker, as well as at his fresh face and extreme youth, found a jingle from Richard Barham's *The Ingoldsby Legends* running through his head. . . .

> But now one Mr. Jones
> Comes forth and depones
> That, fifteen years since, he had heard certain groans
> On his way to Stonehenge (to examine the stones
> Described in a work of the late Sir John Soane's),
> That he'd followed the moans,
> And led by their tones,
> Found a raven a-picking a drummer boy's bones.[6]

The meeting at Number 10 was both good and bad for the country. In one way it was providential, since it ensured maximum effort against the German devices. In another way it was harmful. For, certainly, quite unintentionally, Jones by his evidence had wounded, at any rate in Churchill's view, the prestige of the country's finest defense scientist, Tizard. Tizard had been dubious in his assessment of the possibility of such beams (as had Cherwell, until Jones showed him Eckersley's graphs). We have seen how vital Tizard was in the development of radar, and at this moment in 1940 his potential as a war winner was still boundless. At the Prime Minister's shoulder sat the subtle and implacable Cherwell. And whatever exactly transpired in the unrecorded meeting, Tizard decided that after it his position as Scientific Adviser to the Chief of Air Staff was impossible. He went to his club, the Athenaeum, and in that high and formal edifice, austere and rather dusty because of the wartime shortages of staff, he wrote a letter of resignation. He carried the letter to his chief, Sir Cyril Newall, that same evening, and Newall, appearing to agree with him, accepted it. . . .

In less than a month Sir Henry Tizard was asked to lead

the vastly important scientific mission to the United States that he had been advocating for nine months. He carried with him great gifts in the form of British secrets, including that of the war winner, the cavity magnetron tube.[7] It was an honorable task, and nobody could have been more worthy of it than he; yet most British scientists, had they known him to be out of the country, would have felt the weaker for his absence. And when he returned his services were parsimoniously used.

On leaving the meeting at Number 10, Jones returned to the Air Ministry where, in the office of the Director of Signals, Air Commodore C. V. Nutting, he happened to meet the Marconi expert Eckersley. That morning, basing his evidence partly on Eckersley's paper, he had convinced the country's leaders that the Knickebein danger existed. But *Eckersley himself now doubted.* Then what about that series of graphs? Jones asked. Oh, those graphs! Eckersley renounced them. He now felt that he had been stretching theory. He now honestly doubted if radio signals on the 30-megacycle band would curve round the earth.

While Jones was ruefully considering this reversal and balancing it against his other evidence, the significance of Eckersley's denial had not been lost on the others present. Indeed, the Deputy Director of Signals, Air Commodore O. G. W. G. Lywood, had his hand on the telephone. He thought that Blucke's third flight in search of the German beam could be canceled.

"Although I was shaken by Eckersley's statement," Jones says, "I staked everything on the flight. I told Lywood that the Prime Minister had given orders for the flight, and that if it were cancelled I would see that he knew who had stopped it. I then went home and spent one of the most miserable nights of my life. . . ."[8]

As Jones left the Air Ministry to catch a train to Richmond, Flight Lieutenant Bufton and Corporal Mackie were flying from Boscombe Down to Wyton, prior to the start of their night's search.

8

During his listening watch in Paris on January 24, 1942, the Free French agent Robert Delattre, whose code name was "Bob," took down two messages from headquarters in London. That evening, in a rented flat in the Avenue de La Motte-Picquet, Bob's chief, the legendary Rémy, decoded the messages with the help of his wife, Édith.[1] Open on the table before them lay Michelin Map No. 52, which placed in its long rectangle the towns of Le Havre, Rouen, Beauvais, Abbeville, and Amiens. It was rare for an important agent such as Rémy to decode messages; but Rémy was an unusual man, and furthermore he, like his wife, had a passion for codes. At last they read:

> 24.1.42   TO RAYMOND   CODE A   NO 49
> need information indicated questionnaire message that follows stop inform us within fortyeight hours delay necessary obtain this information observing following conditions firstly do not act yourself nor gravely risk members your organisation secondly do not compromise success operation julie stop to deceive boches in event your agent taken he be ready to reply same question not only for place chosen but for three or four other similar places on coast stop to follow. . . .

Rémy was addressed as "Raymond" in coded messages. "Operation Julie" was the code name for the Lysander pick-up of Rémy himself in the next full-moon period. He was wanted in London for consultation with "Passy" (Major André Dewawrin) who commanded the Bureau Central de Renseignement, et d'Action (BCRA) of General de Gaulle. The continuation message was:

24.1.42   TO RAYMOND   CODE A   NO 50
questionnaire firstly position and number machineguns defend-
ing cliff road at theuville repeat theuville on coast between cap
antifer and saint jouin latter being seventeen kilometres north
le havre secondly what other defences thirdly number and state
preparedness defenders stop are they on qui vive stop firstclass
troops or old men stop fourthly where are they quartered fifthly
existence and positions barbed wire [message] ends

Rémy (Gilbert Renault) was one of the most remarkable
of the Frenchmen who joined De Gaulle when France fell
to the Germans in June 1940. At the outset of war the French
Army, to Rémy's fury, had rejected his services as a com-
batant—he was middle-aged, had four children, and was
wanted for propaganda and bureaucratic work.

When Paris fell he and his family were staying with his
mother at Vannes. A fortnight earlier Édith had told him
that she was carrying his fifth child. But they agreed that it
was his duty to join De Gaulle.

He took with him his youngest brother, Claude. Five days
after leaving Vannes, the pair landed from a fishing boat
at Falmouth and at once made for London and General de
Gaulle's headquarters in St. Stephen's House.

Rémy intended to make up for those frustrating months
at the beginning of the war when they had refused to let him
do anything. He at once volunteered for a secret mission and
was accepted, he says, because his passport was covered with
Spanish visas dating from a period of his life when he had
been preparing to make a film about Christopher Columbus.
He was quickly sent back to France through Portugal and
Spain, but not before seeing Claude commissioned in the
Gaullist forces. The selection of Rémy was a brilliant one,
even by Passy's standards, because he was a genuine and
talented person, with the luck of the devil.

A modest man, supremely friendly, whose religion moti-
vated his every calculation, decision, act, Rémy thus describes
his beginning as an agent: "I would never have been able to
carry out this assignment in a foreign country or for a less

righteous cause. But I was on my own soil, among Frenchmen with whom the enemy could not ingratiate himself, and
whom he could not intimidate. . . . From the day when Jean
Fleuret, former union leader of the Pilots of the Port of
Bordeaux, had agreed to work with me"—note that Rémy
says *with* rather than *for*—"I realised that my task would be
easy. I only had to find, in the ports, the railways, the factories, the administrations, men and women of good will
—and I would receive a mass of valuable information which
would surpass all hopes. So, mesh by mesh, was woven my
network. My part consisted simply in convincing people who
were eager to be convinced for their country's sake, then in
holding all together. *Naturally, my family were among the
first to join our ranks. . . .*" And they were destined to
undergo great suffering. After a long imprisonment in Fresnes,
Romainville, and Compiègne, his mother and his sisters
Hélène, Jacqueline, and Madeleine were freed, but his sisters
May and Isabelle were deported to the female concentration
camp of Ravensbrück. His brother Philippe, also deported
by the Germans, was killed in Lübeck harbor a few hours
before the British Army arrived there in 1945.

Convinced that he and his followers were a brotherhood of
men favored by God, Rémy called his group the CND (Confrérie Notre-Dame). When he left London, General de Gaulle
had taken him by the hand and had said firmly, "Au revoir,
Raymond, I am counting on you." It was a tall order; Rémy
had been given the whole Atlantic side of France to cover,
from Hendaye up to Brest. He had accomplished wonders in
that enormous area over a period of a year when the equally
important Réseau Saint-Jacques network, run by his friend
Maurice Duclos and covering the north coast of France from
Brest to Dunkirk, was infiltrated and totally destroyed. From
London, Passy asked CND to take over the latter network's
information services. He began to build again, cleverly sim-
plifying all moves and problems. He describes his task as
"putting living tile upon living tile." Some of his "tiles" were
sent from London, like the French radio operator Bob, who

had been trained in the schools of SOE.[2] Most were recruited in their home areas from the professional classes (many were architects), from the officer class, from the aristocracy and the bourgeoisie, from the peasants, and from those in commerce.

One of Rémy's recruits in the area taken over from Duclos was Roger Dumont, an officer of the Armée de l'Air. Inspired by Pol Roger champagne, Rémy "gave him the code name 'Pol' and told him he would lead our Luftwaffe section." Shortly after taking over this work, Pol had laid before Rémy a detailed report from his friend Roger Hérisse which described closely guarded German radio installations just north of Bruneval.

Pol was in Paris on January 24 when Rémy received the two code messages from London. He summoned Pol, and together they pored over the two "Theuville" messages and the Michelin map. The text of the second message, they decided, knocked out the theory of air attack. Apparently, "they" were thinking in terms of a raid either with commandos landed from the sea or with parachutists. What was there at Bruneval, or Theuville, that was so important to "them" in England? Thinking this over, Rémy was of the opinion that nobody should attempt to get near the actual German installations.

Rémy decided against trying to understand the two messages. Instead, he instructed Pol simply to get the information "they" requested, cautioning him to exercise extreme discretion. The mission, Pol estimated, would take about two weeks.

9

If it went to work at night, Bomber Command had been expected to find its targets by dead reckoning and astral navigation, an uncertain procedure. Flight Lieutenant Bufton therefore administered a profound shock at the Air Ministry when, on the morning of June 22, 1940, he described to very senior officers and defense scientists the clarity, power, and narrowness of the German beam.

Churchill refused to be dismayed; he had at his elbow his scientist-confidant Cherwell, who assured him that any radio beam sent from 260 miles away was itself vulnerable. The first thing to do was to create a defense unit with complete civil and military authority, facilities, aircraft, and all the scientific help it could use. The unit, 80 Wing, established itself at Garston Aerodrome and under Wing Commander E. B. Addison set about a defense task that, with some frankness, was code-named "Headache."

Short-wave sets established on top of the Chain Home towers could pick up the German beams. The occupants of those alarming crow's nests were connected by telephone with Wing Commander Blucke, now climbing in rank as his duties multiplied. He sat in the center of the web, Fighter Command Headquarters, Bentley Priory. "When about dusk the German beams were switched on, the men on the towers would be able to pick them up and let us know, for instance, if a beam was going between Tower A and Tower B," Blucke has explained. "That would give us a clue to the beam's position, and one of our chaps would go up in an Anson and fly back and forth until he picked up the beam, which could then be plotted."[1]

After the fall of France, British Intelligence had been caught in a vacuum from which it instantly began to emerge when it became clear to Europe that the war was not yet lost. Within three weeks of Bufton's discovery flight, Dr. Jones knew about Knickebein stations near Cherbourg and Calais; a third, near Dieppe, began testing on August 23, 1940.

A first solution might have been bombing, but although the aerials were massive, the transmitters were the smallest of targets and bombing, then as now, was by its very nature imprecise. As to defense against Knickebein, electrodiathermy sets used in British hospitals to cauterize wounds were requisitioned and altered to transmit on Knickebein frequencies. They were then installed in police stations where twenty-four hour watches were kept. The policemen only switched on when asked to do so by 80 Wing. Then Lorenz blind-approach transmitters were modified and strategically placed. They were thought to have a certain usefulness in distorting the beams over a short range. In addition, 80 Wing set up jamming beacons, or "Meacons." In Germany, the Low Countries, France, and Norway the Luftwaffe could navigate on more than eighty radio beacons. The Meacons, strategically sited in Britain, were set daily to German frequencies and served to complicate matters for Luftwaffe navigators.

Something more positively effective, however, had to be designed and built in quantity. This problem was passed to the Research Establishment, formerly at Bawdsey and now in Dorset. A team led by one of the Establishment's outstanding young scientists, Dr. Robert Cockburn, worked on a Knickebein jammer called "Aspirin." Cockburn was destined to be a leading figure in the radio war now beginning. He had been a science master at West Ham Municipal College in London until 1937, when he was persuaded to join the radio staff at Farnborough to help develop Fighter Command's VHF equipment.

Imagine a Knickebein as two transmitters side by side, the

one on the right sending out a long beam of dots, the other, a beam of dashes. In the middle the beams narrowly overlap to form a third beam which is aimed at the target, and in this beam the dots exactly key in with the dashes to give a continuous note. (It helps to visualize this if one imagines square dots and rectangular dashes.) Aspirin could transmit on any Knickebein frequency, but it churned out only dashes. They flooded the German beam because Aspirin was powerful. When the German pilot flew into his own dash zone he would veer to find the central beam, but in it he would still get dashes—Cockburn's dashes. So he would go on turning until, in the dot zone, he got a tangle of dots and dashes —again they were Cockburn's dashes—that occasionally synchronized into a false beam note. Cockburn had worked out a system for bending the Knickebein beams. But the Aspirins proved so successful that they were set up to guard most important targets. Captured Luftwaffe officers and men began to complain of the "unreliability" of the beams that had formerly kept them on target. Crews who relied on Knickebein, they said, would find themselves flying around in small circles.

By accident or by Aspirin, a few bombs fell on London. In reply, Churchill asked for a night raid on Berlin. And then Hitler and Göring could not be held back. It was tempting for them to imagine that Britain might be defeated by a continuous and massive bombing of the capital. The decision to martyrize London by day and night bombing meant the end of their chance of winning the Battle of Britain because it relieved the pressure on Fighter Command, which daily grew stronger while the Luftwaffe got relatively weaker. The first daylight attacks on London were so costly to the Germans that the continuation had to be confined to the dark hours. Serious night bombing of London began on September 7, 1940, and until November 13 (with the exception of only one night of storm) an average of 160 bombers attacked the capital in every twenty-four hours. London, near the coast and with the silver snake of the Thames laid across its vitals, was the easiest of targets to hit in any weather. The town played its full part in the defeat of Germany not only because of its spirit but also because of its enormous spread. Had the Knickebein square system worked as it was meant to—or had it not been interfered with—each night 160 bombers would have dropped into a selected target area of the town *one bomb every seventeen yards*. The results would have been lethal.

Before the Knickebein threat had been met, Jones had been preoccupied with X-Gerät (X-apparatus), whose code name in the Air Ministry files was "Ruffian." He had learned that X-Gerät receivers were fitted only in the Heinkel He 111 bombers of a single, elite, independent squadron, Kampf-gruppe 100. KGr 100 had been brought into the Battle of Britain earlier than some of Göring's advisers thought wise. On the night of Eagle Day, August 13, half the squadron (twenty Heinkels) had performed a meticulous exercise against a Spitfire shadow factory on the outskirts of Birmingham. Eleven bombs were direct hits and the remainder were very close indeed. (Thanks to Jones's department, RAF monitors were familiar with KGr 100's call sign—6N).

Shortly after Eagle Day, a radio-search aircraft of 80 Wing piloted by Flight Lieutenant Bufton was doing a routine flight off the Cherbourg Peninsula—not usually a comfortable locality. "We had one of the first centimetric receivers, but we also had one of the old 100 mc/s (megacycles) sets," Bufton said later.[2] "On that set we found ourselves in a maze of signals on the 70 mc/s band, apparently radiating from several transmitters. . . ." The pilot who had found the Knickebein beam had also found the X-Gerät multiple beam.

What was X-Gerät? As early as 1933 Dr. Hans Plendl, a specialist in Hertzian radio developments, began to experiment with an idea for a blind-bombing aid. Telefunken, the German radio manufacturers, were working on the same problem and came up with Knickebein. Plendl saw that

Knickebein could be interfered with by a skillful enemy. His own scheme was more complex, and it says much for German thoroughness that it was persevered with at a time when German air superiority was never in question. X-Gerät consisted of a parent beam that could be aimed at any chosen target and three cross beams. The parent beam, "Weser," was, as Bufton had discovered, transmitted from Cherbourg, while the three cross beams, "Rhein," "Oder," and "Elbe," came from Calais. In order to achieve an exceptionally accurate target beam, Dr. Plendl had surrounded it with a sheath of parallel beams. The aggregate formed a wide highway, which KGr 100 alone could follow.

In mid-September Cherwell wrote a memorandum to Churchill, describing the activities of KGr 100 "stationed at Vannes; home station Lüneburg, and reserve station Köthen. . . . Bombing accuracies of the order of twenty yards are expected. With the technique they are developing this does not seem impossible." Lines of action, he suggested, might be to wipe out the squadron by a concerted attack; to bomb the beam stations, which would be all but impossible because they were almost invisible targets; to destroy the stations by special commando operations; or, finally, to devise radio countermeasures.

An operation mounted by SOE to assassinate the KGr 100 pilots in an ambush between Vannes and their airfield was a failure. Bombing sorties aimed at the transmitters also failed. However, work was soon progressing day and night at the Research Establishment. The jammer devised for X-Gerät was code named "Bromide."

Throughout September the X-beams were often warmed up during the day, and 80 Wing sometimes knew what orders the German bombers at Vannes were getting for that night. Then, at the beginning of October, there was an alarming change in KGr 100's tactics. Instead of dropping their usual 250-kilo high-explosive (HE) bombs, its Heinkels dropped incendiaries. The implication was that KGr 100 was going to lead the ordinary bomber squadrons and mark out the target for them by lighting fires in its center. This was the beginning of the "Pathfinder" system of bombing which the British were later to develop.

KGr 100 took off from Vannes on November 5, 1940, to bomb Birmingham. Early the following morning one of its Heinkels was hopelessly lost over southern England. Beguiled by a Meacon operating near Bridport in Dorset, the pilot thought he saw the French coast ahead, and as he was all but out of fuel, he attempted to put the aircraft down on the beach, which was in fact Chesil Bank, a steep stretch of shingle near Bridport. As the Heinkel came down at the edge of the surf and undertow, one German crewman was killed and two were injured. The wrecked machine was surrounded by armed British soldiers. They secured a rope round the fuselage, which displayed the letters "6N + BH" and the squadron's device, a Viking ship.

While the troops set about salvage, a Royal Navy inshore patrol vessel came on the scene and demanded to know what the Army was doing. As the aircraft was in the water, salvage was a Navy matter. The Army was displeased and disappointed, but the Navy took the rope aboard and dragged the aircraft into deeper water before securing it to a derrick and hoisting away. The rope broke and the Heinkel vanished into the sea.

"It is a very great pity," Cherwell wrote to Churchill that same morning, "that interservice squabbles resulted in the loss of this machine, which is the first of its kind to come within our grasp."

However, the X-Gerät receivers were recovered and were rushed to Farnborough where Jones and Cockburn were among those who examined them. As the examination proceeded, it was realized that X-Gerät was very difficult to beat. It worked on five frequencies and had three further stand-by frequencies available to evade jamming. The eight frequencies were chosen each night from twenty that the system could use. In addition, there were both radio and audio frequencies. Jones, who was always interested in the dated inspection stamps that were a feature of German military equipment, with its excellent routine servicing, noted that the earliest date he found on the receivers' stamps was pre-war, 1938. It was frightening to think that the Germans had possessed so sophisticated a device before the war. And particular interest was aroused by the number of jamming safeguards built into the sets.

Jones had got wind of a German plan, code-named "Moonlight Sonata," to wipe out three English industrial cities beginning, weather permitting, on November 14/15, 1940. He thought that the targets would be Wolverhampton, Birmingham, and Coventry, but he did not know in what order the attacks would be made. The defenses were short of time and jammers, and there was a hectic rush.

"We did not know on the morning of November 14 that the target was Coventry," Jones says. "Addison [commanding 80 Wing] telephoned me at six that evening, and neither of us, nor anyone else in England, knew what the target was to be. We *all* knew that something big was on, and there had been some wild guesses by members of the Air Staff and others which further muddled the issue.

"Addison appealed to me to interpret the results of our listening flight, so as to tell him which frequencies to set the jammers on. It was a nasty problem, with five beams to jam and only three jammers available. It could just be done, if we picked the three most vital beams and got their frequencies right. It happened that I had recently broken the coding system for the German frequencies, and knew that, with one exception, they must all be either whole numbers of megacycles or whole numbers plus a half between 66.5 and 75.0. None of the measurements Addison telephoned to me squared up with this, and so I had to guess. I gave him my guesses, and then went home."[3]

That night, taking off from Vannes, the target-marking Heinkels of KGr 100 kept well on the outside edge of the wide Weser beam to avoid British night fighters, which were

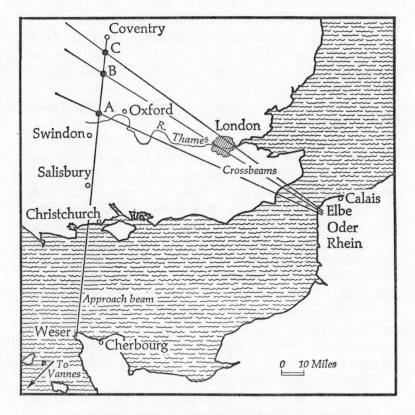

X-GERÄT TARGET COVENTRY
ON THE NIGHT OF NOVEMBER 14, 1940

1900 hours GMT—KGr 100 crosses Thames.

A—1906 hours. German pilots cross Rhein beam and close on to narrow bombing beam (Weser). They fly on for thirty kilometers to—

B—1917 hours. Oder signal. Observers push first buttons to start bombing clocks. A further fifteen kilometers and at—

C—1922.30 hours. Elbe signal. Observers push second buttons. Clocks' first hands stop; second hands start moving. Five kilometers to center of—

Coventry—1924.20 hours. Hands on bombing clocks overlap and incendiary bombs automatically released.

beginning to be dangerous, especially in moon periods. They crossed the British coast near Christchurch. Their next landmark was the soaring and so-English spire of Salisbury Cathedral. At Swindon, in Wiltshire, where the rails glinted dull silver in the marshaling yards, the Heinkels began to edge in for the bombing beam. They crossed the Rhein cross beam just after 7 P.M. That was the signal for the pilots to close on the narrow Weser bombing beam and hold to it, flying straight and level for twelve miles. The German aircrews heard strong radio interference on that night's frequencies, but they could just pick out their own signals. Each observer started his bombing clock as they swept through the Oder cross beam while the pilot concentrated on flying within the bombing beam. One hundred and fifty seconds after Oder they flew into Elbe and each observer pressed the second button. The pilots continued straight and level while the two hands of the bombing clock in each Heinkel began to converge. Fifteen minutes after midnight the German incendiaries, directed from far-away Calais, fell in the center of Coventry. Already the bomber squadrons were winging in for the kill. They came over Sussex and Hampshire and over the Wash. Bombing conditions were perfect and they had been well briefed on the main industrial targets in Coventry, nearly all of which were smashed.

At dawn the sky, from which such horror had poured, was serene, while below the citizens and their ready helpers from outside strove to save the entombed and the desperately wounded and to cope with threats of shortage in drinking water, broken gas mains, fires.

Jones's first thought on waking was of the night's possible events.[4] He quickly learned of Coventry's ordeal and thought that his "guesses" for Addison about the three Midland target cities had been wrong. "Actually," he thought, "it would have been a fluke if they had been right." But in the postmortem that quickly followed, Jones's "guesses" proved to have been correct. What had gone wrong was that one man in the countermeasures organization had made a mistake in his measurements, and as a result, while the British jammers were bang on in other respects, they were set to produce the wrong audible note, which was lower than the German one—1,500 instead of 2,000 cycles. A costly mistake.

Bomber Command and the War Cabinet, examining the chaos that one short night had brought, saw that the German Pathfinder system had worked well and judged that this form of aerial holocaust on the center of an industrial city was the most effective form. What the British tacticians possibly failed to consider was that soon after the holocaust the industrial production of Coventry *rose*. As for the Germans, their Intelligence services wrote Coventry off the map of England, and so the Luftwaffe did not ram home near-destruction by a timed succession of attacks—a failure noted by those in England who thought the war could be won by aerial bombing of Germany.

Next on the "Moonlight Sonata" program was Birmingham. But now the audio-frequencies error in the jammers had been rectified, and the incendiaries, and the bombs fell south of the target center and in many cases outside the city boundaries. Jones had made great efforts with Antiaircraft Command to get major reinforcements of guns and searchlights around Wolverhampton, the third target. The defenses waited, the guns silent, and Jones, had he been less confident in his own sources of information, would have felt embarrassed. But within three or four weeks confirmation came through that Luftwaffe Supreme Command had canceled the Wolverhampton raid because a German day reconnaissance flight that was to have preceded it had shown the increase in the defenses.

By the end of 1940 Plendl's X-Gerät had been controlled, indeed mastered, by 80 Wing and the scientists. But Jones and his new assistant, F. Charles Frank, a young physical chemist, were on the track of yet another German blind-bombing device. In June, Jones had learned that new transmitters, code-named "Wotan," were being set up near Cherbourg and Brest. He deduced from the name "Wotan," signifying the one-eyed Teutonic god, that the new transmitters were to operate a single-beam system. Such a system, oddly enough, was the only one mentioned in the 1939 Oslo Report, where it had been described with fair accuracy. (One curious aspect of this is that Plendl told Jones after the war that he had not even thought of that particular system until 1940.) Jones's information was correct, even if the "one-eyed" lead was not accurate, for the new transmitters comprised Dr. Plendl's second system, "Y-Gerät." The German code name for X-Gerät was Wotan 1, and that for Y-Gerät, Wotan 2. The British had two names for the latest menace, "Wye" and "Benito."

At first the British failed to analyze the new beam, and small wonder. Even German General Martini had taken two whole hours to explain Benito to Göring, who at the end of it announced that he was completely flummoxed. He said it sounded too complicated, and in a way he was right.

When Cockburn put the beam on a cathode-ray tube, he and his friends grasped its nature. The beam radiated three directional signals every second. Each Y-Gerät-equipped German bomber carried an electronic analyzer, by means of which certain emissions from the ground station in German territory were returned to it from the aircraft. The ground station could thus know the aircraft's exact distance away, along the beam, and when the aircraft was over the target, the ground station told the bomb aimer to release his bombs. It was a fantastic invention. It was possibly even more accurate than X-Gerät, and its operation needed only a single ground station; these could have proliferated along the French coast. But thanks to the Oslo Report and the strength of the scientific opposition, Y-Gerät's usefulness was ending before it had been used—while it was still being worked up by the Heinkel 111s of KG 26 flying out of Poix, using Wotan 2s at Poix and Cherbourg.

Cockburn named his Y-Gerät jammer "Domino." His first Domino began operating at Highgate, in North London, in February 1941, and very shortly the second was ready at

Beacon Hill on Salisbury Plain. When the second one got going, the Germans slashed in with a precision air attack on Beacon Hill that was nearly successful.

Dominos picked up the Y-Gerät ranging signal from the German bomber, and the BBC television transmitter at Alexandra Palace in London reradiated the signal on the Wotan 2's frequency. This canceled out the German system. There were feints and evasions. The Germans set up new ground stations and altered and realtered frequencies. But only eighteen times were bombs dropped out of eighty-nine Y-Gerät bombing sorties.

Then, on the night of May 3, 1941, KG 26 lost three Y-Gerät Heinkels over England. When he analyzed and tested the resulting mass of captured equipment, Dr. Cockburn saw that, "Unlocking the Wye beam was a bit of cake. The Germans had fallen into the trap of making things automatic. All one had to do was to radiate a continuous note on the beam's frequency. This filled in the gaps between the signals, unlocked the beam analyser, and sent the whole thing haywire . . ."[5]

Cockburn had a new jammer, "Benjamin," in operation on May 27. He knew that a single additional circuit in Y-Gerät would have protected it from the attentions of Benjamin. But the circuit was not fitted. And the Luftwaffe was being called away, unit by unit, with increasing momentum—to Russia.

10

"Charlemagne," a Confrérie Notre-Dame (CND) agent in Le Havre, was a garage proprietor whose real name was Charles Chauveau. In late January 1942 he came to Paris in a Simca 5 to pick up Pol at Rémy's request. As soon as they reached the border of Seine-et-Oise, Charlemagne drove into a wood and changed his false number plates for authentic ones corresponding with his permit to drive in Seine-Inférieure. The risks of such a journey at that time were great.

Pol's assignment was to study the coast north of Le Havre and its approach roads in the area of Saint-Jouin and Bruneval. Here Charlemagne would be invaluable, for he knew every twist and turn like the back of his hand.

Charlemagne took rooms in a seedy Le Havre hotel where no questions would be asked and no identity cards needed. The unheated room was so cold and the sheets so damp that Pol gave up all idea of sleeping. He spent the night shivering on a hard chair, fully dressed. In the morning Charlemagne borrowed two wheels with chains for the Simca. He had been warned that the steep roads around Bruneval had ten inches of snow on top of ice.

It was wiser for Frenchmen in those days to keep off the main roads, particularly in that heavily garrisoned Channel area. As soon as he could, Charlemagne left the Le Havre-Étretat road, N. 40, and drove through Heuqueville and Saint-Jouin. Another two and a half kilometers and they were at the Calvary road junction at the eastern end of Bruneval hamlet. The first house on the left was the Hôtel Beauminet.

The proprietor, Paul Vennier, Charlemagne explained

while he parked the car in virgin snow behind the hotel, was one of the best; so was Mme. Vennier, even though she was Swiss. (There was a feeling in France during the war that Swiss people might be pro-German.[1]) The two of them would tell Pol all he wanted to know.

He was right. The Venniers were only too glad to talk. They knew the number of Luftwaffe men stationed in the big square of farm buildings at Le Presbytère (or Theuville), but they had not heard of the lone *château* on the cliff being occupied. Of course, it was a military area and no civilian had been up there for a long time. Food and other supplies had been delivered at Le Presbytère, but never at the *château* nor in the radio station near Cap d'Antifer lighthouse.

Then there was the guard post in a villa, Stella Maris, down by the beach. It and the machine-gun posts running up from the Bruneval road were not, the Venniers thought, completely manned all the time. But they certainly could be manned at a few minutes notice, and there was always a guard of about ten soldiers mounted there. The Bruneval garrison was an infantry platoon under a sergeant, an efficient and energetic soldier; they were all quartered, to the Vennier's shame, in the hotel. The troops seemed good, neither young nor old, and they were kept on their toes, since the whole countryside swarmed with German units, some of them armored.

At the end of a long and amicable conversation Pol suggested to Charlemagne that they take a look at the sea. The beach, Vennier warned, was mined. But Pol was insistent.

An icy wind tore up at them as they walked downhill between a row of rather grim houses, northern-French gable-end romantic, their doors and windows sadly in need of paint. Just before the barbed-wire entanglement across the road, the cliff path climbed almost vertically on their right towards the radio station. On Pol's left now was the seaside villa, Stella Maris, peeling cement. A tall German sentry emerged from the doorway and looked sadly at them. Charlemagne was very friendly.

"Good morning, Fritz," he said in German.[2] "Just taking a
stroll with my cousin here. He's from Paris, you know. Feels
he must see the sea before he goes on home. Shut up in a
dark office all day long, you see. You know how they get,
desperate?" The sentry was smiling. Charlemagne seemed to
be mellowing him. "Lucky you're here," Charlemagne continued. "Without you we wouldn't have dared go any farther.
We've heard there are mines. Imagine that!"

"Ja, Tellerminen."

"Nix gut. I wonder if I dare suggest—would you accompany
us down the shingle, just for a second? It would give this
dear fellow so much innocent pleasure, I assure you."

"Jawohl," the sentry replied pleasantly. He pulled aside a
"knife rest" gate to make an opening in the barbed wire,
and they went through. He shut it behind them and made
them follow him closely on the path through the supposed
minefield.

Soon they were on a short length of beach overhung by
cliffs. It was a steep beach of round pebbles bigger than
chestnuts. Even on the calmest day it seemed likely that a
swell would break there. Charlemagne knew it from peacetime, and confirmed that there was an undertow. An uncomfortable place for bathing. How about underwater obstacles?
The tide was low, and there was no sign of anything like that.

While Charlemagne gave their German friend a cigarette,
Pol stood by, apparently dreaming. He allowed himself the
luxury of thinking that the English shore was only 150
kilometers across the sulky-looking water. Then he turned to
look up at the machine-gun emplacements, one to the south
of the Stella Maris villa and not far above its roofline, and
another similar post but higher up, on the north side. He
could actually see the snout of a machine gun at the south
side. Pol shivered. He saw one soldier up there, wearing a
forage cap, not a steel helmet, and, judging by the look of
him, several greatcoats. A boring station. No wonder the
Boches were often hitting it up at night in the Beauminet

. . . What else? Barbed wire? None in view beyond the rather dense barrage across the road to the beach.

On the way out, Pol noticed that the obliging German crossed the supposed minefield with no sign of caution. The "mines" were a myth to discourage the curious; the enemy obviously believed the place impregnable without them. Pol shared their belief.

They walked briskly back to the hotel, and there Charlemagne found some of his regular customers. Garage owners were in great demand in Occupied France. The gas- or charcoal-driven cars of ordinary people needed constant tinkering; and tires were scarcer than gold, since nearly all of them went to the occupying forces or to Germany itself. After a glass of calvados and thirty minutes of business talk, which was excellent cover for their visit, Charlemagne drove his "cousin" to the Hôtel des Vieux Plats in the agricultural village of Gonneville-la-Mallet, seven kilometers inland. There the couple treated themselves to a delicious luncheon at an immoral and immodest price and without official restriction of any kind. It was the sort of black-market restaurant that existed in every corner of France during the war; it was also the type most likely to be patronized by the higher-ranking and richer German officers. With the coffee (real coffee) and calvados, Pol called for the visitors' register. From it, when they were alone, he copied the names of all German military, knowing that their units could be traced in the German Army lists that were in London.

While Pol was fulfilling his mission in Bruneval, Rémy, his chief, was some fifty miles away, hidden in the small café owned by the "Guardian Angel" (Marcel Legardien) and his splendid wife, Suzanne. Rémy and a companion were expecting to be picked up by a Lysander of the Tempsford Squadrons that brought supplies to the Resistance.[3] Bob, the wireless operator, was also there. He had installed an aerial in the Legardiens' attic. Rémy had with him a heavy valise filled with incriminating documents destined for the BCRA in

London and a big suitcase holding all the latest military maps of France, which were also urgently wanted across the Channel. But night after night the wind blew and the snow fell. The cloud cover was low. The operation had to be suspended. And when Rémy got back to Paris he found that there was a crisis.

"Hilarion" reported that the German warships *Scharnhorst, Gneisenau,* and *Prinz Eugen* might well be preparing to leave Brest, the great naval port in Brittany. Hilarion (Lieutenant de Vaisseau Jean Philippon) was the CND leader in Brest, and as a spy he was superb. He belonged to a group of fifteen hundred French sailors who, with ten Navy officers and thirty engineers, still functioned in the Naval Arsenal. Only the certainty that some of his companions would pay with their lives for the discovery of his clandestine work tempered Hilarion's daring. His information was technical, detailed, and, so far, infallible. He had become so important to CND that Rémy had, until then, refused to let him risk having a radio operator and transmitter. The radio-detection services of the Germans in Brest and Lorient were known to be even more deadly than elsewhere, and the streets were filled with informers and with representatives of the Gestapo, the Abwehr, the Geheime Feldpolizei (GFP), and, worst of all, the Milice, French criminals released from prison by the Gestapo to infiltrate and destroy the Resistance. Down in the basins of La Ninon, a fortified part of the main harbor of Brest, *Scharnhorst* and *Gneisenau* were hidden by huge nets. Their antiaircraft equipment was manned by squads of German Army gunners imported for the purpose, while the ships' crews slept outside the much-bombed port. Nobody in Brest got enough sleep, since the RAF bombed most nights.

Rémy hated going there. He always feared that his visit might compromise Hilarion. But this time he had to go, taking with him "Lenfant" (André Cholet), a balding, witty, sad-faced radio operator, one of the best. They also carried a set for Hilarion, who had chosen to use his own operator, Radio-Quartermaster Arsène Gall. Gall, a Breton Hercules, was Hilarion's personal assistant in the Service des Jardins, for Hilarion's cover duties (later he was to be an admiral and to command the French Mediterranean Squadron) consisted of growing radishes and lettuce in the Arsenal gardens.

Rémy, Hilarion, Lenfant, and the immense Gall filled Hilarion's small room. Lenfant carefully described to Gall the characteristics of the British clandestine radio service he would have to work with and also the extreme perils of the German listening and direction-finding service. He explained to the quartermaster his allotted "plan," which told him when England would call and listen for his reply and on which wavelengths. He could alter the wavelengths by changing his crystals. And here, on the plan, were his call signs and other technical details. Gall kept nodding impassively. He was not worried. Transmissions, Lenfant went on explaining, were called "schedules" or "skeds," and Hilarion's quota would be high—five transmissions a week. With the way things seemed to be going in Brest, according to Hilarion, England would probably step up that number to one a day or even more, with a lot of emergency standby. Gall nodded. Then Lenfant turned to explaining the code system, Rémy listening carefully. In a danger area like Brest, they both emphasized, messages must never exceed thirty five-letter groups. The skeds must be kept short. And Lenfant warned them that sometimes a sked would go by with no contact at all because, for the safety of the operator, these were sets of low power quite unlike the types Gall had used on cruisers and destroyers.

Meanwhile, the message from Hilarion destined for London, encoded by the four of them, lay on the table beside a pad ruled out in rectangles for the anticipated five-letter groups of incoming message. The set had been grounded to the waste pipe of the wash basin, and its aerial was fixed across the ceiling. The time was approaching; it was very near. Quartermaster Gall settled himself easily in front of the set. At zero hour he began to tap out his call sign lightly, his hand completely obscuring the key. A shrill sound of morse code came to them through his earphones. They were calling him, but they didn't hear him yet. He fiddled with the tuning of his set and then the index finger of his left hand, a finger as big as a banana, began to jerk from letter to letter of the message, while the other hand tapped it out. Every now and then, Lenfant noted, he would be asked for a repeat, his headphones shrilling. Then his message was sent, and he picked up a pencil and began to print letters in the rectangles on his pad. Occasionally he would query a letter. When he laid down the pencil, there was an exchange of signals, and he pulled off the headphones. If it was always as straightforward as that, there would be nothing to worry about. He watched Rémy and Hilarion, who were decoding the message from London. It was brief and congratulatory. Quality of reception, as Rémy well knew, varied from one part of France to another. He again warned Hilarion and Gall of the efficiency of the German direction-finding services. If Gall heard any sudden interference while he was in communication, he should shut down at once, hide the set, and leave the house by his alternative route. He was never to transmit twice from the same house, the same district. Interference often meant that the German "central" was trying to hold the clandestine operator at his set while the direction-finding vans closed in on him.

From then on, Hilarion took to riding about on a bicycle, accompanied by Quartermaster Gall. They carried bits of transmitter in their pockets, others strapped to their carriers, and they never transmitted twice from the same place. Hilarion thus was able to report to London the Germans' secret preparations for taking the warships to sea. Other CND agents in the northern sector reported Luftwaffe fighter squadrons and wings moving to the Channel airfields, including several of those now flying the deadly Focke-Wulf 190 fighters.

Back in Paris on February 9, Rémy had an appointment with Pol at Jeff's. "Jeff" was Mme. Lucienne Dixon, a Frenchwoman married to an American. She lived at 1, Rue General Largeau, near the Porte d'Auteuil. Pol was ready with his report on Bruneval (or Theuville). They worked on it together, trying to condense it, for the sending of any message —let alone an unusually long one—was incredibly dangerous in Paris. Rémy went off to his own flat where he checked and double-checked the coding. He was there, sitting with his wife, Édith, and the children, when Bob arrived.

Warning him to be careful, Rémy handed over the flimsy bit of paper. And that same evening, as though it were the most natural thing in the world, as though Paris were not swarming with radio-detection units, Bob informed Rémy by telephone, that the Bruneval transmission had safely passed to London.

I I

Worth Matravers looks over the edge of the Dorset Downs to the tidal swirl of the Channel near St. Alban's Head. The village's largest house is the modest vicarage; its inn, the Square & Compass, is discreetly sited on the left as the lane enters the village. The ground, chalk and flint, is not rich, but it gives a swept feeling of durability, of calm; the sky is vast at Worth. The nearest town, squatting under the cliffs and invisible from the village, is the small one of Swanage.

It was to this corner of ageless England that the radar men came in 1940 to get on with their work. In 1938, Bawdsey's brilliant Robert Watson-Watt had been promoted to London, and A. P. Rowe took his place as superintendent. But at the outbreak of war the politicians feared that the supposedly omniscient Germans would instantly wipe out Bawdsey, killing its essential scientists. (However, the Nazis had so little respect for scientists and for Germany's wealth of scientific talent, much of which had seeped away before the war to America, England, and Sweden, that they were drafting young scientists into the armed forces in the hope that they would meet an early and ennobling death.) In any event, the Bawdsey establishment was banished to the safety and isolation of Dundee, on the coast north of Edinburgh. Everything went wrong from the beginning. The Air Ministry had forgotten to notify those it had designated to arrange for the Bawdsey group's arrival, with the result that nobody in Dundee expected them and their gear had to stand out in the mist and rain, protected only by packing cases. The climate proved quite unsuited to the flying side of their work, and the isolation was a serious problem, for it was part of the wartime scientist's make-up that he worked best in the thick of things. Wisely, the Air Ministry listened to Rowe's complaints, and on May 5, 1940, the group moved south in convoy, to settle in and around Worth Matravers. Six months later it was given the three-letter name TRE (Telecommunications Research Establishment) which became known and admired, not by the general public who heard nothing of it, but by those in England and, later, America who were running the war.

At Worth Matravers the scientists, whose numbers kept increasing, worked in huts, protected against bomb blast by earth banks. Their presence on the headland when the Battle of Britain began quite soon after their arrival, was advertized by two radar towers, one 350-feet tall, the other 240. The scientists now found themselves disturbed by air-raid warnings, so they dispersed locally into an empty private school, Leeson House, between Worth and Swanage, and then into another school, Durnford House. Leeson House stables, which they used as a laboratory, overlooked Swanage and Swanage Bay, with a view eastward to the Needles and the entry to the Solent. Still the expansion continued. TRE overflowed down the hill, moved into Swanage, and began to recruit assistants there.

Rowe learned that the scientists were perfectly willing to work in the most unlikely and unsuitable corners and at all hours, provided they were given enormous supplies of electric power. At the start there were no holidays, no weekends, no days off. Left alone, Rowe decided, they would work until they became jaded and stale. He decreed that Saturdays would be holidays.

On Sundays there were meetings which came to be called the "Sunday Soviets." These played a significant part in the development of TRE. They had begun at Bawdsey which, with its cricket pitch, its beautiful grounds, and the variety of its wartime staff—most of them young—had a university-like atmosphere. Then, too, it was near Cambridge University, which, in the Cavendish Laboratory, held the remarkable pool of scientific talent created there by Ernest Rutherford. There was much mixing between the two centers, which possibly was why the Sunday Soviets got off to such a good start. Now they were held in Swanage, and their importance became increasingly recognized. Senior and junior officers, members of the Cabinet, scientists, politicians, VIPs from industry, all jaded by the week's worries in London, would get themselves down to a Swanage hotel by Saturday evening and on Sunday morning would be in Rowe's office, where there was a general free-for-all. The senior officers could name their needs in the way of equipment, while junior ones, many of them straight out of action with Fighter or Bomber or Coastal Command, could point out faults and ask for improvements. As well as learning from their guests, the scientists of TRE were able to explain and to "sell" their newest ideas. The Soviets were an immense time-saver. There was nothing remotely like them in any other service-connected establishment in England or in any other country.[1]

When Rowe became superintendent at Bawdsey there were a few draftsmen in a small drawing office and some twenty skilled mechanics to make experimental equipment. By the end of the war Rowe was superintendent of a TRE that employed two hundred draftsmen and five hundred men of various skills in its model shop. Swanage was soon unable to accommodate TRE's new engineering unit, which was built at West Howe, near Bournemouth. As well as inventing, testing, and improving, TRE understood that its task was to shorten the period between the birth of an idea and its full-scale use in operations. Consumer reaction was studied and was molded. Aircrews were informed of devices in the works and were taught how to use them by means of electronic simulators made by TRE. TRE made its own instructional films. Its small radar school set up in Swanage grew until thousands were passing through it. Rowe remembers "a front row of Air Vice-Marshals and Air Commodores, sitting at the feet of flannel-bagged lecturers. . . . This could not have happened in Germany."[2]

Apart from helping technically in the Battle of the Beams, TRE's first pressing task at Worth Matravers was to produce an efficient means for RAF night fighter to get within range of Luftwaffe night bomber.

Airborne radar, in which Britain had a lead over Germany, had been initiated by E. G. ("Taffy") Bowen in the autumn of 1936 at Bawdsey. At the start, Bowen's work was supervised by Watson-Watt, who said that airborne radar must be designed to throw out a long, narrow beam; but to create such a radar, much shorter wavelengths were required. Bowen's first air interception (AI) set worked on a 6.8-meter wavelength, but he soon had one working on 1.5 meters. Tizard and Dowding, both realists, knew that in concentrating on Britain's day defenses they had left their country open to enemy night attacks, but there had not been time to do more. They felt that if they had not concentrated on being able to beat off daylight air attack, the night attacks might never have come. From the outset they gave Bowen every help. In 1938 a special RAF flight was attached to the Bawdsey unit to work with him. The flight had gone north with the scientists and now, its numbers increased, it had settled at Christchurch, about twenty-five miles northeast of Swanage. Soon it got too big for the airfield there and moved to Hurn (now Bournemouth Airport).

By July 1940 Bowen had an AI set, the Mark III, working in a Blenheim bomber. The Blenheim was too slow for a night fighter, and the Beaufighter, which was to be its replacement, was giving a lot of development trouble. As to the 1.5-meter AI set, its maximum range was two miles, which was on the short side, and its minimum range was eight hundred feet, which was on the long side.

It was understood that the 1.5-meter AI sets could never be entirely satisfactory. They were vulnerable to enemy jamming, the beam was far too wide for accuracy, and much of its energy spilled to the ground. This could have been improved by having aerial clusters on the noses of the fighters (such as the Germans fitted later in the war on the noses of their Junkers Ju 88s). But such aerials had a sorry effect on the speed and handling of the aircraft. What was needed in those small airborne sets was a *very* short wavelength, ideally one of ten centimeters. To achieve that, an electron tube of small size which produced fantastic power would have to be devised.

A great deal of the credit for achieving the wonder electron tube must go to the Admiralty, which, before the advent of radar, was the most tube-conscious of any of the services. In 1938 Dr. C. S. Wright, its Director of Scientific Research, had predicted correctly that the side that developed electron-tube power on the shortest wavelength would win the war. After a sticky start in radar, the Royal Navy had two ships, *Rodney* and *Sheffield,* fitted with experimental early-warning sets by the end of 1938. And that year the energetic man who had built up the Admiralty's scientific power in the thirties, Sir Frederick Brundrett, more or less cornered, and therefore unified, electron-tube production. In the face of opposition from the Air Ministry, Brundrett organized the setting up of a single interservice organization, which he ran himself (with a committee). At the outset of war he called together the major electron-tube manufacturers, whose production was being hampered by industrial and scientific security. Brundrett persuaded them to forget their inhibitions about exchanging secrets—for the good of their country.

Having got around the manufacturers, Brundrett called for major research. He got teams going at the Cavendish and Clarendon laboratories (at Cambridge and Oxford respectively), and at Birmingham and Bristol Universities. At Birmingham an Australian, Professor M. L. E. Oliphant, headed an impressive group of young men, most of them nuclear physicists. Oliphant and some of the others set to work to develop an electron tube called the "klystron," which had been recently produced by the Varian brothers at Stanford University, in California. The Greek word "klystron" means, charmingly, "incoming waves on a beach," and in the tube electrons were driven along a passage past or through resonators. Two of the Birmingham physicists, John Randall and Henry Boot, neither of whom was engaged with Oliphant on the klystron, had the notion that the waves-on-a-beach electron principle might be applied to another instrument, the magnetron, which had originated in America in 1921.[3] They designed such an electron tube, the cavity magnetron, and they built it in proper Rube Goldberg fashion. Air was drawn from their experimental model by a continuously working pump. The ends of the tube were closed by embedding halfpennies in sealing wax. A clumsy laboratory electromagnet was used to provide the magnetic field.

They tested the tube on February 21, 1940, and the cavity magnetron in one burst exceeded all expectations. Two car headlights connected to it flared and shattered. Two bigger headlights could not take the power. Low-pressure neon lamps were connected, and they showed that the halfpenny-and-sealing-wax contraption was producing 400 watts on a wavelength of 9 centimeters. Brundrett at once reinforced this success with support from the Admiralty, the General Electric Company (GEC) at Wembley, and the British Thomson Houston Company at Rugby, as well as from the other universities. When the GEC Research Laboratories under C. C. Paterson developed the first production model, it produced ten *thousand* watts.

TRE experiments with this new marvel began in July 1940 under P. I. Dee, another prewar nuclear physicist. The ledge by Leeson House stables with its view away eastwards was an ideal ground site for experiments with centimetric radar. "Soon," Rowe says, "there was a line of trailers there . . . each with a metal parabolic mirror overlooking the town [Swanage] and the sea. This became known as 'Centimetre Alley.'"[4] An experimental airborne AI set using the magnetron detected a "hostile" aircraft at a range of six miles in August 1940. But it was not until March 1941 that a prototype centimetric AI set went up in a night fighter. Through the long earlier stages of the night battle the pilots had to make do with blunter tools.

It may seem odd that if radar could work in daylight, it did not readily work in the dark. But during the day Chain Home and its ancillaries could put fighters on to their targets with height errors of a couple of thousand feet and distance errors of a couple of miles; the fighters scrambled and the human eye, added to the human brain, canceled the errors. Without vision, however, man is one of the more helpless animals. Then there was an extra problem in that the Luftwaffe (like the RAF in the early stages of their attack on Germany) favored dispersed night-bombing attacks. TRE calculated that during an average night raid over England in 1940–41, there was one German bomber to every nine hundred cubic miles of darkness.

There were two factors in catching them. The pilot of the night fighter had to "see" the enemy with his AI set, but before that, he had to be directed to within AI range by controllers on the ground. Here Rowe explains:

"The solution was reached with the Plan Position Indicator, which was installed in a new form of radar set known as the GCI (ground-controlled interception). The controller had before him the screen of a cathode-ray tube similar in size to that of a domestic television. Marked permanently on this screen was a map of the surrounding area up to distances from him of about fifty miles. Positions of the hostile bomber and the friendly fighter were shown by bright spots on the tube face which, in addition to the map, was marked in grid squares. By calculating the speed and direction of flight of the enemy, the fighter could be directed by the shortest route. The IFF (identification friend from foe) set carried in the fighter caused the friendly spot to give a characteristic signal every few seconds."[5]

(IFF was developed at Bawdsey in the very early days and was subsequently improved. It was carried by all RAF aircraft. There arose among British bomber crews a superstition that if they kept IFF switched on over Germany and Occupied Europe, the set interfered with the ice-blue radar-controlled German "master" searchlights, which probed their blue fingers vertically into the sky and then, with demoniac speed, fixed on an aircraft. If you were located by one of these, a team of ordinary searchlights caught you in a cone, and escape from the consequent flak was hideously difficult. Keeping IFF on over Germany—although it had been devised for the return trip to England—became a habit that, rather than giving protection, cost British lives: German night fighters were fitted with a device later in the radio war that could home on IFF.)

The first GCI set was built at Worth Matravers in the spring of 1940 and began its series of tests; TRE agreed to put through a crash program to produce twelve of them before the end of the year.

"During that lovely summer," writes Rowe, "we often saw hostile day bombers passing over us. One day we counted seventy-two of them. . . . There were times when, during paper-bag lunches on the cliffs by St. Alban's Head I saw aircraft with smoking tails take their last dives into the sea. But these events were little concern of ours, for our eyes were on the coming night-bombing war. We had a GCI set from which fighters could be controlled; we had the co-operation of AI-fitted night fighters at Middle Wallop; and we had enemy night bombers. After our day's work many of us went to our GCI station, hoping that this would be the night on which civilian scientists working as controllers at a research station would be the means of bringing down a night bomber. . . . Bomber and fighter would be tracked and their heights assessed. When the fighter had been put on the tail of the bomber, the GCI station would give the signal 'Flash weapon!' and the fighter crew would switch on the AI set. . . . It is sad to record that those who had evolved AI failed to obtain a kill. They were replaced by RAF controllers who, in fact, did the job much better."

On October 16, 1940, the first GCI set was delivered by TRE for service and the last of the twelve sets was delivered six days after the New Year. The sets, Rowe says, "were often hand-made with odd bits and pieces. . . . There was still, that winter, a period of frustration and training before results came. Then enemy losses increased month by month until in May 1941, 102 night bombers were shot down by fighters and 172 were assessed as probably destroyed or damaged. During this period the casualty rate suffered by night bombers rose from less than half of 1 per cent to more than 7 per cent. . . ."

Bomber Command's three navigational aids of the war (the Command began it with none) were devised and developed by TRE at Worth Matravers. The first, "Gee," a system of navigational pulses, was soon jammed by the enemy but remained invaluable as a navigational guide. (Someone in the Navy suggested that D-Day should have been called "Gee-Day"—the ships used it too.) The second system, called "Oboe," was the child of Alec H. Reeves, an inventor in the pulse-techniques field, who joined TRE at Swanage from Standard Telephone. If Reeves had not had the enthusiastic support of the distinguished operational pilot H. E. Bufton, Oboe might never have been used, since it and Reeves roused fierce opposition. For example, a "high-ranking official" in the Ministry of Aircraft Production wrote, "I regret having to do this, but I am sure it is time to say quite bluntly that these disquisitions from TRE on Oboe are becoming ridiculous. If they came as inventions from the outside public and not from official sources, they would be rejected without hesitation. . . . If I had the power, I would discover the man responsible for this latest Oboe effort and sack him, so that he could no longer waste not only his time and effort, but ours also, by his vain imaginings." The letter was passed to Rowe by its recipient, a "higher-ranking official" in the same Ministry—and Rowe drafted more staff to support Reeves. Oboe, which worked with two ground radar stations, was the most accurate navigational aid of the war, though its range was very limited—a maximum of 270 miles.

It was Oboe, carried in another remarkable invention, the Mosquito fighter-bomber, that brought destruction to the Ruhr.

The third system, H₂S, came from the Leeson House stables above Swanage. For when Dee and Lovell tried their experimental centimetric AI sets there, they registered ships entering and leaving the Solent. Dee took a set up in one of his Blenheims and had the aerial looking slightly downwards instead of ahead. The set's revolving arm blocked in a radar map, and on the display appeared Southampton. This meant that with H₂S, a bomber could carry a self-contained navigational aid, one that could reveal to the aircrew an actual map of their target. There was one snag, and it was a horror. The cavity magnetron was a solid block of copper in which the highly secret cavities had been hollowed out; it appeared to be indestructible. This meant that it could be retrieved intact by the enemy from a downed plane. Farnborough tried in vain, and with live experiments, to destroy it. In the course of one such experiment a ten-foot hole was blown in the fuselage of a captured Junkers 88. When the experts examined the remains of the magnetron on the ground, they saw that it was still possible to understand how it worked.[6] Surely it was unthinkable that this incredible device should be virtually handed over to the Germans?

There is a story that Lord Cherwell invented the name "H₂S," but this is incorrect. . . . Dr. R. V. Jones found that TRE was working on a new aid which they called "TF." Jones correctly guessed that this stood for "town finding" and that it related to Dee's vastly successful experiments with centimetric radar. He pointed out to Cherwell the insecurity that arose from TRE's frequent practice of naming devices by the initials of words that described their purposes. Cherwell acknowledged this and said he would get it altered when he got down to Swanage (he was going to a Sunday Soviet). When he returned he said that he had been successful and that the new name was "H₂S." He enquired if the remarkably perspicacious Jones could guess the connection. Jones could not.[7]

"It's very clever," Cherwell said. "It stands for 'Home Sweet Home.'"

When Jones next visited TRE the change of code name cropped up in conversation, and he found that the new name's derivation was a scientific one. When Cherwell had asked them to change the name "TF" they had considered it over lunch, and one of them had recalled an incident of a year or so earlier. . . . Cherwell had been shown the possibilities of a certain device, but had not seemed interested. On a subsequent visit, after being shown everything else, he asked what had happened to that particular device. In the meantime, relatively little had been done about it, precisely because Cherwell had shown no interest. They did not think it polite to tell him that, in so many words, and they tried to give other reasons for the lack of development. Cherwell became extremely annoyed and said he was thoroughly upset by such prevarications in a scientific research establishment in time of war. "*It stinks!*" he exclaimed. "*It positively definitely stinks!*" The TRE executives at lunch therefore enthusiastically received a suggestion from one of their number that "TF" be renamed "H2S." What they did not reckon with was that Cherwell should at once ask, "But why H2S? What is the connection between H2S and this device?" There was an awkward silence until one of those present imaginatively suggested "Home Sweet Home."

Yet another operational question had to be answered. Should not centimetric radar be reserved for the U-boat war? When Taffy Bowen was developing AI in 1937 the early set's weakness—the return of strong echoes from the ground—showed him its possibilities over the sea. The marine version of the set was called "ASV" (air-to-surface vessel). By the summer of 1940 Coastal Command aircraft had Mark II ASV, which was technically capable of locating a surfaced submarine at four miles range and homing in on it. At that time the Germans had comparatively few submarines. However, the U-boat fleet was quickly increased and its main operating bases were on the French Biscay coast. The U-boats had to surface to run their diesels for recharging their batteries. If they surfaced in daylight, the British aircraft could, and did, catch them in the bay, using ASV. The first German answer was to surface at night. The British replied with the airborne Leigh searchlight, which was bright enough for the aircraft, having located the submarine by ASV, to mount an attack. But all that the Germans had to do, the British realized from the start, was to put in each U-boat a simple radio-listening device which would receive energy from the wide beam of the 1.5-meter ASV. This could give visual or aural warning, or both, when an ASV-equipped aircraft approached, and the submarine could dive to safety. (The U-boats were so noisy when surfaced that the crews did not hear approaching aircraft.) But if the cavity magnetron could be kept exclusively for Coastal Command, there was no reason why it should fall into German hands, and the U-boat war would be won, since the Germans' radio device, though effective against ASV, would be useless against H2S/ASV.[8]

It seemed clear to the majority of scientists and war leaders who knew the problem—the indestructibility of the cavity magnetron—that Coastal Command could make more valuable use of H2S than Bomber Command. But Lord Cherwell, with what Jones has described as "his emotional commitment to make bombing more scientific, combined with his inclination to attack rather than defence," insisted that the bombers as well as the antisubmarine patrols have it.[9] He won the day, and one of the first bombers fitted with it, a Stirling of No. 7 Squadron, was shot down on February 2, 1943, near Rotterdam. The aircraft was an 80 per cent wreck. Two of the crew had survived but "both have obstinately and consistently refused to make any kind of statement," Engineer-Colonel Schwenke, the German captured-equipment expert, stated in his interrogation report.

Dr. Plendl and General Martini were called to the inquiry

into "Rotterdam," the German name for H₂S. Telefunken was ordered to make six radar sets of the same centimetric type and two additional sets, the first, "Naxos," a detector, and the second, "Korfu," a direction-finding receiver to be fitted in night fighters. All this took German technicians and scientists weeks and months. It was not until May that Gö-ring read the final assessment of Rotterdam. He said: "We must admit that in this sphere the British and Americans are far ahead of us. I expected them to be advanced, but I never thought they would get so far ahead. I did hope that even if we were behind, we could at least be in the same race."

The first Rotterdam salvaged by the Germans was soon completely lost in a bombing attack on Berlin in which the Telefunken works was badly mauled, but that same night the Germans obtained a second H₂S set when one of No. 35 Squadron's Halifaxes was shot down over Holland. Care-ful interrogation of RAF prisoners, too, gave results. German scientists and the German electronics industry reacted with customary energy to the stimulus of their enemy's scientific lead, a lead they were never able to diminish. As for the British scientists who had developed H₂S, few of them were aware that the device had fallen so rapidly into German hands, let alone that the Germans had been so quick to ana-lyze its significance.

12

Bomber Command had discovered early in the war that, until long-range first-line fighter aircraft could be produced as escorts, daylight raids on Germany were too costly. The prewar designers in England, Germany, and the United States had assumed that bombers with powered gun turrets would be able to defend themselves in daylight by flying in formation and giving mutual support with cross fire. Eventually all three nations learned that, in the face of strong fighter opposition, such tactics meant death.

It was an expensive lesson, proving that designers should work, as TRE tried to do, with the airmen or soldiers or sailors for whom they design and that they should work under war conditions. Between the two World Wars the bomber designers saw their aircraft as swift, defendable "flying fortresses" (to borrow an American proprietary name). These aircraft were splendid on paper. They captured the imaginations of politicians and flying men. But the designers had not foreseen how rapid was to be the improvement in fighter aircraft or, inversely, how severely the bomber was to be handicapped by its size and weight. The fighter pilot, secure in his speed and balance, aimed *his whole machine* at the target and hose-piped a stream of observable tracer fire into it. The gunner in a bomber's powered turret was infinitely at a disadvantage. He was more vulnerable, he was probably much more uncomfortable—sometimes almost frozen to death—and his mentality was that of the defender rather than the attacker. In addition, the turret gunner had (as any civilian shooting sportsman will readily understand) immensely difficult problems of skill and prognostication. Supposing, for the sake of simplicity, that the turret gunner's aircraft and that of the enemy fighter were each flying at 300 miles per hour; he might, though it would be unlikely, have an easy broadside target, or he might, more probably, have a target coming at him at an angle and at a speed approaching 600 miles per hour. Clearly, the solution was to achieve air superiority with the bombers and to give them fighter defense. That was what the Germans were able to do at the beginning. That was what the Allies did in the latter stages.

For the English the lesson came soon after midday on December 18, 1939. Twenty-four Wellingtons were on patrol near Wilhelmshaven, on the northwest coast of Germany, with orders to bomb any German naval unit found at sea. (Bombing of the German mainland was at that time prohibited by the British Government.) The Freya radar on Wangerooge, in the East Frisian Islands, had picked up the Wellingtons at a range of more than seventy miles and sent out the alert. German fighter pilots were sitting down to lunch, but as the Wellingtons neared the Freya, fifty fighters, Messerschmitt 109s and 110s, climbed above them into the cloudless sky. Maintaining their diamond formation, the Wellingtons were turning toward England when the cannon-firing Messerschmitts swooped on them. The British lost 58 per cent of their aircraft—only ten Wellingtons got home. Strangely enough, the Luftwaffe did not learn from that afternoon's work; they did not learn until August 15, 1940, in the Battle of Britain, when General Hans-Jürgen Stumpf, commanding Luftflotte 5, sent his unescorted bombers to England across the North Sea.

So, with such resources as it could muster, Bomber Command began to attack by night when Churchill, in May 1940, lifted the ban on bombing Germany. Within a month, more than two thousand bombing sorties were flown with minimal losses. By the standards that were later to prevail, the raids were small and inaccurate because the British as yet had no radio bombing aids.

Nevertheless, the attacks had a disproportionate effect in

Germany. First, they constituted an unpleasantness that was plainly going to get worse before it got better. Secondly, although Göring himself had declared that not a single bomb would fall on the Ruhr, he began to demand more D/T radar production. And the same kind of helplessness under night bombing that the British had experienced now had to be endured by the Germans. Something had to be done, and Colonel Josef Kammhuber, aged forty-three, was called in to do it. Göring promoted him to major-general, told him to take twenty-four hours or so to study the matter and then to get on with building an effective defense. He would have priority in D/T apparatus, searchlights, guns, and fighter aircraft.

Kammhuber considered the situation as he found it. The type of aircraft used as night fighters were the Me 110, the new fighter version of the Ju 88, and some Me 109s. The twin-engined Ju 88 and Me 110 fighters were useful gun platforms for dealing with slow bombers, but the fast single-engine Me 109 was making the majority of the kills in the "helle Nachtjagd"—floodlit night hunt. The fighters waited until there was a warning from the Freya outpost line. They then orbited their airfields' radio beacons until the German search-lights and flak, or the fires started by their bomber foes, illuminated or silhouetted the bombers; then they closed and attacked. The stupidity there, Kammhuber saw, was that the enemy had probably already dropped their loads and the German night fighters were operating in their own flak areas.

His answer was to lay a defense line across the British air approaches to Germany, running from the northern tip of Denmark to the Elbe estuary, then west by south along North Germany and Holland, and then down through Belgium and France to the Swiss-Italian frontier. The line was to consist of a series of equally spaced defense stations, or radio boxes, each box with sides some thirty kilometers in length. The code name for such a radio box was "Himmel-bett" (four-poster bed). By putting four-posters on the Frisian and other islands, Kammhuber planned from the start to strengthen the line at crucial points and deepen it strategically. He increased the number of early-warning stations along the coasts and he also, in collaboration with General Martini, obtained a build-up in the German Signals' monitoring service. This proved to be invaluable when faced with such an intense, and at first indiscriminate, user of radio as RAF Bomber Command.

Because the defense operated in a series of identical boxes, it is fairly simple to explain. Each box had two Würzburg radars and one Freya. They were sited in a triangle with sides of less than one kilometer. In the center were station headquarters and the control room with its Seeburg table.

The Seeburg was a two-storied structure made of wood that represented on a small scale the whole cube of that particular Himmelbett. One operator at the table operated the red (bomber) Würzburg simulator while the other operated the blue (fighter) one. The Würzburg simulators (copying in small scale what was happening in the kilometers of space around the radars) were at floor level and their red and blue pencils of light came through the table and shone up, a small blue circle and a small red one on the ground-glass "ceiling" above. At the upper level of the table the fighter controller stood, looking down on the ground-glass grid plan of the sky, the "roof," so to speak, of the Himmelbett.

When early warning came through that RAF bombers were approaching, one night fighter in each Himmelbett took off and orbited the Himmelbett's radio beacon, which was in contact by radiotelephone with the Himmelbett's controller. The German fighter was followed by the station's blue Würzburg.

The station's Freya picked up some of the raiders which, in the early stages of British night bombing of Germany, as in the German bombing of Britain, were dispersed and traveling individually to their target or targets.

If a British bomber came toward or near the Himmelbett, the red Würzburg, helped by the Freya, fixed on it while the blue Würzburg continued to track the night fighter. Each

1. Sir Robert Watson-Watt, KCB, LLD, FRS, the pioneer of radar in Britain.

2. Lord Cherwell (left), Winston Churchill's scientific adviser. To his left stand Air Chief Marshal Sir Charles Portal, Admiral Sir Dudley Pound, Prime Minister Churchill, and Major-General Kenneth Loch.

3. A. P. Rowe, CBE, presiding genius of the Telecommunications Research Establishment (TRE). (Over his shoulder, his opponent, Reichsmarshall Hermann Göring).

4. Major-General Josef Kammhuber, creator of the Kammhuber Line which proved so costly to Allied bombers.

5. Professor R. V. Jones, CB, CBE, FRS, behind-the-scenes genius in Britain's radar war effort.

6. Major John Frost, now Major-General J. D. Frost, CB, DSO, MC, who led the Bruneval Raid.

7. Flight-Sergeant C. W. H. Cox (right), the radar expert who stole the Würzburg, pictured at a Bruneval commemoration ceremony, flanked by a parachute sergeant.

8. Britain's round-the-clock sentinels: a typical Chain Home radar station.

9. A Würzburg radar abandoned by the Germans. This one was used to provide fire-control data for a flak battery and displays a claim of three aircraft shot down.

10. The ground reconnaissance: Rémy, head of the Channel coast Resistance network, pictured while taking oath at trial of a spy who destroyed his network.

11. The air reconnaissance: Flying Officer Tony Hill's "dicing" oblique shows the small (ten-foot diameter) Würzburg and the Lone House at Bruneval.

12. Bruneval, during an Anglo-French commemoration service. In the background, the cliff on which the Würzburg stood (to left of building). In the middle ground, the gully from which the German machine gun fired up the hill.

13. Bruneval: the beach seen from the Würzburg site. In the foreground, the hill down which the withdrawal had to be made; on the left, the Bruneval road.

14. One of the assault landing craft bringing back the Bruneval raiders.

15. Back at Portsmouth, the motor gunboats are secured alongside *Prins Albert*.

16. Wing-Commander Charles Pickard, who led the flight of Whitleys which dropped the paratroops, examines a trophy of the Bruneval Raid.

17. One of the German prisoners from Bruneval is handed over to the Military.

of the two Würzburgs was connected by direct line to an operator inside the lower (ground level) stage of the See-burg table.

The Himmelbett controller was in constant communica-tion with his fighter pilot on the radio telephone and, while watching the blue blob and the red jolting across the grid, talked the fighter into contact. If the fighter pilot failed to find his prey, he returned to orbit round the radio beacon. It was a simple and ingenious scheme. It worked.[1]

As the Himmelbett line increased and as, with practice, the pilots and controllers made speedy improvements, Kammhuber altered the siting of the German searchlight belt, to give the crews a greater chance of catching bombers that had slipped through. The belt was made out of bounds to all German aircraft save night fighters. In the autumn of 1941 the Himmelbett searchlights were removed by the or-der of the Luftwaffe Supreme Command and taken from Kammhuber's control, to operate with the flak and to be con-centrated around towns and "areas of premier defence." He tried to prevent it, but when the searchlights had gone he found that the proportion of bomber kills rose, because the line's fighter pilots ceased to rely on anything other than radar and their controllers' vectors.

Kammhuber's main concerns were, first, to improve on the Würzburg and, second (as with Dowding and Tizard in Eng-land), to get a workable AI radar in his night fighters. The efficiency of each station in the Himmelbett line depended on its Würzburgs, because the Freya did not give the altitude of the incoming bomber. The Würzburgs did, but their range of twenty miles was too short and they were liable to suffer from ground reflections if the bomber flew lower than six thousand feet. Kammhuber lost no time in throwing these defects at the manufacturer, Telefunken. Unlike Britain, Germany still had plenty of slack to take up in her manufac-turing industry, and Telefunken came up promptly with an improvement. Before the winter of 1941 it was experimenting with a new Giant Würzburg, and very shortly this began to replace the standard machines inside the Himmelbett boxes. The Giant was not readily transportable. Its bowl-shaped skeletonic reflector was twenty-five feet in diameter as opposed to its small parent's ten feet. The Giant threw a narrower beam and it had double the range—forty miles.

As to airborne radar, the British had a long start, and also, though the Germans did not yet know it, a tremendous superiority with their new electron tube. Still, Telefunken did wonders. By the end of January 1942, just before the Bruneval raid, four Junkers 88 night fighters were working, carrying the new Lichtenstein AI set. The Lichtenstein was heavy and operated through a clumsy jut of aerials on the Junker's nose, but it had a maximum range of two miles, similar to that of the early TRE models, and a very good minimum range of two hundred meters. There was, however, strong pilot resistance to the Lichtenstein; this was partly because there was great confidence in the Himmelbett system of controlled interception and partly because the proliferation of aerials all but ruined the fighter's handling and performance.

So the situation in early 1942 was that the British were building up their bombing campaign, and their aircraft industry was turning out, particularly in the Lancaster, better long-range bombers than the Germans had or would have; but Bomber Command had still to apply science if its night bombing was to develop accuracy.[2]

Meanwhile, Germany, although engaged on several fronts and particularly in Russia, where the initial thrust had gone in very deep, was reacting with speed and brains to the Allied bombing threat. German fighter production, spurred by the obvious need for night fighters, had at once risen dramatically, and there was scope for a steady expansion, which continued until the end of the war. The British were already losing night bombers on an average of about four out of every hundred. Some of these losses were attributable to the German flak with its blue master-searchlights, but at least two thirds of the victims, it was learned in de-briefing at RAF bomber bases, had been shot down by night fighters.

If the Germans were not using radar, how were their night fighters managing to do so well? Dr. R. V. Jones had not forgotten the "radio detection stations along the North Sea Coast" mentioned in the 1939 Oslo Report. He, like the German-trained Lord Cherwell, had kept an open mind, but it was difficult to find anybody in England in 1939 or even 1942 willing to consider the possibility that Germany too might have radar. Now British aircraft were falling over Germany, and it was the Germans, rather than Jones and his Intelligence colleagues, who had the priceless advantage of crew interrogation. British radar had involved the erection of huge masts and towers; if the Germans did possess radar, they must have another variety that did not require such formidable structures.

Back in May 1940 Jones had noted that a German prisoner had mentioned a radio gunlaying and ranging device used by his Navy; he had also spoken of the Luftwaffe's radio warning system. Then, in July of that year an Intelligence source in northern France sent over a section of a German report in which a "Freya warning" was mentioned, together with the fact that it had been able to put German fighters on to intruding British aircraft. Jones had at once asked that any further information on Freya be given priority. In due course, a report came of a Freya station that had been set up at Lannion, a small port in the northwest corner of the Côtes-du-Nord department. Jones could think of no direct significance in Lannion itself, and there were no reports of secret works there; but an early-warning station there would make sense, since Lannion was on an air route to Brest and the Biscay ports of France, which the enemy would obviously turn into his most important submarine bases. It must be significant, Jones reasoned, that the Germans had established a Freya there only three weeks after entering France. Also, according to the French agent, it was under a twenty-four-hour armed guard and had its own flak protection. What then was a "Freya?"

Turning back into mythology, Jones noted that the goddess Freya had betrayed her husband in order to possess Brisingamen, a magic necklace. The necklace was guarded for Freya by Heimdal, servant of the Gods, who could see for a hundred miles in every direction, in daylight and in the dark. Would the Germans have been so obvious, Jones wondered, as to name a radar device "Freya?" If so, it must be comparatively small. The air photographs of Lannion showed nothing significant. Jones immediately wrote a memo to the Prime Minister.

"Heimdal himself would have seemed the best choice for a code name for RDF [radio direction finding]," Winston Churchill read. "It is difficult to escape the conclusion that the Freya-Gerät is a form of portable RDF. Freya may possibly be associated with Wotan—she was at one time his mistress—although it would have been expected that the Führer would have in this case chosen Frigga, Wotan's lawful wife."

Churchill at once ordered General Ismay to ascertain if any British RDF sets had fallen intact into German hands at the time of Dunkirk. The gist of Ismay's findings was that one radar set had been left behind by the RAF but that it had probably been destroyed first. The general pointed out that the Germans might have obtained very complete information about RDF from the French, to whom all things, even RDF, had been vouchsafed before the debacle.

A further Intelligence report from France soon reached Jones at the Air Ministry. Another Freya station was said to be located on Cap de la Hague, northwest of Cherbourg. On July 25, 1940, this Freya had, in fact, guided German dive bombers to the destroyer H.M.S. *Delight*, which they sank, and *Delight* had done nothing to reveal her position. To the British her loss had been inexplicable. Now Jones thought it might be connected with Cap de la Hague. It looked as though Freya was an efficient long-distance instrument. From Paris, too, Jones had been sent a copy of Daily Orders at the headquarters of Luftflotte 3. Freya was mentioned. It was a part of German air defenses and must exist in large numbers.

German radar was first heard and recognized in England because Jones was on another of his radio-navigational trails. He had always wondered if the Germans, like his own people, were working on centimetric techniques, and he therefore paid close attention to evidence from the Continent that a German apparatus existed called "Knickebein Dezi." The standard Knickebein worked on a wavelength of some ten meters. Was it not reasonable to suppose that Knickebein Dezi might be a similar thing but working on a wavelength of a few decimeters? Further, he heard of a German technician making an alteration of thirteen centimeters in one of the beams.

"I was able to get Prime Ministerial pressure applied to a search at these wavelengths," he says. "Although I myself regarded this particular deduction as a slender one, I was convinced that a search ought to be made on general principle. As it turned out, the deduction was false; *Knickebein Dezi* certainly proved to be a decimetric installation associated with the *Knickebein* system. But it was the communications link which tied the system into the German signals network. . . . Moreover the mention of thirteen centimetres had referred simply to the moving of a monitor aerial used as a siting target for directing the beam. The radio search which was instituted on these false premises, however, proved to be fully justified. . . . It revealed to us that the Germans had a Radar system surveying the Straits of Dover. . . ."[3]

Derek Garrard, who had been working on radar at TRE, was to be attached to Dr. Jones's staff at the Air Ministry. As part of the search mentioned above, he was encouraged to take a few days off somewhere between Swanage and London and to do some beam hunting on the short wavelength. He packed a lot of TRE equipment into the back of his car and drove east along the chalk downs of southern England. From near Dover he heard strange signals on 375 megacycles. Further, he discovered that the transmissions were connected with the shelling of British ships passing through the Straits. They were being attacked by the German coastal batteries, and the radar emissions Garrard had discovered were those of the shore-based German Seetakt, the naval gun-laying unit.

Garrard's discovery was soon being digested at Swanage and in London and was investigated in every way that could be imagined. It made people uneasy. They would have been yet more uncomfortable had they realized that Seetakt was operational during the Spanish Civil War and that a report on its aerial array had been in Admiralty files for eighteen months. Naval Intelligence had noted during the *Graf Spee*'s tour of duty in Spanish waters a large shrouded aerial above the bridge. When, after a running battle with three British cruisers in December 1939, the German captain saw fit to scuttle his pocket battleship in the shallow mouth of the River Plate, a British radar specialist, L. Bainbridge Bell, joined the boatloads of sightseers who went out in small boats from Montevideo to examine the stranded and damaged monster. Bell had climbed up to the aerial and reported to London that it could have belonged to a radar unit used for ranging the battleship's guns.[4] Bainbridge Bell's supposition was shelved in the Admiralty. He had no *proof* that it had been a radar unit.

It began to seem to scientific intelligence that the Germans not only had radar, but sophisticated radar. If so, the British were working in a dangerous vacuum. But now a new aid in their search for the elusive Dezimeter Telegraphie was coming to hand; the aid was an improved kind of aerial photography devised by an Australian.

13

On September 14, 1938, Alfred J. Miranda, an American businessman, cabled F. Sidney Cotton, an Australian businessman with offices in St. James's Square, London. Miranda said he would arrive the following day, and he urgently wanted Cotton to accompany him to Paris. Miranda dealt in many things, including aeroplanes and guns, whereas Cotton's business at that time was in a new type of film, Dufaycolor. In Paris Cotton met Paul Koster, Miranda's agent, "a man of seventy, but spry and animated."[1] In the course of two meetings, Koster sounded out Cotton's reactions to the rising menace of Nazi Germany. He received Cotton's assurances that he would be ready to take part immediately in the inevitable war with Germany. Koster told him he would be contacted on his return to London.

One day shortly after Cotton's return to London, the telephone rang. The speaker said he was "a friend of Paul's" and asked permission to come round right away. Two minutes later Cotton's secretary brought in the visiting card of Major F. W. Winterbotham. "I looked up to see a man of about my own age," Cotton, then forty-four, says, "dressed in a grey suit which toned with his grey eyes and greying hair. There was a look of determined discretion about him."[2]

Winterbotham told Cotton that he represented official intelligence organizations in England and in France. Now that Germany was expanding in all military ways and at the same time had clamped down the strictest peacetime security yet seen anywhere, what was needed was a privately owned aircraft able to take clandestine aerial photographs of German and Italian fortifications, airfields, and factories. Cotton,

well known as a flying man on the Continent and with bona-
fide business interests there, would be ideal for the job.
Would he be willing to let Winterbotham buy him a suitable
aircraft, and if so, what type would be the best?

A Lockheed 12A, Cotton said. He picked up a telephone
and asked to be put through to Miranda in New York.
Miranda agreed to buy him a Lockheed at once.

What remuneration would Cotton require for such work,
Winterbotham asked. None, Cotton answered, so long as his
out-of-pocket expenses were met. He was somewhat less than
pleased when Winterbotham proceeded to explain that Cotton would only be the official owner of the spy aircraft,
because the clandestine flights were to be made under the
aegis of experts in the French Deuxième Bureau, who had
"a predominant interest" in the flights.

In January 1939 the new Lockheed 12A arrived in England
—a twin-engine six-passenger aircraft. Cotton at once flew it
solo and was delighted with it. He was more reluctant than
ever to hand it over to the French, who, in his opinion, produced clumsy pilots and photographers whose methods and
equipment caused Cotton's hackles to rise. There was a
nightmare flight over the Rhine with a Deuxième Bureau
cameraman astern in the cabin. The Frenchman had established contact with Cotton in the pilot's seat by attaching
long strings to each of the Australian's elbows. Responding
to the tugs and wondering where the German fighters were,
Cotton wove a zigzag course across the map. He demanded
to see the resulting photographs and was dissatisfied with
what he saw. He proposed to the French that he should take
over the photographic side, which he understood as well as
anybody in Europe, including the Germans. Instead of their
one slow and massive camera he would make a framework
that could hold three of the RAF's F.24 cameras, two angled
outwards and the third looking straight down, thus covering
several square miles at each exposure. He knew that the RAF
results with the F.24 were disappointing, but he also knew
he could improve on them dramatically by using Leica film

and fine-grain developer and by playing warm air around the cameras and thus cutting out condensation. The French vetoed his proposition, so he turned over the Lockheed to them and told Winterbotham that he was telephoning Miranda to buy another one. When it arrived he would get to work in earnest. There was not much time. Winterbotham agreed.

The second Lockheed, even better suited to his purpose than the first, reached Southampton early that May and Cotton made some alterations with his remarkable blend of ingenuity and thoroughness. Extra fuel tanks were fitted, and "tear-drop" windows so that the pilot could see below and astern (one of Cotton's own patents). Airwork, a private firm at Heston, near London, made him "secret emplacements" for five cameras. Metal slides, almost impossible to detect, covered the embrasures when the cameras were not in use. There were three F.24s in the belly and a Leica mounted in each wing. All controls for the cameras were electric and were connected to the pilot's seat. The cameras and films and even the portable oxygen equipment could be packed away in suitcases which were covered with travel labels to make them look like innocent luggage. Lastly, the color was changed. One day at Heston he watched the maharaja of Jodhpur's private aeroplane taking off; when he looked up a few seconds later, he could not see it. He deduced that the maharaja's color, a pale duck-egg green, was wonderful camouflage. He had the Lockheed painted just a shade paler and patented the color under the name "Camotint."

Cotton's first assignment from Winterbotham for the gorgeous new spy plane was a long one, covering the Italian military scene outside Italy proper. Cotton chose Bob Niven, a young Canadian, for his copilot. The Lockheed, with full tanks, was refused a certificate of airworthiness by the official air inspectors. But Cotton, always difficult to thwart, decided that "I could hardly be blamed if some of the tanks were filled in error." All were filled, and he and Niven took off with plenty of lift, contrary to the inspectors' predictions and room to spare. On June 14, 1939, in Malta, Cotton recorded: "Introduced today to a five-foot-four RAF pilot named Shorty Longbottom—a fine young pilot with a slide-rule mind, keenly interested in my ideas on aerial photography."[3] Shorty could only get leave to do a brief flight with Cotton and Niven over Sicily. They photographed Comiso, Augusta, Catania and Syracuse, with excellent results. "Very glad," Cotton wrote, "to have Shorty with me, as he checked over the working of the cameras and gave me many useful tips on their operation." Cotton flew on for eleven days, staying only in the best hotels, and carrying out the required photographic coverage of the eastern Mediterranean, North Africa, and Ethiopia. It was time, then, to return to England and go to work on Germany.

Most conveniently, the Germans were genuinely interested in Cotton's color film. Dufaycolor's agent in Berlin had flown in the Richthofen Circus with Göring in World War I and knew all the senior Nazis. When Cotton first arrived at Tempelhof Airport, on July 26, 1939, there was a jack-booted guard of honor. And for a short period in which he took many clandestine photographs, Cotton and his *"kolossal"* Lockheed were frequently seen in and over the Reich. Both were nearly sequestered at the beginning of the war.

In August 1939 Cotton had proposed a plan to bring Göring to England to convince him that if Germany attacked Poland, the English would fight to the death. Göring had at first agreed to a swift journey over in the *kolossal* Lockheed, which had, in German eyes, assumed an almost ambassadorial status. Prime Minister Neville Chamberlain and Lord Halifax, Foreign Secretary, had consented to such a meeting and had made plans for a reception at Chequers. But Winterbotham hated the notion of the trip. He had reason to believe that the German invasion of Poland was being expedited, and if this became certain, he said he would send Cotton a warning telegram:

MOTHER IS ILL

MARY

That telegram was delivered to Cotton at the Adlon Hotel in Berlin on August 24. The following day, when a secret order to begin the attack was issued and then withdrawn (because Mussolini's disapproval of the intervention and the signing of the Anglo-Polish pact), a further telegram arrived:

MOTHER VERY LOW AND ASKING FOR YOU

MARY

In the end, after interminable delays, Cotton and Niven were allowed to take off from Tempelhof in the Lockheed. They had to follow a narrow prescribed route out of Germany, but while east of Groningen, Cotton saw the German battle fleet anchored in the Schilling Roads, outside Wilhelmshaven, and photographed it.

Sidney Cotton was a big man—he weighed a good two hundred pounds—with the bristling self-assertiveness of a small man. The strongest bent in his character was one of absolute independence. Characteristically, after a good record in World War I as a pilot in the Royal Naval Air Service, he quarreled with his commanding officer over what he claimed to be a bad decision by the latter, and resigned his commission.

By far the most noteworthy event in Cotton's war career was his invention of the "Sidcot suit." One cold day in France in 1916, when Cotton, then twenty-two, was working on the engine of his fighter, a Sopwith one-and-a-half strutter, there was an enemy alert. He took off as he was, in oily, greasy overalls. When he got back to the Mess he found that he was quite warm, whereas his brother pilots in full flying kit, had nearly frozen solid in their open cockpits. That started him thinking. He got leave and asked Robinson & Cleaver, a London department store, to make him a one-piece flying suit of his own design with a fur lining, a layer of airproof silk, and an outside layer of Burberry material. The neck and cuffs were lined with fur "to prevent the warm air from escaping. I had deep pockets fitted just below either knee so that pilots could reach down into them easily when sitting in cockpits. I asked Robinson & Cleaver to register my design, and for a name I took the first three letter of each of my names. . . . My father had drilled it into his family that none of us should ever try to make money out of our country's need in war, so I never made a penny out of the Sidcot suit, nor did I make any kind of claim after the war."[4] This despite the enormous success of his suit, which was adopted by the then Royal Flying Corps. Baron Manfred Von Richthofen, greatest fighter pilot of that war, was wearing a Sidcot suit when he was at last shot down, in 1918. And there was hardly a man who flew for the RAF in World War II who did not wear a Sidcot at some time.

Between the wars Sidney Cotton frequently mixed successful business activities (for a period he sold American inventions to the British and British inventions to the Americans) with flying adventures. When still a young man, using capital he raised personally, he flew the Newfoundland mails, organized an aerial survey of the island, and acted as spotter for the sealing fleet. His description of his work there reads like something out of a novel by Nevil Shute.

For his aerial survey of Newfoundland he got backing from Lord Northcliffe, from Sifton Praed of St. James's, map makers, and from a Welsh mining syndicate. Then, quite suddenly in 1923, Cotton sold out his stake in Newfoundland, where he had five operational aircraft, a sizable working yacht, shore establishments, and a big timber business. The decision to sell was made when he was flying an Avro on a seal-spotting trip; two hundred miles from land the engine began to falter. "No one knew what route I was on and I had no radio. I'd been taking this sort of risk for three years and so far I'd been lucky, but now the prospect of freezing to death brought me to my senses." He managed to nurse the ailing Avro back to his base at Botwood and left Newfoundland.

When war came Cotton's association with Winterbotham

continued. "The RAF are having camera trouble," Winterbotham said one day. "The first Sea Lord wants some photographs of foreign ports, the RAF can't get them, and everybody is raising merry hell." He asked Cotton to go next morning to talk with the Director General of Operations, Air Vice-Marshal Richard Peck.

While Peck was extremely diplomatic, Cotton sensed hostility in the atmosphere. Bad feeling existed between the Admiralty and the Air Staff on the subject of photoreconnaissance. At interservice meetings in Whitehall, the bluff sailors were apt to make insidious comparisons between the consistent early failures of the RAF in that field and the almost nonchalant ease with which "that fellow Cotton" seemed to get excellent pictures—a civilian in a civilian machine! Peck now asked Cotton if he had any special equipment. No, Cotton answered. Then how did he explain the excellence of his pictures when the cameras in the Blenheims were freezing up all the time? Cotton explained that it was not the cameras that froze, but the condensation round them.

Peck arranged a further meeting in his office, and there Cotton met an even higher-ranking officer, the Vice-Chief of the Air Staff, Air Marshal Sir Richard Peirse. After many introductions to bland-faced officers in RAF blue, Peirse told Cotton that aerial coverage was urgently needed of the Dutch ports of Flushing and IJmuiden. RAF crews had tried repeatedly to get it and had failed. Could Cotton make any suggestions?

"Lend me a Blenheim and I'll get you the pictures right away."

Peirse was appalled at the thought of a civilian flying around in a military plane. If Cotton were shot down and captured, he could be executed as a spy. Cotton replied that he wouldn't mind taking such a risk—he'd been taking it for some time before war was declared. Presumably he had been sent for as the photographic specialist that he was. Couldn't they let him get on with the job of taking the pictures? It would save a lot of talk and would show whether he could produce or not. But the only thing that was decided was to have a further meeting in Peck's office next morning, with some of the Blenheim pilots present, as well as an expert from the Royal Aircraft Establishment (RAE), at Farnborough, to "disprove" his condensation theories.

Depressed by all the talk while pictures were urgently needed, Cotton stood in his office looking out over St. James's Square. "The morning mist had cleared. It was a lovely warm day. I watched the fleecy clouds as I pondered a means of breaking the deadlock. . . . It was one of those days when anyone who loves flying longs to get airborne. . . . Why not? I rang Bob Niven at Heston and asked him to get me a flash weather report for Holland. The weather there was much the same as London, and the big woolpacks of cloud would give us the cover we needed. I told Bob to get the Lockheed out and warm her up ready for take-off, and as neither of us had had lunch, I asked him to get the airport restaurant to pack us a hamper. I rang Winterbotham and asked him if he knew of any German fighter patrols along the Dutch coast. He said it was quite possible if there were German naval movements. We had no photographic processing facilities at Heston, so I asked Winterbotham to arrange for Farnborough to develop and print some pictures later in the day, warning them it was a rush job, and they might have to work through the night."[5] Cotton then told his secretary to inform any callers that he would be unavailable until the following morning. Kelson, his chauffeur and personal servant, drove him to Heston. The streets and roads were empty, and the Lockheed was only just warmed up when they arrived. Cotton and Niven took off less than an hour after the ending of the second unsatisfactory, indeed hostile, meeting in Air Vice-Marshal Peck's office.

Immediately after take-off, Cotton asked Heston Control to tell Fighter Command that White Flight, his normal protective code for the Lockheed, was going out to sea off the Kent coast on a test flight and returning to land at Farnborough. Because of the low altitude of the protective "woolpacks," he flew at only eleven hundred feet. Crossing the coast at Ramsgate, he set course for the Scheldt estuary. Cotton and Niven found ideal cloud cover and between the clouds perfect photographic weather over Flushing and IJmuiden. They flew right across both targets with all five cameras running, then turned back for Farnborough, where the photographic section worked like heroes well into the early hours.

Kelson drove Cotton back to his flat in Arlington House in time for him to get two hours sleep and an hour for bath and breakfast before the meeting with Peck and his RAF experts. Peck opened it promptly at ten o'clock and there was a repeat performance of the day before—a lot of senior officers prepared to put *Mister* Cotton in his place. After listening for half an hour, Cotton opened his briefcase, took out the album of photographs, and asked, "Is this the kind of thing you want?"

Air Vice-Marshal Peck examined each print and praised them all. They had been enlarged to twelve-inch squares and each was covered with a transparent Kodatrace on which place names and other details were marked.

"These are first class, Cotton," he said. "But we wouldn't expect this sort of quality in wartime." He handed the album round. One of the officers looking at it asked when the pictures had been taken.

"At three-fifteen yesterday," Cotton said.

For a few seconds the others registered incredulity. Then, according to Cotton, there was "indignation as the truth went home. The commotion rose to such a pitch that I wondered what crime I could have committed. 'You had no right to do such a thing . . . flaunting authority . . . what would happen if everyone behaved like that? . . .' Somebody even said I ought to be arrested. I could stand such nonsense no longer, and decided to get out of the room before I told them what I thought of them . . . I walked slowly to the door and slammed it as I went out."[6]

Next morning a conciliatory Air Vice-Marshal Peck telephoned Cotton. He wanted to know when it would be convenient for Air Chief Marshal Sir Cyril Newall, Chief of Air Staff (CAS), to call on him. Cotton replied that he could not possibly put Sir Cyril to such trouble. He would call on the CAS at the latter's convenience.

"Would you be prepared to help, Cotton?" Newall asked him over luncheon at the United Services Club.

"Of course I would."

"Then take charge of the RAF's photographic section."

"That wouldn't work, sir. The regular officers would resent my intrusion; they already do." Cotton gave his opinion that that side of the RAF's work was still unsatisfactory because Lord Trenchard, who had been CAS 1918–29, had insisted that there should be no specialists in the service and because the professional aircrews had regarded photographic reconnaissance as too tame. He insisted that the best solution was to allow him to form a special unit and to give him the necessary aircraft and processing facilities. He would like to start at Heston, with his present nucleus of picked men.

"But Heston is a civil airport."

"Exactly, sir. Nobody would suspect that secret work would be done from there."

Cotton was commissioned as a squadron leader, with the acting rank of wing commander. The new unit was to consist initially of Cotton, five officers, and seventeen NCOs and enlisted men. At Heston Cotton requisitioned the hangars and offices of Airwork, the flying club, and part of the Airport Hotel. Shorty Longbottom, just home from Malta, Bob Niven, and Cotton himself made up the "planning triumvirate." At the beginning the section depended on the developing and processing department at Farnborough, but Newall had agreed that a photographic section should be built at Heston. Cotton's contact with the CAS was through Air Vice-Marshal Peck, and his contact with Peck was through Winterbotham.

Cotton now turned to the question of aircraft. He determined that his section must have Spitfires, stripped, un-armed, polished, and tuned so that nothing aloft could catch them. The experts told him that Spitfires were not suitable and that, in any event, they were unobtainable for such a lowly purpose; he had damned well better make do with the two long-nosed Blenheims they delivered to him. Cotton knew the Blenheims would not do, but he flew the two air-craft to Farnborough, where the Chief Superintendent, Mr. A. H. Hall was most interested in his ideas. Cotton's modifications increased the Blenheims' top speed by eight-een knots, but he still said gloomily that it was far too slow. However, this "Cottonizing" of the Blenheims came to the notice of Sir Hugh Dowding, now Commander in Chief, Fighter Command. Forced to use Blenheims as long-range fighters, he had found them to be hopelessly slow for that task. Dowding turned up at Heston and satisfied him-self that Cotton really could increase a Blenheim's speed. And when the Air Ministry told him they had no facilities for Cottonizing his Blenheim fighters, Cotton promised that if Dowding would requisition another hangar at Heston, he, Cotton, would be able to Cottonize Blenheims at the rate of eight per week. He kept his promise. "We painted the Blen-heims the same pale green as my Lockheed," Cotton says, "and this became standard camouflage for RAF fighters."[7]

The grateful Dowding invited Cotton to take tea with him at Bentley Priory, a hospitable gesture that turned out to be fraught with danger. Cotton left the tea table with the promise that two Spitfires would be delivered at Heston at nine next morning. They were. Trouble immediately ensued and not only for Cotton. A mark was chalked up against Dowding (who later was to be removed from his command immediately after directing the RAF in winning the great-est and most important battle in English history). As for Cotton, he was told that he had had no authority to get new aircraft, particularly Spitfires. How was Cotton going to serv-ice them? they demanded. They needed trained Rolls-Royce staff. Did Cotton intend to pinch those as well? (He did.)

His official reply was that his unit was attached to Fighter Command and that the reallocation of Spitfires was a domestic matter inside the Command. In any event, while the row blazed on, he had already converted his Spitfires, and merely by disarming them, Cottonizing them, and polishing all external surfaces into a hard gloss, he increased their speed from 360 to just under 400 mph. Next he intended fitting a thirty-gallon fuel tank under the pilot's seat to increase the range to 1,250 miles at thirty thousand feet. The RAE experts said this would shift the center of gravity too far aft. Cotton produced his calculations. They compromised on a twenty-nine-gallon tank. ("I let them get away with the odd gallon.")

When he announced his intention of fitting cameras weighing sixty-four pounds immediately astern of the new tank, the same argument arose. But where aircraft were concerned, Cotton was an impossible man to argue with. He knew too much. Calling for a screwdriver, he opened an inspection panel in the rear end of the Spitfire's fuselage and showed the RAE experts lead weights amounting to 32 lbs. These had been put there by the manufacturers to counterbalance the extra weight of the new three-bladed steel propeller. The cameras were fitted and worked well.

At last he was ready to begin taking pictures, though with only two Spitfires, one of which had to be used for training a unit destined, he knew, for expansion.

14

There was a vast amount of photoreconnaissance to be done on the German frontier whenever the weather was suitable, and Sidney Cotton, of course, lost no time in late 1939 in getting to work from RAF bases in France. If his relations with the Air Staff continued to be strained, he was soon on excellent terms with Air Marshal Sir Arthur Barratt, who commanded the RAF in France. The Belgians, afraid of annoying the Germans during the "phony war," refused to allow Anglo-French aerial reconnaissance over their territory, and as the Belgian maps were considered inadequate by Lord Gort, Commander in Chief of the British Expeditionary Force, and his staff, Cotton was asked unofficially, to get a complete aerial coverage of the country. The more "that fellow Cotton" was asked to do, especially if it seemed a little contrary to regulations, the more eager he was to tackle it.

Exposed film poured in from Shorty Longbottom, who did many of the initial flights, and Cotton had difficulty in getting it interpreted and processed. "By the end of the war," he says, "the Allied Central Interpretation Unit employed 550 officers and 2,000 other ranks, providing 80 per cent of our intelligence on the enemy. At the outbreak of war our interpretation capacity consisted of two RAF officers at the Air Ministry, two Army officers, and a small nucleus at the Admiralty."[1] Nor could the Air Ministry interpret his film easily, since although its quality was good it was taken from thirty thousand feet instead of the ten thousand usual with the RAF and the French Armée de l'Air. Cotton insisted that the task of maintaining a watch on Germany had to be done from thirty thousand feet, that reconnaisance from ten thousand was suicidal. "We must learn to interpret from that height. And we must get better cameras."

He found an unofficial way to obtain interpretation, and at first he financed it out of his own pocket. "Lemnos" Hemming had worked with Cotton in Newfoundland and was now running an aerial survey business at Wembley called the Aircraft Operating Company (AOC). Hemming, knowing that his business would have a valuable part to play in the war, had done his best to get it taken over by the Air Ministry, but the Ministry refused to consider such a step. Cotton took the matter up with Air Vice-Marshal Peck but could not convince him of the value of Hemming and his trained interpreters, who worked stereoscopically and used a large and extremely sophisticated Swiss calibrating and measuring machine known as the "Wild" (pronounced "vilt").

Swamped by his growing backlog of uninterpreted film, Cotton privately took over Hemming's firm, swearing every member of it to secrecy. As a consequence, the standard of interpretation was raised and Cotton was able to prove that his thirty-thousand-foot photographs could be read by trained technicians. Hemming also produced a camera with a twenty-inch focal length, which gave a scale of 1/18,000 at thirty thousand feet, as against 1/72,000 for the five-inch camera. Cotton's unit successfully used both cameras until the Air Ministry produced the F.52 which gave a scale of 1/10,000 from thirty thousand feet and became the standard air camera of the war.

Although during his prewar clandestine work Sidney Cotton had not found working with the Deuxième Bureau easy, he now found the French helpful. General Joseph Vuillemin, French Chief of Air Staff, in return for certain photographic favors, gave him access to French airfields. Cotton found these more secure and more comfortable than RAF fields in France, where station commanders might resent Cotton's two duck-egg green Spitfires, his non-military Lockheed, and his perfect manservant driving a large private car with an illuminated Union Jack on the back. Vuillemin had a special hangar built for Cotton at his own field, Coulommiers. It could house the Lockheed, and two Spitfires and was roofed in straw thatch to resemble a haystack. (It escaped, as few hangars did, the German attacks on French airfields in May 1940.)

RAF and French aircraft had been trying for weeks in the autumn of 1939, and with severe losses, to photograph the Ruhr industrial area of Germany. Bob Niven stood by for days, waiting for better visibility over that smoke-palled area, until December 29, when, in less than half an hour of Spitfire flight, he covered the whole southern half. During the next few clear days he photographed Cologne, Düsseldorf, and much of the Siegfried Line. Even this—and despite Cotton's loud and forceful protests—did not induce the Air Staff to keep their promises to him. He should by now have had eight Spitfires, a trained RAF staff officer to take some administrative weight off his shoulders, and two photographic trailers to work with his section in France. Most of all, he wanted Hemming's AOC to be officially recognized and incorporated with his Photographic Development Unit (PDU).

But Cotton now had help from an unexpected quarter. He was introduced to a Colonel Lespair, who commanded the French School of Photographic Interpretation at Meaux. "I was shown beautiful dossiers of photographs. It was plain from the detailed annotations and analyses that the French were a long way ahead of the RAF in interpretation and that even Lemnos' men could learn a lot from them."[2] Cotton arranged for one of the AOC men Douglas Kendall, to be allowed to take the French course (Kendall eventually became one of the leading photographic interpreters of the war). Meanwhile, Cotton also used the French school to process some of his unit's film. Lespair was at first astonished, then fascinated by Cotton's theories; and when he heard of Cotton's difficulties with the British Air Staff, he produced a chart which (summarized in words) showed:

1. The RAF had photographed twenty-five hundred square miles of German territory in three months for the loss of forty aircraft.
2. The French Armée de l'Air had photographed six thousand square miles for the loss of sixty aircraft.
3. Cotton's unit had photographed *five thousand* square miles in three flights *without loss*. (And these figures did not include twelve thousand square miles of Belgian territory which, at the request of Lord Gort, the unit had secretly photographed, also without loss.)

Cotton flew Lespair's figures to Peck in London. He guessed, as he watched Peck studying the paper, that the figures were "about right." He was taken straight in to see Air Marshal Peirse, and the following day he was told that the Air Council had approved the expansion of his unit. His reply was tart: it had been approved much earlier by the Chief of Air Staff, Sir Cyril Newall. Nine days later the first of his new Spitfires touched down at Heston. He made another vain attempt to get Lemnos Hemming's AOC recognized and to obtain the administrative officer that, with his businessman's passion for clarity and order, he craved. However, Air Marshal Barratt soon produced the latter, in the person of Wing Commander Geoffrey Tuttle, one of the best officers on his staff in France. This was a momentous appointment.

Cotton's next real tussle with the Establishment came on February 6, 1940, when Commander Charles Drake of Naval Intelligence telephoned Cotton that there had been a report that the German battleship *Tirpitz* had put to sea, but that the RAF had failed to get photographic or visual proof, one way or the other. The weather was thick and remained so for three days. But at eleven o'clock on the morning of February 10, Shorty Longbottom took off for Wilhelmshaven. Cotton telephoned Lemnos Hemming in Wembley to keep some of his staff on duty all night.

"It was a cold, clear day. The Spitfire, stripped of all armament, streamlined to our pattern, and polished till it shone, climbed rapidly away from Heston. At three-twenty that afternoon Shorty was safely back, having photographed Wilhelmshaven and Emden. . . . I took the film straight to Hemming at Wembley but the special processing for ship recognition took some hours, and it was two on Sunday morning before the film was ready for interpretation."[3]

Michael Spender, a Clarendon physicist and brother of Stephen Spender the poet and of Humphrey Spender the painter, was the photointerpreter of ships. He had joined Hemming's firm in 1939, and when it came under Sidney Cotton's direction he was one of the first to grasp that air intelligence could inform in time as well as in space. In other words, if the Spitfires could photograph Kiel regularly and the results of each reconnaissance were compared with those that preceded and those that followed it, the interpreter should get a good idea of what the enemy was *doing* there and of what might *happen* there—not just of what *was* there. If photographic intelligence is read in depth of scene, context, war background, then it becomes possible to penetrate the enemy's thoughts and know his plans.

That Sunday morning, in the early hours, Spender was able to state that *Tirpitz* was still in dry dock. It seemed essential to Cotton that a Royal Navy specialist should also, and at once, examine the pictures. He telephoned the Air Ministry and was told to take the processed film there. He must not contact the Admiralty. Cotton drove straight to the Ministry and delivered a complete set.

By Monday evening the Admiralty were getting desperate for information. They had not yet been shown the pictures and had heard from the Air Ministry that there were sixty submarines at Emden. (Michael Spender had correctly recognized these as a group of barges, not submarines.) Cotton decided that "the play had gone on long enough" and sent Naval Intelligence a set of prints with Spender's interpretations on the traces. The Admiralty realized that it could have had the correct interpretation thirty-six hours earlier. The result was that Churchill listened with mounting wrath to the complaints of the First Sea Lord, Admiral Sir Dudley

Pound, and Cotton was ordered to attend the War Room meeting that night. Churchill had intended to be there to sponsor him, but he was not; he had been summoned unexpectedly to Buckingham Palace. To make things worse, Pound settled himself in his high-backed chair and motioned Cotton brusquely to take a similar chair on his right, the place of honor normally occupied by Air Marshal Peirse. Peirse had at once inquired on entering the room, "What are *you* doing here, Cotton?" The admiral had intervened, "Sorry about this, Peirse, but we sent for Cotton in rather a hurry, and there wasn't time to get permission from the Air Staff. We particularly want him here tonight."

Shorty's pictures were passed around with the annotations by Michael Spender, including the Wild measurements of the German ships (and barges). Peirse asked how these had been obtained. Cotton answered, "With a special photographic instrument, sir."

"Why weren't Air Staff told about it? We'd have requisitioned it at once."

Cotton says that he had in his pocket a copy of the Air Ministry's latest refusal to do just that, but he kept quiet with an effort, and "accepted the rebuke."

Sparks then flew between Pound and Peirse. According to Cotton,[4] the next part of the meeting went like this:

POUND   We have pressed for information on the whereabouts of those ships and have been put off for one reason or another. We are not prepared to accept that situation any longer.

PEIRSE   I thought we had made it clear that this is a most difficult task and that some of the best brains in the Air Force are working on it.

POUND   Perhaps you'd get better results if you tried some of the lesser brains . . . (*turning to Cotton*) Cotton, you've heard what we've been discussing. Can you get us this information?

COTTON   Yes sir. Quite easily.

PEIRSE   (*Jumping from his chair*) I do not accept that, just because Cotton says it. There are scores of difficulties he probably hasn't even thought of.

COTTON Surely the proof of the pudding's in the eating, Air Marshal. May we not try?

POUND Sounds reasonable to me. What about it, Peirse?

PEIRSE How do you propose to carry out this operation? I shall want to know a lot more about it before I'm convinced it's feasible.

Some technical argument followed between Cotton and Peirse and then the latter arranged that they would "work out the details" the following morning. "And bring me the information on the equipment you mentioned earlier," Peirse added.

Pound leaned across toward the air marshal. "Are you going to requisition that equipment *now*, Peirse? Because if not, we propose to do it ourselves." And the air marshal answered, "Yes, I should have been told about it before."[5]

A week after Cotton's little victory in the War Room (which was not in the end a victory except for Hemming and the Wild machine), he heard from the Admiralty that coverage was urgently needed on the German ports. The Air Ministry told him they were making regular flights over Helgoland and obtaining the necessary information. Checking back with the Navy, Cotton found they had only been given visual information obtained by moonlight. He also learned that in carrying out those sorties three Blenheims had been lost out of five. "I regarded this slaughter as unnecessary and little short of criminal," Cotton says. And he said so openly, that being his nature. He could not help "exploding," as he put it, at the "shocking waste" of sending Blenheim bombers on tasks for which they were not fitted and the "criminal aspect" of losing splendid aircrew on such impossible tasks. At the Admiralty's request he went on photographing Helgoland and all other German targets given him by Naval Intelligence.

It was now his turn to attack the Air Ministry. Earlier he had recommended Bob Niven and Shorty for the Distinguished Flying Cross. The Ministry's press release on the announcement of the awards said that the pilots had been engaged on developing a new kind of photographic intelligence. Cotton naturally felt that this was "a disturbing and annoying lapse of security." He had come to believe "that jealousy of my unit's reputation was mounting. I was aware that there were men in the Air Ministry intriguing against me . . . but apart from repeated requests for speeding up the expansion of my unit, I took no action except to appeal to senior officers not to listen to gossip, but to back us up fully."[6]

On March 2 Niven took off in a Spitfire only delivered a few days previously from the Supermarine Aviation Works at Southampton. It was fitted with Cotton's new wing tanks and had a range of two thousand miles. From thirty thousand feet Niven took a complete set of pictures of the whole Ruhr. At the end of his traverses, three German fighters rose to intercept near the Luxembourg frontier. Niven opened up the Merlin engines to maximum permissible revs. It seemed to him that he just slid away from his three pursuers, as if they had been flying in glue. After half a minute he cut back his revs to save gas. Niven's pictures were so good that Cotton had them made into a single mosaic. When he opened this out in front of Air Chief Marshal Sir Edgar Ludlow-Hewitt, Commander in Chief, Bomber Command, he in his turn put forward a request that Cotton's unit should belong to Bomber Command. This Cotton opposed, on the grounds that "it was unwise for a major customer to run the show."

On the day following Niven's triumph, Cotton experienced his Black Sunday. "First, one of my new pilots crashed our training Spitfire, which seemed tragic enough at the time. Then real tragedy overtook us with the news that Dennis Slocum's Hudson had been shot down over Kent by Spitfires from Biggin Hill . . . Slocum was killed, and so was the wireless operator lent to me by Ludlow-Hewitt." One of Cotton's more delightful characteristics was his sense of identification with his pilots. "Slogger" Slocum, a former airline pilot, first flew in "Cotton's Circus" as a free lance on short leaves from his own RAF squadron, which was stationed in Scotland. When he managed to get transferred, he came up even to Cotton's standard. On his first long-range flight, over naval targets including the North Sea ports of Cuxhaven and Brunsbüttel, his cameras caught German submarines surfaced. The pictures were so remarkable that the Admiralty decided to show them to the King. "Cotton could always pick 'em," his unit used to say. They also picked Cotton, as was shown by Slocum and others like him.

That March Cotton was given sensible advice by three high-ranking airmen, Ludlow-Hewitt, Barratt, and Air Commodore Douglas Colyer, then air attaché in Paris. He had earlier had the same sort of advice from such men at the Air Ministry as Tedder. They all told him to stop fretting himself into a frenzy at the slowness of the Air Ministry, to stop tilting at windmills, to appear to obey all orders, and at the same time to push his unit ahead quietly. But Cotton was incapable of following such advice. His frustrations boiled over, and as he had said to Chief of Air Staff Newall, he was an Australian who talked not of spades but of bloody shovels. He enjoyed taking the Admiralty line, for example, on the radar defense system. He carried no IFF (identification friend from foe) in his Lockheed "simply," he says, "because no one had ever suggested it."[7] While admitting that his "White Flight taking off" warning had always been given to Fighter Command and that his Lockheed was a civilian aircraft and easy to recognize, he felt that if the early-warning system worked at all, he should have been buzzed quite often by British fighters. His attitude toward British radar was more deprecatory than Churchill's "M'yes," and he was unwise enough to use the Lockheed in Admiralty probes to test the system. To the Air Staff his conduct there seemed disloyal. The reason he aroused no defensive reaction from British fighters probably was that though the Chain Home screen picked up the Lockheed, the air defenses were not set in motion for one isolated aircraft that in any event would be recognized by the Observer Corps for what it was. Later in the war the Tempsford Squadrons, which did the parachuting and clandestine landings in Occupied Europe, were to prove that single bombers could fly through or under the very effective German radar screen, do their work, and return unchallenged.

Interpreting for Cotton's unit in France on May 7, 1940, Douglas Kendall (his French training completed) saw from the record of a Spitfire sortie that there were German tank units hidden in the Ardennes forest. Cotton took the still-wet negative to Air Marshal Barratt, who asked for an immediate low-level sortie. This showed that there were some four hundred German tanks *visible* in quite a small area. Barratt was alive to the significance of the discovery. The Allies were expecting the main German attack to come across the Belgian plain, and it was generally believed (though some experts ridiculed the theory) that the German armor could not pass through the Ardennes.

Unable to get any reaction from London that he considered strong enough, Barratt asked Cotton on May 9 to take his photographs to the Commander in Chief, Bomber Command, in England. If the British "heavies" (there were now some two hundred of them) bombed that section of forest with incendiaries and high explosives, the enemy's gasoline and oil and munitions dumps as well as his armor would certainly be in hazard. Cotton flew himself to Heston and drove without delay to Bomber Command Headquarters at High Wycombe, where his friend Ludlow-Hewitt had been replaced by Air Marshal Sir Charles Portal.

Although Cotton was an unofficial emissary, Portal received him. "The interview proved an unfortunate one," Cotton says. "He clearly regarded me as a nuisance. . . . I showed him the photographs, but I could see that my task was hopeless."[8] Cotton knew, of course, that Barratt had no power to call in the heavies, though when real war began he would be able to ask Bomber Command for assistance. What Barratt asked for now was a bombing attack on a German target before the Germans had actually started shooting. Even had Cotton convinced the War Cabinet, there would hardly have been time. The Panzer divisions, seven of them, began to roar out of their forest base early the following morning, May 10, and their thrust pulverized Western Europe.

With the outbreak of the shooting war, Cotton was told that the Air Ministry had decided to expand his PDU at an unprecedented rate. But on May 16, after the Dutch had surrendered and Churchill had flown to Paris to see Premier Paul Reynaud, Cotton learned that the unit had been ordered to leave France. "Naturally, though, they were waiting for my orders." He signaled them to stop where they were, pending his arrival, and piloted the Lockheed over to Meaux. He was soon with Air Marshal Barratt whom he found, "like everyone else, looking very tired." Cotton persuaded Barratt that now more than ever he needed the services of the only reconnaissance unit that could and would survive the German onslaught. As for the evacuation of his people and their gear demanded by London, Cotton assured the air marshal that with their Hudsons even his ground staff were completely mobile, that he would guarantee their safety, and that none of them should fall into enemy hands.

The following day there were more orders from London to leave France. Cotton sent back all the men he could spare in one of the Hudsons. Meanwhile, he and the unit continued to operate under Barratt for a further three weeks. On June 14, when his Spitfires had at last been withdrawn from French bases and the rest of the section were on the move south to Poitiers, Cotton flew to London. Geoffrey Tuttle warned him then that the Air Ministry had belatedly awakened to the merits of his methods and were planning to take over the unit and sack him. Cotton would not believe it. He asked his friends in Air Intelligence if it were true, and they denied it. That same afternoon he took off again for Poitiers. The unit had increased its transport by salvaging an abandoned but airworthy Fairey Battle light bomber. Before he and Bob Niven left for England in the Lockheed, all his people having been safely dispatched home, they picked up two stranded waifs, an English girl secretary and her collie. Cotton noted, "the dog seemed to enjoy the flight."

They flew into thick fog over the English coast. Cotton accordingly turned back for Jersey and took rooms for himself and his passengers (including the dog) in a hotel, which was machine-gunned by the Luftwaffe early next morning. Expecting German aircraft to be active over the Channel, Cotton filled up the Lockheed's tanks and flew out into the Western Approaches before turning up north and coming in over Bristol, and thence on to Heston. As he stepped from the Lockheed he was handed an official letter. He was puzzled by the address, since his initials were incorrect and he had been credited with a decoration he had never won. He read:

> Air Ministry, Dept. OA
> London SW1
>
> 16 June 1940

SECRET[9]

S.58864/S.6.

Sir,

  1. I am commanded by the Air Council to inform you that they have recently had under review the question of the future status and organisation of the Photographic Development Unit and that, after careful consideration, they have reached the conclusion that this Unit, which you have done so much to foster, should now be regarded as having passed beyond the stage of experiment and should take its place as part of the ordinary organisation of the Royal Air Force.

  2. It has accordingly been decided that it should be constituted as a unit of the Royal Air Force under the orders of the Commander-in-Chief, Coastal Command, and should be commanded by a regular serving officer. Wing Commander G. W. Tuttle, D.F.C., has been appointed.

  3. I am to add that the Council wish to record how much they are indebted to you for the work you have done and for the great gifts of imagination and inventive thought which you have

brought to bear on the development of the technique of photography in the Royal Air Force.

I am, Sir,

Your obedient servant,
Arthur Street

Wing-Commander H. L. Cotton, AFC
Royal Air Force Station,
Heston, Middlesex.

Sir Arthur Street was Permanent Under-secretary to the Air Ministry.

At last Cotton's enemies, while his major ally Air Marshal Barratt was still busy with the French defeat, had thrown him out. The Admiralty, which had been responsible for some of his unpopularity with the Air Council, was too lazy (or too discreet) to stand up for him. And when, later, Their Lordships offered him employment they were told sharply by the Air Ministry that they might not employ him, that if they did so it would be considered a hostile act; meekly they acquiesced.

Cotton's efforts to get back into his own unit were politely quashed. Every effort he made to do something to help win the war was smothered by the remorseless and sound-proof blanket that the Establishment can drop over any unwanted or resented person, particularly in time of war. The services of this one energetic, patriotic, and brilliant individual were made taboo by a Ministry that knew his brilliance had made it look foolish.

Cotton was a man of many interests, and he did not lie down and die. His consolation was that his unit and the nucleus of officers and men, including Geoffrey Tuttle, whom he had personally chosen, went from success to success. The views he had postulated on high-speed photographic reconnaissance and scientific stereoscopic interpretation in depth, views which had been laughed at, ridiculed, resisted, were now the official views. And the unit, now that he who had conceived it and who had raised it up had been sacked, was one of the brightest gems in the Establishment's regalia.

15

As Cotton was always delighted to declare, his successor, Geoffrey Tuttle, made a remarkable success of the Photographic Reconnaissance Unit (PRU); and he rose to be an air marshal and to receive a knighthood. Yet when he met Cotton at any time after the latter's dismissal, it was the senior regular officer who called the junior reservist "sir." Tuttle amply showed that in choosing him Cotton and Barratt had been wise. He cemented and increased the virility of Cotton's unit and injected into it an element of dignity and effortless discipline. "There might easily have been a disastrous drop in morale after Cotton left," writes Constance Babington Smith,[1] herself a full-fledged member of "Cotton's Circus" on the interpretation side. "But Tuttle had the good sense to accept the flying club atmosphere, and not to try to regularize things all at once. He was quite prepared to overlook a pilot's blue suede shoes if that pilot was getting good photographs."

With the fall of France the unit had become vital to the country, and though for a long time Spitfires were necessarily in short supply, expansion was rapid. Later, a move was made to Benson, in the Thames Valley, as Heston Airport became too small and too insecure.

Under Tuttle the PRU continued with its high-speed high-altitude cover, and Cotton's interpreters, with their stereoscopes and the Wild machines, were in the center of the scientific branch. "Lemnos" Hemming had succeeded in enlisting the services of Claude Wavell, a mathematician who had worked with him on a pioneering air survey of Rio de Janeiro. The tendency with high-grade interpreters was specialization, and this, sensibly, was encouraged. Michael Spender, for example, continued to specialize in German ships and harbors, Constance Babington Smith in German aircraft (and later rockets), and Claude Wavell became a specialist in German radio and radar installations, a department that drew him much into close contact with Dr. R. V. Jones, Charles Frank, and Derek Garrard.

"Early in 1941," writes Miss Babington Smith,[2] "not long after Peter Riddell[3] had asked me to start an aircraft section, the Photographic Interpretation Unit [of the PRU] moved to a safer and more pleasant spot. Its new home was a large pseudo-Tudor mansion called Danesfield, a pretentious edifice of whitish-grey stone with castellated towers and fancy brick chimneys, which looks out southwards from a magnificent site between Marlow and Henley. When Danesfield became an Air Force station it had to be given an official title and it was named RAF Medmenham, after the little riverside village nearby. From then on the name Medmenham . . . was identified with Photographic Intelligence . . . The distance that separated Medmenham from the [PRU] airfield at Benson was a gulf that was not very often crossed, which was a great pity. Whenever any of us did get over to meet the pilots, or when, during spells of bad weather, some of the pilots came over to Medmenham, it always left one feeling, Why can't this happen more often? Both our own work and the pilots' seemed to get a tremendous boost from it."

That was not the only boost that PRU pilots were getting. They had learned the technique called "dicing" in RAF slang. When close-up photographic cover was urgently wanted of any place or object, the pilot would streak in low, very low indeed, and try to take the target as he shaved past it. Dicing was becoming so important that Tuttle had had the Spitfires painted pale pink, since that color had been proved on trials to be better (low down, at least) than Cotton's duck-egg green.

R. V. Jones, as one would expect, was extremely methodical and liable to hang on to any clue. Having learned in July 1940 that a Freya radar unit on Cap de la Hague had been responsible, or partly so, for sinking H.M.S. *Delight*, he had asked PRU to cover Cap de la Hague and the village at its southern end, Auderville. And he had asked Claude Wavell to bring him any pictures they had already. On November 22, 1940, Wavell turned up at Jones's office in London with prints which showed a couple of rather odd circles west of Auderville. He thought they might be "cow pens." But according to the Wild measurements, the "pens" were only twenty feet in diameter, which did not look the right size for cows. They might, Wavell suggested, be flak-gun sites.

By this time Jones had established a technique for identifying Knickebeins in photographs by comparing the shadows of their big aerials as they rotated. When the Auderville pictures had come in, and while Jones was still talking with Wavell, Charles Frank put two similar pictures in his stereoscope and, following Jones's technique with Knickebein shadows, looked carefully at the "cow pens." It seemed fantastic, but he saw that the two pictures did not quite match up. A shadow inside one of the pens had fractionally widened. Exactly what time had elapsed between the two frames? Nine seconds. During those seconds, it seemed to him, some thin structure, perhaps high and quite wide, but thin, like a playing card standing on edge, had turned a bit on its central vertical axis. It could be a radar aerial. Had they found the villain that had finished off *Delight*? Jones agreed with Frank; it looked like a breakthrough. PRU was asked to lay on dicing sorties over the "cow pens" west of Auderville.

There was a prolonged delay. Photoreconnaissance was overextended on anti-invasion assignments, and some of the senior officers running the war were very annoyed with Jones. He was always being a prophet of doom. Now he was claiming that the Hun had radar! Even if true, did it matter so much? Radar, they argued (they thought as the Germans had), was defensive; it did not kill people. But the Prime Minister was excited about it, and a high-powered committee under Air Marshal Joubert de la Ferté had been set up to get at the truth.

The first PRU dicing sortie was a failure. The pilot photographed the field next to the "cow pens," which took him right over an antiaircraft gun. Jones was told that what he had taken to be enemy radar was in fact a gun. But Jones sharply called for another photograph, this time on target. So, on February 22, 1941, another Spitfire pilot, Flying Officer W. K. Manifould, made the second attempt and came back with a wonderful oblique (the low-level, close-up photograph achieved in dicing).

One can imagine with what intense excitement—rather like Holmes and Watson on first seeing the Hound of the Baskervilles—Jones, Frank, and Garrard examined Manifould's work of nerve and skill. So that was what a Freya looked like: beautiful! beautiful! What was more, that same day they picked up the Freya pulses from Auderville on a frequency of 120 megacycles. Garrard put them on a cathode-ray tube and broke them down into a perfectly intelligible signal. He noted that the signals were different from the Seetakt emissions that he had originally picked up on the cliffs of Dover.

The next day, February 23, had been fixed in advance by Air Marshal Joubert for a meeting of his committee of inquiry. When Dr. Jones arrived with his double proof (pictures *and* sound), the air marshal wondered if Jones had not been stacking the cards in order to make a point. However, the previous day's date on Manifould's oblique and Garrard's report proved that this was not so. The inquiry was ended; the question was answered. The Germans, beyond any possible doubt, had radar.

Information now came in from Belgium and France. Freyas were much smaller than CH towers, but turning aerials could not always be concealed. Also the British, by radio and PRU searches, were able to plot the Freyas around the length of Colonel Kammhuber's Himmelbett line. A piece of motion picture film was sent to England which showed Luftwaffe signalers working a Freya and tracking British aircraft. So much for Freya; but that there was another type of German radar set, complementary, perhaps more important, the British had also learned.

"Ferret" Wellingtons of 109 Squadron in their radio-search sorties reported from the Freya sites different signals of shorter range, on a frequency of 570 megacycles. One Wellington, on a coastal tour of Brittany on May 8, 1941, plotted nine of the 570-megacycle emissions. It was particularly maddening that nothing showed on any photographs of those places. Agents, requested to list all known sorts of German radar in the occupied territories, spoke of "FMG" and "Freya." The British did not know what FMG meant (actually the letters represented *Funk Messgerät*—radio-measuring apparatus). Jones learned that four FMGs were operating in Vienna, of all places, by the end of 1941. As Vienna seemed unstrategic, though emotionally important to Hitler and the Germans, Jones inferred that FMG was an integral part of German aerial defense and had been produced in considerable numbers.

Two unusual leads now, in late 1941, came through to London, one from a United States source and the other from a Chinese. Jones received a photograph taken by "a well wisher in the American Embassy in Berlin." The photograph showed in the distance, above treetops, a new German flak tower, and on the tower was a metal lattice aerial shaped like a saucer on edge. There was no foreground to the picture and nothing to give scale to the aerial. But a few weeks later a Chinese scientist sent in a report. He had been walking near the Berlin Zoo and had seen the same flak tower. He described what he took to be a directional and ranging device for the ack-ack guns in the tower; it was, he said, paraboloid in shape, and the diameter of the bowl was at least twenty feet.

His description puzzled the British. (He was, of course, describing one of the new Giant Würzburg sets that had been produced in response to Kammhuber's complaints about the original set.) If scores of 570-megacycle radar installations existed round the coasts of German-held Europe, why were they invisible if they were as big as the one near the Berlin Zoo? Could they be underground or camouflaged in some special manner?

However, there were now more opportunities for photographic coverage and Charles Frank was looking at a new batch of aerial photographs when, once more, he thought he noticed something. It was on a medium-level photograph of a Freya station on the cliffs north of Bruneval, between Le Havre and Étretat. Near the Freya station was the prominent lighthouse of Cap d'Antifer. Inland was a large farm complex around a square. That was where the signalers operating the station would be quartered. There were flak guns, well sited as usual. Between the big farm and Bruneval village, down below in its gulch, stood an isolated house. It would be officers' quarters, presumably, or some kind of headquarters. There were trees around the farm and inland, and trees around Bruneval. But the headland surrounding the isolated house was bare, its turf eaten short by cattle. The paths or tracks from the Freya station to the farm and from the farm to the house showed up clearly on the photograph. But the equally well-used path from the station to the house was indirect. It led south to a small black dot, and from the dot it went up to the house. Frank conceded that the dot could be anything from a latrine to the entry of an underground dormitory. But there was a chance that it was the missing link, the radar whose 570-megacycle signals the "Ferrets" had heard. Dicing was the only solution. Jones asked for low obliques of Bruneval "through the regular channels," but whether by accident or design, he also let Claude Wavell know about it.

Jones had paid close attention to "Cotton's Circus" and its development into the official Photographic Reconnaissance Unit. He had seen, as Cotton and only a few others had, that when the country was on the defensive and when it went into the attack, photography with proper interpretation could tell more than a thousand agents. No part of PRU was without interest to him.

Jones had first heard of Tony Hill when he was told that there was a PRU pilot who was keen on taking low obliques (dicing) but who always somehow muffed the camera shot, so that he just missed the vital object. Jones was interested. He made a point of meeting Hill, whom he found to be a most likable young flying officer, modest, shy, half-wild, dedicated. Over a pint of beer together in a Thames Valley pub, they discussed dicing. Hill explained that he was by nature "a bit slow" and seemed unable to manage the camera. So the scientist and the pilot took the problem to bits and put it together again. The timing was, in fact, very difficult, because the camera was behind the pilot, pointing broadside and a little astern. The pilot therefore had to dive on the target and watch it disappear under that shark-like Spitfire wing and flash up on the other side. At just which moment he pressed the button depended on his personal reactions, his nerve, and a few other factors. He simply had to learn by trial and error. When Jones and Hill had talked it all out, they had reduced it virtually to a technique, like golf or tennis, with the result that Hill went to work intensively, got the knack of it, and went on to take some of the best photographs of the whole war.

At this stage in the hunt—late 1941—there occurred one of those "rare but precious visits" of PRU pilots from Benson in Oxfordshire to their Intelligence Wing at the wisteria-draped Danesfield, fifteen miles away. Gordon Hughes, one of the PRU Spitfire pilots, drove over with Tony Hill. Hughes made his way to Claude Wavell's office, where Wavell at once showed him his newest gadget. He had called it, rather grandly, the "Altazimeter," and he had designed and made it himself. Its function was to work out rapidly and accurately the actual heights of objects seen on aerial pictures. Height, he explained to Hughes, equaled shadow length times the tangent of the sun's altitude. It followed that the only data needed were latitude, the scale of the photograph(s), the orientation, and the date.[4] It was merely an application of the principles of spherical trigonometry. That was the kind of thing that Gordon Hughes came to Danesfield to hear. He found it both elevating and restful. But now Wavell changed the subject.

He took from his desk two photographs of a length of cliffy French coastline and put them in his stereoscope. As Hughes looked, Wavell explained. It was felt that the speck where that path to the isolated house suddenly changed course might be the paraboloidal installation that the scientists were all so keen to find.

Hughes suddenly remembered that Tony Hill was waiting for him below, and Wavell suggested that Hill be asked to take a look at the pictures. When Hill was sitting opposite him, Wavell began to talk about German radar. It was different from the English variety and its origins were as old or older. He laid another pair of pictures under the stereoscope and showed Hill the one-millimeter variation in shadow that had put Charles Frank on the track of the Freya. That piece of inspired deduction, he said, had led to *this*. . . . He produced the Manifould oblique which had finally convinced people that the Germans had radar. The oblique was proof, and it showed the equipment to be very sophisticated. It wasn't funny. Bomber losses over Germany were getting worse, and the enemy radar plainly had much to do with it, especially, it was thought, the as yet undiscovered set that worked on 570 megacycles. He changed the photographs again, putting the first two back on top. Was the dot the paraboloidal installation? . . .

Hill spoke. "Where exactly is this place Bruneval?"

Wavell told him.

"I'll get you your answer tomorrow."

Next morning Wavell saw on the PRU operations' board:

ÉTRETAT—HILL

and he was worried. The flak would be hot. He telephoned Benson. Would Mr. Hill be good enough to call him at RAF Medmenham as soon as he got back from his mission?

His heart turned over when the telephone rang.

"Tony Hill here. You were right. It must be a paraboloidal whatnot and the Jerries were round it like flies."

"You saw it?"

"Clearly. It's like an electric bowl heater and about ten foot across." Hill then apologized. His camera had failed. There were no pictures. "But don't worry. I'll have another go tomorrow."[5]

There was a rule that no pilot might fly the same dicing sortie two days running. The risks were great the first day, and on the second, with an alerted defense, they could be expected to be many times greater. But Hill was determined to photograph the "bowl heater," and nothing was going to stop him. He had no authorization, and as luck would have it, Jones's official request for low obliques had gone to another squadron, three of whose aircraft were warming up, also at Benson, as Tony Hill got into his Spitfire. A senior member of the PRU ground crew came and challenged his right to go. Hill sent a message across the airfield to the other pilots, saying that the Bruneval job was his and that if he saw them within twenty miles of the target, he would shoot them down (he did not specify what with). In any event, he swooped again over Bruneval, shaving the edge of the cliff and the lone, ugly house, the scream of speed in his head, the surge of the Merlin at his knees. The low oblique he brought back to Benson was just what Jones wanted. Hill had brought the Giant Würzburg to life.

Hill's next great pictures came after the Bruneval Raid. They were of two Giant Würzburgs on the Dutch island of Walcheren. Jones's office had had news of a German night-fighter station there and high-level photographs indicated one Freya and two Berlin Zoo-type Würzburgs. Hill swept down in a low curve along the Dutch coast and his sideways-aimed camera took from point blank range first one Giant and then the other. They were facing different ways as he passed, so the German apparatus was taken from two angles. He also caught one of the Luftwaffe Signals crew of the second Würzburg, who was just climbing to the cabin and who "froze" on the metal ladder as the *Engländer* passed.

That was in May 1942. In October of the same year Hill diced an aircraft factory at Le Creusot. He was not satisfied with his first flight, so again, as at Bruneval, he repeated it the following day—and was shot down.

"We had become very good friends," Jones said. "And I think I felt Tony's death at Le Creusot on 21 October, 1942, more than any other during the war. He was very much my idea of what a schoolboy's hero should be. As soon as I heard that he was down we organized a rescue operation. But he was too badly injured to survive."[6]

16

February 1942 had begun badly for the French agent Rémy. His impending Lysander flight from France to England had been so frequently postponed that it seemed as though it might never come off. Yet it was always hanging over him and it disrupted his other activities at a time of more than usual difficulty for the Confrérie Notre-Dame. True, he had been cheered by Pol's luck with the Bruneval report, and it had seemed too good to be true when the irrepressible Bob, on February 9, transmitted the report to London.

But on the evening of the twelfth Rémy bought a *Paris-Soir* and read with disgust the main news story. *Scharnhorst*, *Gneisenau*, and *Prinz Eugen* were said to have left Brest the night before and to have steamed up-Channel for Germany without being challenged by the Royal Navy or the Royal Air Force. Rémy was enraged. The escape seemed to set at naught the achievements and sacrifices of his CND agents who had worked in Brest, particularly those of Hilarion and "L'Hermite." L'Hermite (Bernard Anquetil) had been killed by a firing squad the previous October at the prison in Mont Valérien. He had refused to utter a single word that might have incriminated CND or any of its host of fringe helpers. Had he died in vain? It truly seemed so. Had the English paid absolutely no attention to accurate information gleaned by Hilarion from the radish patches of the Arsenal garden in Brest? It would seem so. Had Pol's reports of sudden moves of German fighters to the Channel airfields been regarded as so much eyewash?

On the other hand, Rémy was ruefully aware that the English, thanks to the Japanese and to the Germans with their submarines and their Afrika Korps, were all too busy elsewhere. Everything seemed to be going wrong with the right side. And the Nazi-controlled French newspapers, apparently happy to take their lead from Dr. Goebbels' Propaganda Ministry, trumpeted out each Axis advantage, hailing every skirmish as a major victory. As to their panegyrics on the escape of the three German ships from Brest, anyone would have thought, as Rémy pointed out, that Nelson had lost the Battle of Trafalgar. He argued with any of his friends who had the heart to discuss so sore a subject that the German warships had been blockaded in Brest for close to a year. And now, instead of surging into the Atlantic to prey on Allied shipping and shoot it out with the Royal Navy, they were scampering east to the comparative safety of their home ports. And it was indeed comparative only: the British had shown and were showing that they could bomb all Germany. Casting about for excuses, Rémy also pointed out that the German Navy had picked very thick, typical Channel weather. The English spy plane of Coastal Command that always shadowed the three ships, for so long stationary, had caught just one glimpse of them sneaking out through the Goulet de Brest, probably at the very moment his radio had chosen to break down. How unlucky could one be? All the same, even Rémy had to admit that the Germans had conceived a dangerous operation and had carried it through successfully. They had sent the three ships up-Channel under a tremendous Luftwaffe fighter cover. Where, then, was the RAF, which had been victorious in the Battle of Britain? Where was the Royal Navy? Where the heavy coastal artillery, the submarines, the minefields, the swift motor torpedo boats the English were said to possess?

He would have been surprised (but perhaps not relieved) to know that a small section of English opinion, an increasingly important section—the scientific one—was not entirely displeased, since the German breakout emphasized the importance of science in the coming phases of the war. The general public, the Prime Minister and his colleagues, and the press were even more dismayed than Rémy; *The Times* described it as "the most mortifying episode in our naval history since the Dutch got inside the Thames in the seventeenth century." What there was no way of understanding at the time was that with the escape of the three ships, the Germans had called an end to the radar stalemate, for they had achieved the escape through temporarily blotting out British radar. But in the radar war—a jamming war, a war of electronics—that was to ensue, the British and their American ally were immeasurably the stronger and the more ingenious side.

Again, as Rémy rightly sensed, in moving the three ships into the dubious security of North Sea ports, Hitler had made his first lairlike move of the war. He was drawing into a defensive ring. And the reason was not far to seek: air power. It was no longer good tactics for him to send capital ships marauding. They were too easily found and destroyed from the air. The Luftwaffe, contrary to expectations, had just failed to defeat the Royal Air Force. It was the outcome of the Battle of Britain and Bomber Command's aggression that made Hitler call the three warships home rather than send them out into the Atlantic to blast a huge hole in England's supplies.

The German antiradar moves during the Battle of Britain had been mishandled in a fairly logical way. While CH stations in Britain were attacked, Martini's Signals people on the French coast listened. As they continued to report that bombed CH stations declared destroyed went on transmitting, it came to be thought (quite erroneously) at Luftwaffe Supreme Command that the important control mechanism of each British station must be underground, in bombproof bunkers. Accordingly, Göring decided to discontinue attacking the CH stations and any further bombing was so spasmodic that the defense's remarkable repair services easily coped.

Meanwhile, however, on the Cherbourg Peninsula and near

Calais, Martini had set up cross-Channel jamming transmitters. After their first shock at realizing the extent of the British radar coverage, Luftwaffe Signals had realized that the British Hertzian walls were by no means invulnerable. Many people in Britain held the same opinion. Long before, when A. P. Rowe took over the running of Bawdsey from Watson-Watt in August 1938, he asked Dr. E. C. Williams to try jamming the station. A diathermy set was accordingly fitted in a Sunderland flying boat. When this heavy machine lumbered into Bawdsey's radar twilight the radar screens were covered with pretty dancing lights. Colored filters helped the then-inexperienced operators to distinguish the aircraft's trace, and in subsequent experiments Professor T. R. Merton had developed the "long afterglow" whereby an aircraft's trace remained while the dancing lights died.

In the early days of September 1940 the first German jamming transmitters began their effort. On September 11 they ran at full strength. By using colored slides and waiting for the afterglow, the Chain Home operators, many of them now WAAFs (Women's Auxiliary Air Force) and very much on top of their job, kept going, and the CH cover of the South Coast was never completely at a loss. But that it was seriously interfered with was indicated by the day's results, which were unusually bad. Fighter Command flew 678 sorties, losing twenty-nine aircraft with seventeen pilots killed and six wounded. The Luftwaffe lost only twenty-five aircraft.

Two days later, when the Germans attacked London intermittently by day and fiercely at night, they made another attempt to jam, and three CH stations, Dover, Rye, and Canewdon, were in some difficulty. But the general impression, on both sides, was that the German jammers were not powerful enough. The British felt that airborne jammers would have been more effective. In that stage of the war the German jamming, like their direct attacks on radar stations, had been too haphazard. Nor had the importance of radar been fully appreciated by Germany's leaders. At his conference in Berlin on September 13, Hitler referred to the unusually bad showing of the RAF on September 11. But he did not in any way link it with Luftwaffe Signals' jamming. He merely said that he thought the British defenses were at last cracking. One gets the impression that he thought in terms of a kind of poster art—Nordic heroic youth battering at a more effete type of youth.

This emotional viewpoint was again reflected in February 1942 in the decision to redeploy *Scharnhorst, Gneisenau,* and *Prinz Eugen,* which was, strategically, a bad move. At Brest the German ships had been tying down important British forces and were in a position to exploit any obvious British weakness in the Atlantic battle. However, Hitler could not bear to think of his ships being bombed in a foreign land, and he conjured up visions of a threatening naval power center in the North Sea—including even the Soviet Navy, then stronger on paper than in fact. But if his motives were emotional, there was nothing ill-considered about his orders for the move. Complete Luftwaffe cover had to be given. Göring, nervous about the responsibility, handed it over to Air Field Marshal Milch. Milch consulted with Martini, whom he disliked and despised. Dr. Hans Plendl, the inventor of two of Dr. Jones's headaches—the Knickebein and the X-Gerät —shortly now to be given a senior post in Germany's radar defense organization, was also called in to advise.

A program of analysis, location (with special narrow-angle direction finders suggested by Plendl and with the help of Luftwaffe reconnaissance), and frequency-testing of the British radar service on the south coast of England was rapidly carried through. The Germans were now in close contact with their main ally, the Japanese, and were beginning to understand that their warships could not function unless Germany had air superiority. They now agreed that air superiority had not been achieved over England, but, by decree of the Führer, it *must* be achieved over those three ships for two days. And it was so achieved.[1]

It was found that the British radar cover was limited in frequency variation and could easily be jammed. Proper equipment was set up in two centers in France directly connected by landline to and therefore controllable from a central headquarters. These centers were strategically placed near Cherbourg, to cover the wide part of the Channel, and at Calais, for the vital narrows. A co-ordinated program was worked out with the Luftwaffe fighter units. So, while the fighter screen was gathering in the north of France, the jammers from the two centers began gradually getting the British operators used to spasmodic interference. Then, during the escape, when the three ships were already well up-Channel from Brest, the jammers opened up full blast, and for a while in the southern part of England there was no radar cover.

A board of inquiry was set up in England to ascertain how the German ships had managed to move almost unhindered so close to the south coast. The results of the inquiry were unpublicized. They involved decisions to broaden the frequencies of many British radar services, making them less vulnerable to jamming and, far more important, to become aggressors in the radar war. Up to this point radar had proved itself in a defensive role: Knickebein had been jammed, as had X-Gerät Y-Gerät. It was now time to attack the radar systems on German and German-held territory.[2] Cockburn and his helpers at Swanage had a means ready to disrupt the German Freya system. As for the Würzburg, that would be tackled after the Bruneval Raid.

There was some faint relief for Rémy following the breakout from Brest, since the British bombing there now ceased and Hilarion was no longer in danger of death or, worse, capture. Rémy was still under orders from London to remain in Paris until Operation Julie, that endlessly postponed flight across the Channel, was brought off. He objected to being thus confined, and the news from the Far East made him despondent.

On February 15 Singapore, the British stronghold in Malaya, capitulated to the Japanese. The "island fortress" had held out for only two weeks after the day when all the British forces left in the Malay Peninsula withdrew within its perimeters. Churchill had at once admitted this disaster to be one of the worst in British history. Goebbels was, for once, in enthusiastic accord, and as usual he got a lot of coverage in the German-dominated newspapers of Paris.

Infuriated by all that he had read, Rémy found himself at lunchtime in one of the premier restaurants surrounded by German officers who seemed to him "more arrogant than ever." And, culminating stroke, when he was handed the vast menu he was outraged to read, "fully visible in the middle of the fish and shellfish dishes" the words *Coupe Singapour.* He made up his mind to have a reckoning with the restaurateur after Liberation, which that morning seemed depressingly distant, even uncertain.

17

When Hill's low oblique of Bruneval reached his office in the Air Ministry, Jones decided after careful scrutiny that it was possible to get in there; there was a beach only a few hundred yards from the objective. Almost the next person he happened to meet was W. B. Lewis, deputy superintendent of TRE (Telecommunications Research Establishment). Lewis promised that any proposal to raid the cliff top for samples would have his support. Jones then took his suggestion to the Vice-Chief of the Air Staff, Sir Richard Peirse, and to Lord Cherwell, which was as good as telling Churchill. It would seem that the firm proposal for the Bruneval Raid went from the Air Staff (who were interested in the end result) to Combined Operations (who would have to do the raiding). At a slightly later stage Tizard, independently, had the same idea.

From then on Jones watched, as an informed outsider, the progress of "C" Company's training. What directly concerned him was the Würzburg itself, and that meant a contact with Flight-Sergeant Charles Cox and Lieutenant Dennis Vernon of "C" Company. The date of the raid was drawing very near when Cox and Vernon were granted two days "compassionate" leave in London. Each was told in confidence to report in the afternoon of the second day to the duty officer at the Air Ministry.

"I went home for one precious night to Wisbech," Cox recalls.[1] "When I got to the Air Ministry the next day Lieutenant Vernon was there, in the waiting room. I thought it peculiar, him not being an airman. We were taken to an office. Three men sat behind the desk, two Englishmen in civilian clothes and a Frenchman in British Army uniform, battle dress. He said little. The Englishman in the middle, powerfully built, sure of himself, a good bit younger than me, did the talking, while the third man spoke occasionally when what you would call the technical side of matters was under discussion.

"There was a lot of talk to begin with about what would happen if we were taken by the Jerries. We were only to tell them, of course, the standard things, name, rank, and number. But we must make it clear, if caught on the job, that we were simply a demolition squad out to do mischief to a valuable bit of enemy equipment. We would both come in for special questioning, since I was the only airman in the parachuting party, and Vernon was the only engineer officer. We discussed alibis. The tall man said the Germans often planted an 'English' fellow-prisoner in the cell of a newly captured man. He would be an expert at getting information, and there could be hidden mikes. We were warned too against the kindness-and-generosity treatment: they might put you in a comfortable room with soft music, a box of Coronas, and a bottle of whisky or brandy. . . . I told the Intelligence people I could stand up to any amount of *that* type of interrogation.

"We were given advice on how to escape capture if things went badly wrong with the raid. With the French people in the locality we would be among friends. Granted half a chance, any of the farmers or villagers would hide us and risk their lives . . . just as they were doing for all our boys shot down over France. It might well be, the big man said, that even if things went wrong, we would be smuggled, Dennis and me, fairly quickly back to England, either by boat or in a small pick-up aircraft. But in case we were completely on our own over there, we were given French money, maps printed on fine silk and collar studs with miniature compasses hidden in the bases. We had to memorize three addresses, two in France and one in Switzerland. If we got to any of the three, we had a code password. The people in the houses would do the rest. We would simply be packages in their care.

"Most of the rest of the interview was technical stuff concerning the German RDF [radio direction finding] set, what was wanted from it, and why. Both the Englishmen evidently knew more about radar than we did. Without raising his voice or saying anything dramatic, the main spokesman had made us feel that our job was something really worth doing, and that we were lucky to find ourselves doing it.

"It did not take long. It was very matter-of-fact and reassuring. A WAAF driver took us in a staff Humber to Waterloo Station. When we left the train at Salisbury, another WAAF recognized us, guided us to similar Humber, and drove us to Tilshead. We were beginning to feel quite important people; but we were soon cut down to size, the pair of us, because our lot were still doing those damned exercises with the Navy, and it was too near mid-winter for swimming. (Supposing either Dennis Vernon or I had caught pneumonia, and hadn't been able to go on the raid?)"

Jones's companion at the interview was a radar specialist from TRE at Swanage, D. H. Priest. Dangerous though it was judged to be in view of the known "thoroughness" of German interrogation methods, it had been decided to send one expert on the raid. Priest had been chosen and had been given a temporary flight-lieutenant's commission and a cover story for the occasion. He was to arrive with the landing craft, and his code name was "Noah." It was envisaged that *if* the flight went easily for the parachutists up above on the headland as well as down by the beach, and *if* the landing craft made the beach in good time, and *if* armored German units were slower than seemed likely in arriving at the scene, then Priest might have time to hurry up the cliff path, make an assessment of the paraboloidal device, and supervise its dismemberment. It was a tall order. But they had to think of every eventuality.

To Major John Frost and "C" Company as a whole, the successful breakout of *Scharnhorst, Gneisenau,* and *Prinz*

Eugen on February 11 was upsetting. It appeared to show a certain British lack of control in the Channel area, which did not augur well for their own evacuation after the raid. And the marine side of their training was going badly; indeed, it did not go at all.

"Security" would not sanction a move of the parachute unit from Tilshead to new quarters nearer the south coast. Accordingly, day after short February day, they drove south to the Channel in Bedford trucks, did their watery exercise, and returned in the dark. The Dorset coast which, particularly around Lulworth, has cliffs resembling those at Bruneval, seemed to be favored by the Navy. It is an exposed coast, and the weather was obstinately foul. What had been planned as the final rehearsal was one of the worst of a series of disappointments. The parachutists were to leave their transport on a flat stretch of land near the sea. The Whitley bombers would parachute down to them there the weapon containers and the folding trolley (a light-weight but very strong two-wheeled trolley with a good capacity for stolen mechanical parts, specially designed and made to drop on its own parachute). And after attacking an imaginary objective, the raiding party would consolidate on the beach and call in the landing craft by radio and by radio beacon. As it happened, the landing craft waited off the wrong beach, the Whitleys dropped the containers in the wrong place, and the parachutists got trapped in an actual defensive minefield and were lucky to get out of it without casualties.

When only forty-eight hours remained before the first possible departure on the raid itself, the naval authority at Portsmouth insisted on yet another night exercise. This had to be postponed for twenty-four hours because of heavy weather. It was then held on the night of Sunday, February 22, in Southampton Water; there was still far too much wind outside in the English Channel.

This time "C" Company with all its gear and appendages made a "withdrawal" in creditable silence and good order. Four men pulled and pushed the two-wheeled trolley, carrying a sizable boulder. The timing was correct. Contact had for once been established with the Navy on both No. 18 radio sets. The landing craft were all there—but a long way offshore. The raiders were ordered to wade out to the boats. It seemed pointless to risk their weapons and the trolley, so these were left under guard at the water's edge. For a considerable distance the piercingly cold sea was only three feet deep. Then it crept up to their thighs, then shoaled again. Cox had to make a dash for the boats—his legs were stiffening with cramp. When the hundred and sixteen cursing men were aboard, the landing craft went full astern—and did not budge.[2] The officers jumped overboard, followed by the men. Everybody pushed and heaved. Still, the boats, aground on a falling tide, would not move. The men waded ashore, facing the tedious, too familiar, drive in soaking clothes and drafty trucks, back to the dark huts of Tilshead.

The next four days, Monday to Thursday, were the only days possible for the operation in February, when the moon was full and the landing craft could approach Bruneval on a rising tide.

Orders had now been issued. All the officers had typewritten copies headed:

SECRET   NOT TO BE TAKEN IN AIRCRAFT
OPERATIONAL ORDER "BITING"
By
Major J. D. Frost, Commanding
'C' Coy. 2 Parachute Bn.
Topography—Scene of operation to be explained on model.

In the cellars of Danesfield, below the large rooms where Constance Babington Smith and Claude Wavell and others worked at interpretation for PRU, there was a model-making workshop. The Bruneval model had been accurately put together from blown-up air photographs and the biggest-scale French maps. The Würzburg was there, the ugly house, trees, fences, gates, German pillboxes, all to scale. Since the raid

was to be an operation by moonlight and over complicated
and rugged terrain, the lie of the land had to be familiar to
every man. Few people can "see" a piece of country by looking at a map. A model is different.

In "C" Company's orders, the German defenses round the
beach were described as "Beach Fort," "Redoubt," and
"Guard Room," (the villa, Stella Maris). The house, locally
called the *château*, was "Lone House," and the big farmyard of Le Presbytère was "Rectangle." The Würzburg was
"Henry."

The stated objectives of the raid were: "To capture various
parts of HENRY and bring them down to the boats. To capture
prisoners who have been in charge of HENRY. And to obtain
all possible information about HENRY, and any documents
referring to him which may be in LONE HOUSE."

Frost's doubts as to the merits of the original Divisional
plan had not induced the planners to change it. His force of
120 men was divided into three parties of equal size, each
with its own limited objectives. The parties were to drop at
five-minute intervals, the first groups going down at fifteen
minutes past midnight.

The first party of forty men was code-named "Nelson."
Because it had the longest journey to its objective, it was to
drop first and to move silently and swiftly down to the
beach. When Frost gave the attacking signal up above, this
party was to storm, take, and hold Redoubt, Beach Fort, and
Guard Room, thus securing the whole force's line of retreat.
Nelson consisted of three light assault sections (ten men
each) commanded by Lieutenant E. C. B. ("Junior")
Charteris of the King's Own Scottish Borderers and a heavy
section, also ten men, under Captain John Ross of the Black
Watch. In his section Ross had some sappers with antitank
mines (for the Bruneval road to the beach) and mine detectors and guide lines. As soon as the beach was taken he
was to mark a route through the minefield, establish a check
point, and see that the signalers contacted the Royal Navy.
It was this part of the plan, Frost believed, where most

could go wrong. There was no saying how many Germans would be in the beach defenses after midnight, assuming that surprise was achieved; and if strongly and resolutely manned, they could be all but impregnable. On the other hand, Charteris and Ross were both officers of character and determination to whom the men were devoted. Charteris' sections, mainly made up of Seaforth Highlanders, had tremendous offensive potentiality.

The second party of forty men had to split into four, three with code names. "Drake," with twenty men under Lieutenant Peter Naumoff, was to move towards Rectangle and take up a position west of it to ward off enemy threats to Lone House and Henry. "Hardy," a group of five men under Frost, would surround Lone House, while "Jellicoe," an assault section of ten men under Lieutenant Peter Young, would surround Henry. The Royal Engineers (REs) led by Lieutenant Vernon and accompanied by Cox, totaling five men, would move to Henry when Young's party had cleared it of the enemy, and Young would then protect them while they worked.

The third party, "Rodney," forty men under Lieutenant John Timothy, Royal West Kent Regiment, would drop last, and would act as landward screen, reserve, and finally, rear guard.

The reason the numbers were multiples or fractions of ten was that they dropped in "sticks" of ten, a technical necessity for paratroop drops of that time.

As to timing: everybody was to get into his attacking position as quickly and silently as possible, and when this had been effected, Frost, from the steps of Lone House, would give the signal to attack, four blasts on his whistle.

They all agreed that the dropping zone, due east of a track running north and south on the model, seemed a good one, and so did the forming-up point by a line of trees nearby. They also agreed that it would be a heartening thing to see Noah (the TRE radar specialist Priest) come up the hill from the beach. That would mean that the boats had actually reached the place and that the situation at two key points, the beach and Henry, was under some kind of control. There were surprisingly few questions. One man, looking at Tony Hill's oblique, asked how surprise could be effected if the RAF went flashing cameras in the Germans' faces. "Oh telephoto lens, you know. Taken from miles away," Frost replied. Another asked if they would drop with blackened faces. "Certainly not," was the answer. "The main thing on this party is to avoid confusion. I'll have no black faces. I want to be able to recognize you in the moonlight." And a third man asked, "When you get to the front door of Lone House, sir, and you blow your whistle, what do you do if the door's locked?" "Ring the bell."[3]

On Monday morning, February 23, "C" Company went through their normal routine. At ten o'clock they checked and cleaned all weapons and packed the containers, which were to leave for Thruxton Aerodrome at two. Ross had contrived, without breaking security with the Glider Pilots' Regiment, to get the men a particularly good midday meal, and after it they were urged to have a siesta until tea, at five o'clock. And at teatime a message came through from Division. "Owing to adverse weather conditions" there would have to be a twenty-four hour postponement.

Tuesday, Wednesday, and Thursday were exact repeats of Monday: each morning they repacked the containers, and each evening they unpacked them; the weapons were cleaned, recleaned, and cleaned again. And Thursday had always been named as the very last possible day in February for the raid.

"We are all thoroughly miserable," Frost wrote in his diary. "Each morning we brace ourselves for the venture, and each night, after a further postponement, we have time to think of all the things that can go wrong, and to reflect that if we don't go on Thursday we shall have to wait for a whole month to pass before conditions *may* be suitable. After all, the weather in the English Channel in February and March is not inclined to be 'suitable.'"

Friday morning was bright and frosty. The wind seemed to have dropped. The clouds had gone. Frost expected a message from Divisional Headquarters instructing him to send everyone on leave. But the message was that the other branches of the service involved had agreed to see what weather one more night would bring.

Stand-by again. For the fifth day running they went through the now-tedious morning routine—breakfast, tidying up, packing containers. The men all felt listless except, it seemed to Frost, Sergeant-Major Strachan, who was in high good humor and said he was sure they were going to have some fun at last.

At teatime Friday, General Browning, commander of the 1st Airborne Division, immaculate as usual, arrived to wish them all luck. The raid was on.

As the Royal Navy's participation called for an earlier start from England, Admiral Sir William James, Commander in Chief Portsmouth, had signaled that morning: CARRY OUT OPERATION BITING TONIGHT 27 FEBRUARY.[4]

In the afternoon *Prins Albert*, carrying, apart from her regular complement, thirty-two Welsh commandos—officers and men of the Royal Welch Fusiliers and the South Wales Borderers—slipped out through the boom defenses escorted by five motor gunboats (MGBs) and two destroyers. Each MGB carried a crew of sixteen, and the 2,700 horsepower of its three Hall-Scott gasoline engines gave it a speed of twenty-seven knots. The armament of each MGB was two two-pounders, two pairs of half-inch twin-mounted Vickers machine guns firing tracer and armor-piercing shells mixed, one Oerlikon, and four depth charges. Long after dark, at 9:52, *Prins Albert* lowered six assault landing craft (LCAs) into the sea. Each, in addition to its regular Navy crew, carried four soldiers who were there to give extra firepower with their Bren guns. The Welshmen had blackened their faces and were in the highest of spirits.

Prins Albert turned and headed home.

18

That Friday morning, February 27, Rémy awoke at Saint-Saëns, north of Rouen and about fifty miles inland from Bruneval. He had endured a wretched night, sharing a bed with a grumbling companion, another agent also due to go to England by that unconventional means of transport, the Westland Lysander. Julitte, like Rémy, had been put off many times. He had "*quite* lost hope" and every five minutes or so, he said so.

Rémy himself, a large man, who at that moment was coughing with a heavy cold, was not exactly an ideal bedfellow. But Marcel Legardien's café of the Guardian Angel, which was once more sheltering them, could only offer one spare bedroom with one bed and a mattress on the floor for Bob.

Cautiously parting the window curtains, Rémy peered out at the weather. A leaden sky. Cloud base as low as six hundred meters. Bob had already left his bed on the floor and gone to gauge conditions at the landing ground. On his return he announced that there was not more than twenty centimeters of snow anywhere. It was hard snow, excellent for Lysander work.[1]

Julitte, Bob, and Rémy had had an enormous piece of luck the day before. They had left Paris by train, from the Gare St.-Lazare. Arriving at Rouen, they looked for the bus to Saint-Saëns and, as was usual in those days, found it packed with travelers, the roof smothered in an untidy mass of luggage and bicycles. Rémy, with his natural air of authority, persuaded the driver to find room on the roof for their two pieces of luggage. One of these was Bob's English transmitting set in its standard brown suitcase; the other was a bulky valise filled with Confrérie Notre-Dame documents on their way to England—a risky passage indeed!

Having seen to their luggage, the three men with difficulty thrust themselves into the interior of the bus. Just as the bus was about to start, they saw one of the Guardian Angel's resistance group, Léon, rushing across the square waving his arms. They had taken the bus believing the tires on the Guardian Angel's van to be completely worn out. But now a breathless Léon assured them that the Angel had been able to find new tires on the black market and was waiting for them with his van outside his brother's café. After Rémy had given the furious bus driver a large tip to take down the cases he had had such difficulty in stowing, they walked to the café near the Palais de Justice, finding their luggage heavy but delighted that the Angel had turned up.

Indeed, the Angel's appearance proved to be something of a miracle, for on their way to Saint-Saëns they passed their bus from the Rouen station which had been stopped by a patrol of the *Feldgendarmerie*. The passengers were lined up at the roadside while every bit of luggage was dragged off the roof and searched. (The risks that agents like Rémy thought nothing of running were the more terrible because it was pure luck that saved them from disaster.)

The next morning, Friday, Bob made early contact with London and was told to keep a listening watch.

At five in the afternoon London had a message for him. The Lysander flight, Operation Julie, was on.

But at 7:30 P.M., in the personal messages following the BBC's French Service news, Operation Julie was postponed till the following night, and even the normally imperturbable Guardian Angel, rising to produce a bottle of his miraculous Calvados, exploded over the stupidity of those British—it was, he fumed, a perfect night. Julitte said nothing, but his expression—wrinkles of bitter laughter round the eyes, a venomous droop to his mouth—said, "I told you so."

Tasting the Calvados, his aching eyes shut, Rémy forced

himself to remain calm, good humored. This proposed flight
to London had always seemed to him a waste of time. He
was only going there because Passy (Major Dewawrin), De
Gaulle's chief of counterintelligence, insisted on seeing him.
So much time had been wasted when he could have been
elsewhere in the CND area looking after his own people,
wasted in hundreds of hours of waiting in those dangerous
corners, with far too many radio transmissions. It really was
too maddening—particularly when one had a cough, a tem-
perature, sore sinuses, watering eyes. The Guardian Angel
produced a pack of cards. Oh well, it would pass the
time. . . .

At 9:15 P.M. the Angel laid down his cards and switched
on the radio. The familiar French voice from London worked
through the familiar day's news to . . . "*Veuillez maintenant
écouter quelques messages personnels.* . . ." Julitte laughed
bitterly, and Rémy was distressed to find himself echoing
the laughter. But suddenly the silence in the smoke-filled
room was complete; and there was no time to waste. Their
message had come through. Operation Julie was *on.*

The full moon was early that night. And the rendezvous
had been fixed for between ten and eleven. They dashed upstairs to dress, to grab their luggage, overcoats, gloves. Down-
stairs again, there was just time to kiss Mme. Legardien in
front of the round-eyed maid, and they were outside in the
deserted snowy street of Saint-Saëns. Bob had hurried ahead
with Léon to set up his triangle of lights on the landing
ground. The sky was full of stars.

Now all three—Rémy, Julitte, and the Guardian Angel—
were loaded down, for they had to carry Rémy's trunkful of
papers for London, together with the biggest-scale maps covering the whole of France which Passy had ordered. The
mass of paper had been divided among three sacks. Rémy
carried his on his right shoulder. In his left hand was the
equally compromising and by no means light suitcase con-
taining the transmitter. In order to shield his appalling head
cold against the February night air Rémy had covered his

chest and back with thick pads of thermogenic medicated cotton. This ferocious breastplate was held in place by a woolen undershirt covered by a lumberjack shirt, which in turn was covered by a massive white wool sweater knitted by his wife, Édith. Over this he wore yet another thickness of wool—a tweed jacket which he had buttoned with the greatest difficulty. Enormously thick stockings came up to his knickerbockers. A knitted wool Balaclava helmet covered his Basque beret, and he sported fur-lined gauntlets and a fur-lined leather coat, a Canadienne, then the most popular article of clothing in France. Never a sylph, Rémy admits that that moonlit night he must have looked like a perambulating barrel.

The Guardian Angel led them uphill through snow; the landing ground was at least one kilometer away. Immensely powerful, a countryman, a Norman, the Angel swept on as though the heavy sack he carried were no more than a straw. Rémy, following, stumbled and strained, while behind him he heard the imprecations and the sobbing breath of Julitte. At the top of the hill Rémy thankfully paused. He was sweating "as though in a Turkish bath" and "my sweat had triggered off the action of the cotton-wool impregnated with mustard et cetera. It burned me fiercely, back and front, giving the impression that I moved in a ball of flame."[2] He longed to tear off his carapace, but could not reach it under its layers of wool and leather protection. In any event, it was extremely cold on the snowy plateau, and he could imagine he heard Édith saying, "Don't you dare take anything off."

Rémy's watch showed 11 P.M. German time, the equivalent of nine o'clock Greenwich Mean Time. That was supposed to be the latest limit for the operation. But they waited, thinking of the effort it was going to take to carry all those sacks and cases back to the café. Julitte was beginning to act up again: "What fools to imagine that at last . . ." But the Guardian Angel had held up a hand the size of a suckling pig. He had heard an aeroplane, far away, a single small aeroplane. Rémy suddenly became aware that his terri-

ble cold had completely gone, vanished, blown away! Bob
had switched on the three electric flashlights on sticks and
was sending the code letter in Morse with a fourth flashlight.

Losing height rapidly, the Lysander swept round in a circle, switched on its landing light, touched its wheels on the
base of Bob's triangle, rolled on to the apex, turned and
taxied back to swing into the wind at the base. The door
opened and a figure descended. Rémy had known that an
agent called "Anatole" was coming and that the Guardian
Angel was to give him a bed for the first night. Anatole
proved, though, to be a woman, a young woman with fair
hair. The Lysander's engine still turned. The sacks and other
baggage were flung in. Julitte went up the ladder. The Guardian Angel seized Rémy in his muscular arms and brushed his
cheek with a sharp bristle of mustache. As Rémy climbed
the metal ladder, a bottle of the Angel's Calvados in one
hand, he heard Julitte shouting from the rear cockpit, "Look
out, there's no room in here." But Rémy pushed himself in
and somehow sat down despite Julitte's protests. The Lysander was already taking off. They pulled the plexiglass
canopy shut above them. The aircraft climbed masterfully
over the wood, over fields with the outlines of hedges.

Julitte nudged him. "Look."

They were above what appeared to be an airfield near the
edge of the sea. A light ran rapidly across the surface below
them, from one edge to the other.

"A Boche fighter!"

Seeking to warn their pilot, Julitte hunted in vain among
the piles of their belongings for the intercom. Then they
were out over the Channel. The sky seemed empty save for
themselves. Rémy in gratitude looked at the stars. He began
to pray. . . .

"*Je vous salue, Marie, pleine de grâces. . . .*"

He was half asleep, thinking about his other journey to
England from Brittany, with his brother Claude, in 1940. Sud-
denly a brilliant red light passed the length of the cockpit.
The pilot had fired a flare as a recognition signal and below

them were the chalk cliffs of Dover. The Lysander tilted far over on one wing, straightened, and landed at Tangmere. What Rémy did not know while they flew over the Channel was that down to the westward the Whitleys of 51 Squadron were lumbering in the opposite direction carrying "C" Company with its section of Royal Engineers, Flight-Sergeant Cox, and Private Newman on the Bruneval Raid.

19

After Frost had seen his men off to Thruxton Aerodrome in their trucks, he sat down to an evening meal with the glider pilot officers at Tilshead. He found it hard to say nothing about the speculations and fears that galloped through his mind. He looked round him at the placid faces. Would he ever see them again? Lucky devils! Going soon to bed in their warm hut.

After dinner he went to his room and dressed in full parachutist's rig. It felt even more cumbersome than usual. He returned along the passage and could not resist the impulse to open the door of the Mess and poke his head in. The pilots were dozing peacefully near the fire. His soldier servant waited on the doorstep beside the Humber staff car. They both got into the back seat with some difficulty, bulky as Victorian ladies. The drive to Thruxton seemed pleasantly attenuated.

"The Company was dispersed in huts round the perimeter," Frost recalls. "John Ross and I and Sergeant-Major Strachan and Newman visited each little party in turn. Some were fitting their parachutes, some having tea. There was a lot of talk, and one group was singing. It was a glorious night, an utter change in the weather; the kind of thing that only happens in England. Sometimes an aircraft engine would cough into life, and always in the background there was the rattle of a truck coursing round the edge of the aerodrome on some urgent mission. That truck came round again, and it was looking for me. I was wanted on the telephone. Were they going to call it off again?

"But it was Group-Captain Sir Nigel Norman. 'Just want

to say good luck, Frost,' he said. 'Latest information is that there's snow on the other side, and I'm afraid the flak is lively.'

"So the RAF had been snooping round there again, annoying what we wanted to be a sleeping hive of Germans. They had promised diversionary raids by Fighter Command on neighboring parts of the French coast; it was to be hoped that the weather report came from one of them. As for the snow . . . in a way it was a relief to me. We had been issued with snow camouflage suits but they were back at Tilshead. No, my feeling was that our main difficulty on such an operation was the 'fog of war'—confusion. I thought the snow would make things clearer."[1]

Flight-Sergeant Cox found the night scene dramatic. "We were put in blacked-out Nissen huts. Inside it was warm and the light was yellow. Parachutes were laid out in rows on the swept floor and we each picked one, hoping that the dear girl who'd packed it had had her mind on the job. These were dark 'chutes, camouflaged in greens and blacks. Until then I'd only used white or yellow ones. They pressed bully [beef] sandwiches on us, real slabs, and mugs of tea or cocoa laced with rum. We checked each other's straps, and wandered about wide-legged, like Michelin men. It seemed brighter outside than in the hut, and bitterly cold. We were formed up in our tens, or jumping sticks as we had done so often in training. One saw then what it had all been about. It was reassuring to know exactly where to go and who with. Piper Ewan was playing, and that has an effect on Scotsmen. It brings them to the boil—and they're excitable enough already. I'm not sure that the pipes are healthy. The piper was coming on our jaunt, but leaving his pipes behind."[2]

Ewan played their regimental marches as they moved around the tarmac to the twelve Whitley bombers. Frost was exhilarated by the pipes and impressed by the aircrews. "They were a different breed, at ease, and dressed for what they normally did. By comparison we seemed a lot of clowns. I had a waterbottle of strong tea laced with rum, and I

handed it round the blokes in my stick while we waited to
emplane. Charles Pickard came along to see me, puffing (un-
lawfully I suspect) at his pipe, a reassuring and a wholly
proven leader, and very young at that. I wasn't flying with
him. He was leading the flight, with Junior Charteris' lot.
When he drew me aside from the others I expected some
joke or platitude. But he certainly made no attempt to re-
assure me personally.

" 'I feel like a bloody murderer,' he said."

"I was jumper number six in aircraft number six," Cox remembers. "We put on our silk gloves and crawled into sleeping bags for warmth. The Whitley's ribbed aluminum floor
was fiendishly uncomfortable. Ahead we could hear a kite
revving prior to take-off and then it was away. Others followed until it was our turn. The whole machine throbbed
and bumped and dragged itself off the ground as though it
had great big heavy sloppy feet. Nobody slept in that dim-lit
metal cigar. We had some singing. We sang *Lulu, Come Sit
by My Side if You Love Me,* and *Annie Laurie.* Then, by
popular request, I gave them two solos, *The Rose of Tralee,*
and *Because.* Somehow the engines made it easy to sing.
They came in thrums, noisier one instant than the next."

Corporal Stewart and two others had played cards all the
way over. Stewart was winning as usual. He pulled out his
wallet to put in yet another bank note and said generously
that if he copped it on the raid the bloke next to him must
take the cash and make good use of it.

Prins Albert was steaming fast back to Portsmouth. Her
landing craft, escorted by the motor gunboats, were closing
in on the French coast under their own power. There was as
yet little wind (though more was forecast quite soon—too
soon perhaps), and visibility was good, with a bright moon,
little cloud, and some haze.

When the cover was taken from the hole in the bomber
floor a piercing blast entered. Those who cared to look down

saw the sea, gently moving in the moonlight. Suddenly they were over snow-covered land, bouncing and weaving in anti-aircraft fire. Frost dangled his legs in the hole. His bladder felt ready to burst from all the tea drunk at Thruxton. He was so uncomfortable that he could not wait to get down. His companions were in a similar plight. He swore that he'd never get caught like that on any subsequent operation. Why had they not been told to keep off liquids? Or indeed, why hadn't he thought of it?

"Action stations . . . GO!" One after the other the men shot out. As soon as Frost's parachute opened, he saw below him all the dropping zone landmarks, so easily recognizable from hours spent with the model. They were dead on target. He landed very softly in snow a foot deep. No wind. No German reception committee. Now the aircraft were winging away over France and there was flak from the main radar station, probably firing at the last of the Whitleys coming in.

Cox lay in the slipstream looking up at the dark belly of the aircraft. How fat it was, and how fiery the points of its exhausts! Suspended, now, from his parachute, he felt to check that he had his fighting knife and his Colt .45 automatic. Then he was rolling in the snow. "The first thing that struck me was the hush. I suppose it was reaction to the horrible din inside the aircraft. Then I heard a rustling and saw something outlined on the snow and a light on it." He disconnected the container's light and that of the hand-trolley, which had come down nearby.

Having got rid of the Thruxton tea—"not good drill," Frost commented, "but a small initial gesture of defiance"—they gathered at the line of trees. As they did so, Lieutenant Timothy's Rodney party were coming down in a sizable cloud of parachutes. With such visibility, Frost knew, there was little chance of surprise and, anyway, presumably Henry (the Würzburg) would have tracked them across the cliffs. The one good thing was that, even if a lot of Germans now knew that he and his "C" Company were there, they would have no idea where nor how they were going to be hit.

Everything seemed to be going so well that Captain Ross's news came as a shock. Ross and his heavy section, the organizational rear guard of Nelson, the beach assault party, had landed safely with their gear. So had one of Charteris' three light sections of ten men; it had a special task, and it left immediately to do it. The task was to take and hold the German pillbox redoubt on the north side of, and above, the beach. Should the pillbox be manned, they would need surprise, luck, and dash to take it. Having taken it, they were expected to act as the pivot for the whole withdrawal and also for the assault on the beach defenses. (In the event, they found the pillbox unmanned, but quite rightly remained in it according to orders.) Now Ross reported to Frost that *Charteris himself was missing, along with his other two assault sections, twenty men in all.*

Not for the first or the last time, Frost inwardly cursed the inflexible plan that had been thrust on him. This was exactly what he had feared would happen. Two aircraft had failed to deliver their parachutists as planned. Perhaps they had been shot down, perhaps they had dropped the men somewhere else.

Frost asked John Ross to wait for a few minutes to see if Charteris and his men turned up and then to get on down to the beach defenses and do his utmost with the heavy section. The main problems, Henry and Lone House, had to be tackled first as planned, and as soon as he could Frost would get Peter Naumoff, with Drake, down to help Ross at the beach. Meanwhile Naumoff and also Timothy's Rodney party were needed to hold off any attack on the raiders at Henry, either from Rectangle (the farmyard of Le Presbytère) or from Bruneval village.

Within ten minutes of landing No. 2 Party had formed up into its four components. Naumoff led his Drake people off in the Rectangle direction; Frost, with Private Newman at his heels, led his Hardy party toward the plainly visible Lone House; and Peter Young and his Jellicoe assault section made for the Würzburg, followed at a slight distance by Vernon's RE unit and Flight-Sergeant Cox, wheeling the trolley.

To Frost's astonishment, the front door of Lone House stood wide open. The hall was dirty, empty, quite unfurnished. He could just see that Young's party were encircling Henry. Young, Sergeant Mackenzie, and three others would have hand grenades ready as soon as the whistle went, then charge in with their Stens. Frost blew his whistle four times and darted inside the house. The ground floor was empty, but shooting came from above. They ran upstairs and found only one German there, firing down at the tremendous rumpus going on around Henry. They killed him and searched the rest of the house. It was empty.

Meanwhile, Young and his men had overrun the Würzburg position and those Germans who were able took to their heels. One of them scuttled towards the cliff edge, the moon dazzle on the sea silhouetting him. There had been too much shooting, Young felt, and no prisoner had yet been taken. The German was chased and he fell over the edge of the cliff but managed to cling on and find footing. As he climbed back he was caught and taken to the radar bowl. He was unarmed.

Dennis Vernon had left his own men and Cox kneeling in the snow. He went forward to reconnoiter Henry, and after a few seconds they heard him call, "Come on, the REs."

Cox saw that the barbed wire round the radar pit was low and not much of a barrier. He thought it had probably been kept low to avoid electrical interference with the set. The firing from Lone House had now stopped, mercifully, but more firing was coming from another direction, Rectangle. Major Frost soon appeared at the radar pit and Private Newman was questioning the badly shaken German prisoner. He confirmed that he belonged to the Luftwaffe Communications Regiment and that there were about a hundred of his fellows quartered across the fields at Le Presbytère (Rectangle). They were fully armed, the German said, for defense of the main Freya position and also of the Würzburg. Yes, he said in reply to Frost's question, they had mortars, but, being signalers, they were not in the habit of firing them often. Naumoff and his section were responding steadily to the fire from Rectangle, which was mainly directed at them and at Lone House, rather than at Henry. Frost also heard firing from Timothy's party, farther inland. His own group and Young's took up closer defensive positions.

Cox tore aside the thick black rubber curtain that shielded the entry to the radar set. "Hey, Peter!" he called to Newman. "This thing's still hot. Ask that Jerry if he was tracking our aircraft as we came in." The prisoner conceded that this was so. The Freyas in the main part of the station had picked up the British aircraft far offshore; this set had picked them up at thirty kilometers. As the signaler pointed out, the site was "extremely exposed," and when they learned that the hostile aircraft were making straight for them, they had switched the set off in good time and taken cover.

Vernon began to take flash-bulb pictures of the Würzburg, while Cox made notes and sketches, using his hooded flashlight. The flash-bulbs at once drew German fire, and Frost ordered him to stop the photography.

"Like a searchlight on a rotatable platform [turntable] mounted on a flat four-wheeled truck," wrote Cox in describing the Würzburg. "Truck has had its wheels raised and is well sandbagged up to platform level. Paraboloid is ten-foot diameter and hinged so that radio beam can be swung freely up or down or sideways. Small cabin to one side shelters set's display gear and operator's seat. At rear of paraboloid is container three feet wide, two feet deep, five feet high. This appears to hold all the works with the exception of display. Design very clean, and straightforward . . . We found the set switched off, but warm. The top of the compartment taken up by the transmitter and what looks like first stage of receiver. Large power pack with finned metal rectifiers occupies bottom. Between the TX [transmitter] and the power unit is the pulse gear and the receiver IF [intermediate frequency]. Everything solid and in good order. Telefunken labels everywhere which one sapper removing with hammer

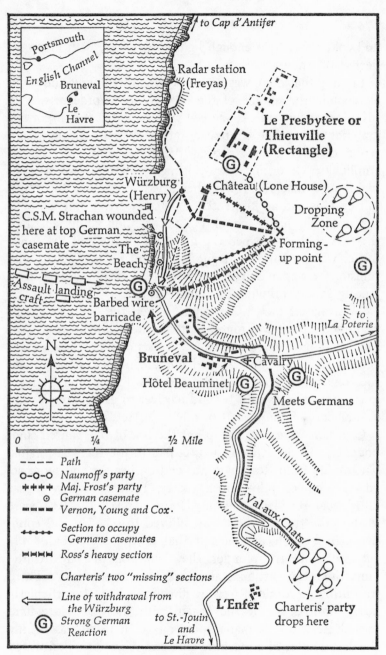

THE BRUNEVAL RAID

and cold chisel. Just enough light to work by, with moon reflected off snow."

Finding that there was no quick way of removing the aerial
element in the middle of the bowl, Vernon ordered one of
his men to saw it off. He agreed with Cox that the important
material was in the container, rather than in the bowl an-
tenna display. They removed the pulse unit and the IF
amplifier in a civilized way, using good tools for a well-
maintained machine. They then tried to get out the transmitter. Cox had an immensely long screwdriver, but it would
not reach the fixing screws. He and Vernon conferred, then
the two of them grasped the handles and body of the transmitter while a third man put his weight on a crowbar. The
transmitter was in a light alloy frame. It came away with a
tearing sound, bringing its frame with it.[3]

"A stroke of luck," Cox says. "When the equipment was
examined later it was found that the frame which we in that
somewhat hasty moment regarded as no more than an en-
cumbrance, something we had not the time to detach from
the transmitter, contained the aerial switching unit that allowed both the transmitter and receiver to use the one aerial,
a vital part of the design of any radar set."

Crowbars were used to rip out the last of the wanted components, and the REs frequently had to use their flashlights.
Enemy fire from Rectangle was getting heavier and more accurate. One of John Frost's party, Private McIntyre, was
killed near the door of Lone House. At last the REs were
loading the trolley, Frost was relieved to see. He had confidence in Vernon, and he felt that now, if they could only
get away with the plunder, they had won the day. At the
same time, the battle situation was one of confusion. There
was firing from nearly every direction. It was particularly
heavy from down by the beach, with the odd white flare
(which must be German) going up. That firing was mainly
the deep stutter of a machine gun, and it was being answered
by one Bren. The firing from Rectangle had increased and

had spread. Obviously the people there had deployed, and soon they would probably advance on Henry and Lone House. Then there was an extraordinary amount of firing that seemed to come from the village itself. Had some of Timothy's men gone berserk and fought their way into the center of Bruneval? Lastly, there was a lot of noise on Timothy's front, but a runner had just come in from there to report that everything was under control except Timothy's No. 38 radio set. That was the main trouble. Frost, except for whistle signals and runners, was without communications, and under the plan laid down he did not have a full complement in his extremely unstatic command post. As for the No. 38 sets, they seemed to be quite useless, since the frequency could not be kept from drifting.

Cox's trolley was loaded.

Frost sent a runner to call in Naumoff at Rectangle—he was to fall back through the main party and lead the way down to the beach. "Remember the password, 'Biting,'" he warned the runner. Young Naumoff had been a supernumerary officer during training. Frost had allowed him to come on the raid because he didn't have the heart to disappoint him. Naumoff seemed to keep very steady, but he had been under fire for some time, and a man who came up from behind might be in danger.

In the meantime, Captain Ross with his heavy section had waited until all of Frost's group had left the forming-up place for their objectives. Then he led his section across ground remembered from the model and down to the road and the entry to the beach.[4] The plan drawn up in England had envisaged a three-point initial attack on the beach. The light assault section that had already gone out was to occupy the important hinge pillbox. Having heard no firing from there, Ross assumed that they *had* occupied it. Ross and his heavy section were to be in reserve in the center, nearest to the road entry to the beach, while Euan Charteris and his two remaining light assault sections (now missing) were to sweep in from the southeast. As Ross slid from the trees down the hill towards the beach entry, a white flare rose from Guard Room (villa Stella Maris). He and the men behind him were at once pinned by machine-gun fire. Lying on the snow, Ross made out that the fire was coming from the inland side of the villa where, slightly above the road, the Germans had made weapon pits with trench communications. Several rifles, probably six or seven, were firing as well as the machine gun. Ross's section replied with rifles and their one Bren. The section consisted of himself and his batman, one reserve sergeant, two signalers with a No. 38 and a No. 18 radio set for contacting the Navy, two sappers with mine detectors and a portable radio beacon, two Bren gunners, and one runner. The Germans had an excellent field of fire, and they were hidden by the villa from the British section in the pillbox to the north. It had not been foreseen that the Germans might dig themselves weapon pits on the landward side. Ross's heavy section was pinned down. The sergeant, dragging himself flat on the snow, managed to get to the thick barbed wire across the road and tried to cut a way through. The Bren gunners and riflemen kept firing. Ross would have given a lot to have a mortar, even a two-inch one.

Mortars were in Frost's mind, too, as he thought of his men concentrating near and on the beach. So far he had heard no bombs, only rifle and automatic fire from the enemy.

In the center of the groups withdrawing across the plateau and down the hill was the trolley, a two-wheeled affair that took some controlling, being heavy-laden. As Naumoff and his section from Rectangle withdrew through the main party, Frost warned him that he would probably have to contact Ross en route and fight his way to the beach. Naumoff got down unobserved, but when the trolley party and its guards came to the German casemate high up on the north side of the gully the machine gun below caught them in full view against the snow and gave them a long burst. Company Sergeant-Major Strachan fell with three bullet wounds in his stomach. Just then Frost's group heard John Ross clearly.

"Don't come down," he shouted. "The beach is not taken yet."

Frost got Strachan behind the concrete jut of the casemate, put field dressings on his ugly wounds, and gave him a morphine injection. A runner came from John Timothy's rear-guard group to say that the Germans were advancing from Rectangle and had already occupied Lone House. Frost accordingly told the trolley party to hold on by the casemate until the machine gun below had been silenced, and, taking every man he could, including sappers, he hurried back to the top of the cliff to counterattack in conjunction with Timothy's group. Whatever was happening down below at the beach, it was vital to keep the Germans above at a good distance. "Fortunately," he says, "the threat did not amount to much. The enemy was confused and did not know what he was up against. They hesitated and withdrew." Frost left Timothy to defend the shoulder of the hill while he hurried back to the casemate and to take control of the fight for the beach. But he found that Vernon, Cox, and two sappers were on the move down toward the beach, skidding and sliding on the frozen path. Strachan, shouting incomprehensible orders, was being half-carried, half-dragged after the radar booty. There had been a lot of shooting down below, but now there seemed to be silence. Frost dashed on down, ahead of the trolley.

When Ross saw the trolley party appearing on the skyline and full in the field of fire of the Germans by Stella Maris, he called out to warn them, realizing that the distraction might be turned to account. His men found a knife-rest gate in the perimeter wire and pulled it aside to make an opening. At that moment, Naumoff and his section reached the bottom of the slope, and as they and Ross's heavy section were about to rush through the wire and assault the German position they heard shouts and firing from the southeast. Charteris! The Scots voices raised in fury and triumph at reaching their objective came clear on the frosty air. The attack from the southeast had turned the enemy's position.

The German machine gun was abandoned and the defenders slipped out of their trenches and off to the southward, to the obscurity of the rough ground at the edge of the sea.

Charles Pickard, who was leading the flight of Whitley bombers, and the aircraft that immediately followed him had been caught in the worst of the German flak near the dropping zone. They had mistaken their landmarks and had dropped their two sticks of parachutists well south of Bruneval, indeed almost halfway between Bruneval and Saint-Jouin. The twenty men landed with their containers in the Val aux Chats, near the small hamlet of l'Enfer. Euan Charteris, their leader, was an outstanding young officer, remarkably intelligent and of the greatest promise.[5] "It was a nasty moment," he said later.[6] For when he picked himself up from the snow he saw at once that their pilots had made a mistake. Where were they? Fortunately, they were able to see the later waves of Whitleys flying in, well to the northward. They soon distributed the contents of their containers and Charteris' two scouts reported a narrow road leading to Bruneval, which, Charteris realized, lay between them and their objective. Putting himself at the head of his men, he led them at a trot along the upper side of the road. As they neared Bruneval they saw German soldiers, but in the half-light they proceeded for some time unchallenged, and when a German joined their line, thinking they were his own people, he was killed silently.

Then the challenge came and they had to shoot their way around the village. This was the firing that Frost had heard while Henry was being dismantled. But if the firing was confusing to Frost, it was still more so to the German garrison, who had little idea where the commandos were or what their objective could possibly be. Now fighting in the half-light, now hurrying on around the village in its sharp valley, now separated, now together again, Charteris' sections shed a man or two here and there. The main raiding party's firing was ahead of them now, and up over the hill on their right.

Charteris led his men at the double across the road leading from the sea to Bruneval and turned right for the German defenses and the beach. They paused a moment to get their breath, then, mad with relief at being at last where their orders had said they should be, they charged forward with a wild yell. Their attack came, by a fluke, in conjunction with the attack from the other side of the valley. The three groups, Charteris', Ross's, and Naumoff's, were through to the beach. At the door of Stella Maris, Sergeant Jimmy Sharp caught a German telephonist coming out and explained to him that he would be making a trip, "*nach England.*"

But would he? Ross's two signalers seemed quite unable to make contact with the Navy on their No. 18 set, and Charteris' two signalers, who had also carried a No. 18, were both missing. As no contact was being made with the No. 18, Ross told one of his signalers to try with the No. 38 set. Meanwhile, his sappers had set up the little portable radio beacon, called "Rebecca," and said it was working properly. It was a gadget so new and so secret that it contained its own built-in demolition charge. Its companion set, known as a "Eureka," was in one of the landing craft. Whether Rebecca was working, the parachutists were uncertain. Then the sappers checked the beach with their mine detectors, getting negative results.

Ross, at his report center, totaled up his losses. There were two confirmed dead—Privates McIntyre and Scott; six missing; and six wounded who had all been gathered on the pebbles. Among them was Corporal Stewart, who had fallen, hit in the head, during the assault on the beach; he called to his nearest comrade, "I've had it, Jock. Take my wallet."

Lance-Corporal Freeman took it and examined Stewart's head. "Och, it's only a wee bit of a gash," he said.

"Then give us back that wallet." Stewart managed to get to his feet.

After consultation with Frost, John Ross fired one green Very light from the north end of the beach and then another from the south, in a final effort to signal the landing craft. Frost "with a sinking heart" called his platoon commanders and began to organize the defenses of an indefensible position. There had been reports from Lieutenant Timothy that headlights were approaching from the east and southeast. Before long the Germans were bound to appear in strength.

Bruneval was, for the light naval units, an easier target than the dark rocky beaches of Loch Fyne or the swelling cliffs round Lulworth. The trouble was, as the Navy was only too well aware, that the deadline for the raid had been extended and the LCAs would now approach a dangerous beach on a falling tide. Another difficulty was the weather itself, which had become, frankly, unsuitable. By midnight, fifteen minutes before the first parachute drop, the barometer began dropping sharply and the breeze, already fresh from the southwest, increased. While they waited in a state of increasing tension, the flotilla of small craft saw enemy ships a mile or so to the seaward, between them and England —two German destroyers and two E-boats or R-boats.[7] The Germans steamed very fast from north to south and apparently saw nothing. Soon after they had gone, the British LCAs saw the white flares fired by the defenders of Stella Maris. By 2:35 the LCAs had closed to within three hundred yards of the beach when "a blue lamp signal was seen, followed by two green Very lights." Two LCAs were ordered to come close into the beach, but as they started inshore, Ross's signaler made contact with his No. 38 set and asked, without authority but understandably enough, that *all* the LCAs should come in.

Frost, his back to the sea and his hopes at zero, heard a cry behind him, "Sir! The boats are coming in . . . God bless the ruddy Navy!" Then the hinterland of the beach, where he was standing and where most of his men were deployed, seemed to the parachutists to be swept by a devastating fire from the Brens in the landing craft.

20

Frost, who had been urging his sections not to stay in the bottom of the ravine, where they would be sitting targets for the enemy above, but to spread out and climb, driving any opposition up and away, went wild when he realized that the Bren gunners in the LCAs were apparently firing into the darkness of the land mass where his men were rather than at the cliff top. He ran out onto the beach shouting and screaming, a tall, jerking figure. The firing paused as, followed by Ross, he bounded and skidded to the water's edge. A Welsh voice said, "We thought you was a Jerry with a suicide wish, but we gave you the benefit of the doubt." The Bren gunners had in fact been aiming at the cliff top.[1]

After he had managed to avert the possible slaughter of his men by their friends, Frost turned his attention to the difficulties of embarkation, which he felt had been increased by the simultaneous arrival of all six boats. However, the abortive exercises on training had taught the parachutists more than they realized. Even with the swell and the falling tide, there were enough of them to hold the boats stern-on to the sea. All who were on the beach got away safely. The total left behind was still eight—two dead and six missing. The first LCAs away took the wounded and Cox and the Royal Engineers with their booty. They were transferred to MGB 312, which then made off at more than twenty knots for Portsmouth.

By three-thirty the remaining gunboats were under way, towing the landing craft and with the parachutists tucked away below decks. In the mounting sea with their tows, they could make no more than seven knots, and at dawn the flotilla was still only fifteen miles from the French coast. The wind had increased on the Beaufort Scale to Force 5. An hour after dawn they were under Spitfire protection. Earlier they had been met by a sea escort consisting of four Free French *chasseurs* (light destroyers)—*Bayonne, Calais, Larmor,* and *Le Lavandou*—and by two British destroyers, H.M.S. *Blencathra* and H.M.S. *Fernie.* On boarding his boat Frost had been distressed to learn that Charteris' two missing signalers had just made contact, using their No. 18 set. They had reached the beach and now would have to attempt to escape to Spain or Switzerland.[2]

An excellent sailor (even in a fast motorboat lurching over a choppy sea), Frost was in the middle of an early lunch at sea ("the sailors certainly upheld the traditions of Royal Navy hospitality; they made much more fuss over us than we deserved"), when a message came for him from Noah (TRE radar specialist Priest) far ahead in MGB 312: "Samples complete and perfect."

Priest had lost no time in examining the bits and pieces of the Würzburg and in questioning Lieutenant Vernon and Flight-Sergeant Cox, who was very seasick. "Once we got home, official opinion had it that the German set was behind our own gear," Cox recalls. "For my part, and I told Mr. Priest so, I thought it a beautiful job, and I've been in wireless all my life. I was particularly struck by the ingenious way it was boxed off in units for easy fault-finding and quick replacement. 'The Jerries must have had RDF as long as us,' I said to Mr. Priest, 'or longer.' 'Well,' he answered, 'as soon as we get your evidence home we should know how long they've been making this Würzburg, and I'm willing to bet the total will be in years, and nearer ten than one. But keep it under your hat, my friend.' When he had done with me I managed to hold down a cup of good strong tea and I went to sleep in the Captain's bunk. Yes! The boat no longer vibrated when I woke, and I found we were alongside *Prins Albert* in good old Pompey [Royal Navy slang for Portsmouth] harbour. Next morning I reported as per instructions at the

Air Ministry. 'Take two weeks leave immediately, Sergeant Cox,' Air Commodore Tait said to me, so I asked his secretary WAAF to send a telegram to Wisbech, saying HOME TONIGHT KILL FATTED CALF. It was near midnight when I got home, but sitting round a big fire there they all were, four generations. 'Hullo family,' I said. 'I've been in France, that's where I've been, and it's in the London newspapers tonight. How about that then?' "

John Frost went on the bridge as they approached Portsmouth. This was a moment that Frost, with a military career in front of him that held more than a fair share of danger and glory, would not forget. The four French *chasseurs* now swept by and saluted the raiders, followed by the two British destroyers; the Spitfire escort, its task accomplished without enemy challenge, flew low over the gunboats before making off inland. At six that evening—February 28—the survivors of "C" Company, its section of Royal Engineers, its RAF flight sergeant, and its German interpreter boarded *Prins Albert*. The ship was crowded with staff officers and journalists. Even Pickard and the Whitley crews were there.

When the Lysander carrying Rémy and Julitte had landed at Tangmere, they were met by "J," a mysterious British officer who had briefed Rémy in Portugal at the beginning of his career as a British agent. He led them to a room where a woman in Army uniform sat jabbing at a coal fire with a steel poker. Rémy and Julitte were given whisky, more whisky, then bacon and eggs, toast, marmalade, and coffee. A black car driven by a woman whisked the three men to London, where J installed Rémy in the Waldorf Hotel under terms of the strictest security. False papers had been made out for a "French Canadian named Georges Roulier." Rémy was ordered to take all his meals in his suite rather than the restaurant. When J at last left him, Rémy plunged into a hot bath, at that time a rarity in France.

Early next morning he was taken to Passy's headquarters

in St. James's Street. His reception was rapturous because all the papers from the Lysander had already been appraised. Rémy permitted the Free French to give him (strictly against J's security instructions) luncheon at L'Écu de France in Jermyn Street. On his return to the Waldorf, J was waiting for him. He handed Rémy as a surprise an early edition of the *Evening Standard* whose headlines and whole front page were concerned with the successful raid at Bruneval.

Utterly delighted, Rémy sat down at the desk in his private sitting room and wrote a message for Pol that J undertook to have transmitted immediately:

TO PACO FOR POL CONGRATULATIONS SUCCESS BRUNEVAL WHICH HAS RESULTED DESTRUCTION IMPORTANT GERMAN INSTALLATION WHILE TAKING AND KILLING NUMEROUS BOCHES

"Paco" (François Faure) was one of the original and most important members of Rémy's Confrérie Notre-Dame. Rémy was bitterly to regret that moment of exhilaration in the Waldorf.

The news of Bruneval, the first successful armed landing in German-occupied Europe, was a tonic for the Allies and a blow to German pride and confidence. Lord Haw-Haw, the English traitor and Nazi propagandist who broadcast nightly from Germany, referred scathingly to Frost and "C" Company as a "handful of redskins." And, possibly for security reasons, the decorations awarded to the parachutists were sparse, even by British Army standards. Major Frost, a professional soldier, and Lieutenant Charteris, whose ambitions were political rather than military, each received the Military Cross, while Flight Sergeant Cox, Sergeant Grieve, and Sergeant Mackenzie received the equally distinguished Military Medal; Lieutenant Young was Mentioned in Despatches; and Company Sergeant-Major Strachan, who lived to fight again but only as a frail shadow of his former self, was awarded the Croix de Guerre.

From the purely military point of view, the recently created Combined Operations under its leader, Mountbatten, had tackled something dramatic and difficult and had carried it through well. Churchill was impressed, and his appetite for raids, always voracious, was whetted. Only one of the Bruneval parachutists took part in the next raid, the extremely gallant and effective one on the naval installation at Saint-Nazaire. "Private Newman" had volunteered his services once more as German interpreter. He was taken prisoner and spent the rest of the war in German hands. So good was his cover story that his real nationality remained a secret, and he survived the war to become a prosperous businessman in England. The third important raid on France before D-Day was that on Dieppe, a ferocious affair of much value in view of the great landings that lay over the horizon.

German reaction at Bruneval during the raid was described in the following report, which revealed that the British had been extremely lucky to have escaped, especially with so few casualties.[3]

At 0055/28.2.42 the German *Freya* station reported aircraft NNE, range 29 km.

The parachutists were sighted by the Army and the Luftwaffe (ground and communications troops) at 0115 [1215 GMT]. The landing was made SE of the Farm and was carried out in complete silence.

All Army and Luftwaffe posts in the area were at once alerted. Scouts sent from the *Freya* position (near Cap d'Antifer) and the Luftwaffe Communications Station (at Le Presbytère) returned with information that the enemy was on the move south of the Farm (Le Presbytère) in the direction of the Château. The parachutist commandos had split into several groups and were converging on the *Würzburg* position and on the Château.

In La Poterie the reserve platoon of the first Company 685 Infantry Regiment had just finished an exercise shortly after 0100 when the parachutists were sighted. The officer commanding at once made contact with the Bruneval guard; the sergeant there had already alerted his men.

The platoon reserve in Bruneval was ordered to occupy Hill 102 to the SE of Bruneval. The officer commanding La Poterie platoon then led his men in a westerly direction towards the Château.

On reaching the Farm building NE of the Château the German troops came under fire from the commando machine guns, and from the W end of the buildings they engaged the British, who were already in possession of the [Würzburg] Luftwaffe station near the Farm. Here one of the commandos fell.

This German platoon encountered fire from the left flank, but the commandos were nevertheless prevented from proceeding with their attack on the *Freya* position. The remainder of the Luftwaffe Communications Station unit quartered in the farm buildings took part in this action.

In accordance with orders, the platoon from Bruneval village divided into two groups and advanced on Hill 102. Outside Bruneval they came under fire from the commandos who had landed N of L'Enfer.

Although this platoon was unable to prevent the commandos from infiltrating between Bruneval and Hill 102, it was because of this platoon's action that individual commandos did not reach the boats in time, and were later taken prisoner. One wounded commando was also captured. It was only because the British objective was not known that this Bruneval platoon did not take part in the action at the Château.

The Bruneval guard, one sergeant and nine men, had meanwhile taken up prepared positions guarding the coast. These [main] defensive positions were so built that they were effective only against attacks through the ravine from seaward. The commandos, approaching from N and NE were able to get close to these strongpoints under cover of the woods. Thus the German guard positions were attacked from the high ground by heavy fire from three or four commando machine guns. After one German soldier had been killed and another wounded the sergeant was obliged to take up new positions. It was not until after one to one and a half hours fighting that the commandos were able to get through the strong-point and the ravine to the beach. With them the commandos took a wounded German soldier and also the soldier who had been on telephone watch at the post. Here another commando fell, and one was wounded. The latter was assisted to the boats, which had come close inshore on the exchange of signal flares.

The commandos embarked just as strong German reinforcements reached Bruneval.

The platoon from La Poterie fought their way to the Luftwaffe Communications Station [*Würzburg*] as the commandos withdrew. It was learned that the Luftwaffe personnel there had put up a stiff resistance, and only after some of them had exhausted their ammunition were the commandos able to break through to the *Würzburg*.

One of the crew had been killed by a British grenade as he tried to set off an explosive charge to destroy the *Würzburg*. The commandos then dismantled parts of the set and also took photographs. On conclusion of this task they obviously intended to attack the *Freya* station. The skillful intervention of the La Poterie platoon, however, prevented this.

The operation of the British commandos was well planned and was executed with great daring. During the operation the British displayed exemplary discipline when under fire. Although attacked by German soldiers they concentrated entirely on their primary task. For a full thirty minutes one group did not fire a shot, then suddenly at the sound of a whistle they went into action.

German losses: Army, two killed, one seriously wounded, two missing. Luftwaffe, three killed, one wounded, three missing. British losses: two killed, one wounded (reached the boats), four captured.[4]

For eighteen months before the Bruneval affair R. V. Jones had been pressing for a complete move from the Dorset coast of the Telecommunications Research Establishment (TRE), whose physical size was now beginning to match its great importance in the Allied war effort, since all the new British radar was under development there. "I believed," Jones says, "that it would be easy for the Germans to detect our new transmissions from a listening post near Cherbourg, and that we therefore ought to move TRE to a site well beyond the range of radio interception. However, Swanage was a pleasant place, and the workers did not want to move. . . . After the Bruneval Raid, however, speculation started about whether the Germans might organise a reprisal; if so, Swanage was a very obvious target."[1]

It was indeed. TRE, like the stolen Würzburg, was on the Channel's very edge, and TRE's position offered a choice of excellent beaches that could be used by the enemy either for assault or for escape.

To TRE itself the notion of any possible move was cataclysmic. As it had grown up around Worth Matravers, expanding to Swanage, to Christchurch, then to Hurn near Bournemouth; it had drawn in and trained its own, now highly skilled, labor. Because the maintenance staff were Dorset people, locally recruited, and because it was located in a holiday area (in peacetime) there was no housing problem, an important consideration in any secret establishment.

"Then came a bombshell," A. P. Rowe says. "There were, we were told, seventeen trainloads of German parachute troops on the other side of the English Channel preparing to attack TRE. The Prime Minister said we must leave the South Coast before the next full moon. A whole regiment of infantry arrived to protect us. They blocked the road approaches, they encircled us with barbed wire, they put demolition charges in our secret equipment, and they made our lives a misery. My own time was spent in discussions as to whether we should die to the last scientist, or run. These events made us co-operate in the task of finding a place where we could get on with the war in peace."[2]

When Jones had made sure that Swanage had been informed "through other channels" of the arrival of a German parachute unit at Cherbourg, he went down himself from London to Dorset with one of his uniformed officers. "We said nothing about the possibility of a reprisal, but we contrived to seem ill at ease throughout the visit, and our conspicuously worn pistols"—Jones was a noted marksman with a pistol—"and steel hats testified to our apprehension."[3]

Malvern College, the boys' school on the side of the Malvern Hills in Worcestershire, overlooking the Vale of Evesham and the Severn Valley, was chosen for TRE's new setting. The perimeter was made secure according to military and scientific standards, new laboratories and workshops were built, power lines and telephones were brought in, and a nearby airfield was enlarged and improved. It was a splendid new base. Great things were to be accomplished there; the triumphant "ghost fleets" of aircraft using "Window" (see below) that made D-Day possible were run from there; King George VI and his Queen visited Rowe and his scientists there. But Worth Matravers and the pale, pure textures of sky, sea, cliff, and grass of the Dorset coast would ever be regretted by the radar men. When they were forced to leave Dorset it seemed that they must leave too much behind them.

"On May 25, 1942," Rowe says, "the TRE people began to move to Malvern by train and in cars mostly so old that it seemed impossible that they could reach their destination. For the last time, I made my auto-cycle journey from

Swanage to unforgettable Corfe [Castle] where, at the Old
Tea House, I had lived for two years. . . ."[4]

One immediate German reaction to the Bruneval Raid was
predictable and a gift to Germany's adversaries. German radar stations on the Channel coast were surrounded with
barbed wire and given all-around tactical defenses. Under
the wire aprons the grass, protected from the tongues of the
omnivorous brown-spotted cattle, grew long and rank, the
weeds proliferated. On aerial photographs, in consequence,
the Freya and Würzburg positions showed up like warts. This
was to be useful before D-Day when it was vital to the Allied
plan that all the enemy radar stations should either be put
out of commission by rocket-firing or precision-bombing aircraft or completely hoaxed so that the enemy might have no
precise warning of the two cross-Channel armadas.[5]

In terms of the bombing assault on Germany and the Germans' characteristically brave and energetic reactions, the
Bruneval Raid had an important effect, and one that had
much to do with TRE's saturnalia of jamming that preceded
D-Day.

TRE specialists, using the captured radar pieces from
Bruneval and the photographs and descriptions of Vernon
and Cox, immediately built a Würzburg at Worth Matravers
and began evaluation exercises. Anxious to inspect the raid's
booty, Jones was twice stopped for speeding when he first
drove down from London to see it. His examination of the
metal labels showed, of course, that the apparatus had been
manufactured by Telefunken (whose factories near Berlin
were then at the outer limit of Allied bombing range). The
lowest serial number brought back from France was 40,144
and the highest was 41,093. Jones thought that, according to
the German practice with armaments, 50 per cent of production would go into spares. The earliest inspection date
(on the transmitter) was November 1940, and the most recent (on the aerial) was August 1941. Jones calculated that
five hundred Würzburg sets would have been in service by

the latter date and that Telefunken would be turning out a hundred a month. (This estimate was accurate; but the firm was also now manufacturing the more effective Giant Würzburg.)

One scientific deduction from the Bruneval capture was as plain as it was unpleasantly controversial: the Würzburg could be tuned over a wide range and was not susceptible to "orthodox" jamming. If the Würzburg was as essential to the German air defenses as seemed likely, there was but one known answer to it, an answer that each side had discovered independently. It consisted simply in the aerial dropping of metal-strip reflectors which, by creating hosts of false echoes or reflections in the enemy radar, would conceal the advancing aircraft.

Each side, believing itself to be the superior in radar and therefore likely to be the more affected by such a blotting-out process, had been horrified by the idea and quietly swept it under the top-secret carpet. Göring had given an order that its German code name, "Düppel," must never be mentioned, even in meetings attended by such persons as himself, Milch, Martini, Kammhuber, Plendl, Galland, and Schwenke, the "captured enemy equipment" expert. By 1942 the Germans were at last, and too late, beginning to realize that they were behind in the radar struggle that must lie ahead. When, in 1942, the British began to jam Freya devices and to attack German ground-to-air communications with two airborne TRE-devised methods ("Mandrel" and "Tinsel"), the already defensively-minded German Air Staff began to wonder in committee when the more important Würzburg system, now controlling night fighters, searchlights, and guns, would be attacked.

In London Dr. Jones, after a visit to Bawdsey Manor back in 1937, had noted that the radar at Bawdsey would detect a piece of wire "half a wavelength long" (a dipole) hanging from a balloon twenty miles away. Jones, who was then researching infrared methods of aircraft detection, expressed this opinion to Cherwell concerning the British radar defense system: "All the Germans would have to do would be to sow a field of dipoles over the North Sea, and our screens would be swamped with echoes."

Cherwell was impressed. "I'll get Winston to raise it," he promised.

When Cherwell had explained dipoles to him, Churchill did raise it, in the important Air Defence Research Subcommittee. He got little satisfaction. Tizard and Watson-Watt admitted to him that scattering dipoles represented a potential way of blinding radar. But in 1937 neither they nor anyone else outside Germany, suspected that the Germans already possessed radar. Both Tizard and Watson-Watt believed that Britain's survival in the coming war depended on developing the Chain Home system and its ancillaries with all possible effort and devotion. And events justified them, showing the Germans to be less aggressive opponents in the radio and radar war than Jones had anticipated. It was this query, however, as to the vulnerability of radar that initially shaded Cherwell's, and therefore Churchill's, early opinions as to its reliability.

In late 1941, only a few months before John Frost and his men dropped at Bruneval, TRE had begun in Dorset the first metal-strip-dropping trials. They were ominously effective. Cockburn came into Rowe's office to report and asked what code name should be given to the experiments. TRE had more than once been reprimanded by Intelligence for being too clever with code names, and since this matter was obviously dynamite, it called for something really pointless. Rowe looked round the room, and said, "How about 'window'?"

TRE's initial experiments with Window were in the hands of a woman, Mrs. Joan Curran. She found that rectangular strips of ordinary tinfoil made the most satisfactory reflectors. The development was continued under another unusually interesting person, a peacetime Oxford physicist and don, Dr. Derek Jackson. Before the war he had ridden his own horse in the Grand National, and during the war, with the

RAF, he had won both the Air Force Cross and the Distinguished Flying Cross as a radar-operating observer in night fighters. In the course of the protracted Window research he nearly lost his life when the Beaufighter from which he was sowing Window was attacked in error by a Spitfire, which shot down the companion Beaufighter, killing its occupants, among them the TRE expert on the new Mark IX fighter radar.

From the day of the Bruneval Raid until the following June, Jones's office was at work familiarizing itself with the German system of air defense—Kammhuber's Himmelbett. At first the system was referred to as the "Main Belt." Then Jones's number two, Charles Frank, came up with the "Kammhuber Line," and the name stuck. "Lines," such as the Siegfried and the Maginot, had been military and journalistic talking points in the early days of the war until it began to turn into a war of movement, a war whose vital forces were in the air and still—to some extent—on and in the sea. Possibly in Jones's office and at TRE, "Kammhuber Line" was the more popular term because they knew that, although the line was scientific and for a time effective, its days were also numbered. Jones himself liked the name; of all his adversaries on the German side, he had taken a fancy to Kammhuber whom he sensed to be honest and patently decent. After the war, when interrogating him, Jones took pleasure in informing his German prisoner that his defenses had been known in England as the "Kammhuber Line." "A warm smile came over his features. I think it almost made up for being in prison," Jones says.[6]

An understanding of Kammhuber's system led to the conclusion that Bomber Command should change from scattered to concentrated formations. Since there was only one German night fighter at a time in each Kammhuber Freya-Würzburg radar box, it would obviously be sound to saturate the box with bombers. Scattered formations were playing Kammhuber's game. Thus began the British "bomber stream," which in time was going to bring the remarkable

German reaction of feeding fighters, like killer fishes, in among the Lancasters, Halifaxes, and Stirlings.

Tacticians in the higher echelon, from Churchill down, argued the pros and cons of using Window against German radar defenses. The more they discussed it, the more reasons were advanced for not using it. Jones, who had been against using H₂S in bombers over Germany (because it meant giving the Germans the chance to learn the secret of the cavity magnetron tube) rather than using it exclusively in the Battle of the Atlantic, was in favor of using Window. Lord Cherwell, who had insisted that H₂S be used at any rate in the Pathfinders of Bomber Command and who had had his way, was determinedly opposed to using Window. On the other hand, Bomber Command's leader, "Bomber" Harris, who had agreed with Cherwell about using H₂S, now agreed with Jones that Window should be used. One of Cherwell's strongest arguments against its use was that the Germans had never thought of it and that to give them the idea would be to invite lethal air attacks on Britain. Jones disagreed. He refused to believe that German research in radar had not independently discovered the effects of scattering dipoles. And in October 1942 he picked up a rumor about the German Düppel experiments in the report of a British agent in Germany based on a chance conversation with a German WAAF in a train. When Jones told Cherwell of this, the latter exploded. Did Jones imagine that air strategy should be affected by what a low-ranking German soldieress had gabbled about during a German train journey? . . . Jones did.

Window was first used over Germany seventeen months after the Bruneval affair, in two of the most deadly raids of the war—target Hamburg. Thanks to the delay in using it, Bomber Command was able to deal the enemy an infinitely heavier series of blows and the German defenses had little time to find an effective answer to the Window techniques. And thanks to Dr. (now wing-commander) Jackson, there was now an efficient way of delivering Window—in bundles weighing only two pounds each that produced the radar echo of a heavy bomber. Also thanks in part to him, to TRE, and to the British and American electronics industries, British radar, both ground and airborne, could itself see through the Window (or Düppel) clouds.

On the night of July 24, 1943, seven hundred and ninety-one British heavy bombers clattered and clawed their way into the sky from their East Anglian bases and thundered over the North Sea. At the end of the usual briefing, a special announcement from "Bomber" Harris had been read to every crew. "Tonight you are going to use Window. It consists of packets of metal strips which produce almost the same reactions on RDF [radio direction finder] as do your aircraft. The German defenses will become confused . . . when good concentration is achieved, Window can so devastate an RDF system that we ourselves have withheld using it until we could effect improvements in our own defenses." At this stage in the war, Bomber Command, unlike the Luftwaffe, did not maintain strict radio discipline. The German listening service, familiar with the British test traffic, had therefore anticipated an unusually heavy raid for that night. German long-range radar had watched the first bombers taking off and had reported the forming of the head of the two-hundred-mile-long stream.

Soon the British began to drop Window, one bundle each minute from each bomber, down the flare chute in the tail. They were flying at nineteen thousand feet in air twenty degrees centigrade below freezing. The advanced defense stations on the islands of Sylt and Helgoland were at once almost blinded by reflections.

At twenty minutes to one in the morning of July 25 the leading bombers crossed the enemy coast. On their H2S screens Hamburg showed like a veined opal set in diamonds. Hamburg, the most ferociously defended city in the world, with its fifty-four Würzburg-controlled flak batteries, its twenty-two Würzburg-controlled searchlight batteries, and its twenty Würzburg-controlled Himmelbetts served by six night-fighter airfields, had been blinded. The city's blue master-searchlights that usually remained vertical until pouncing, spiderlike, on an intruder, were groping about the sky as though demented. Their operators, like the gunners and the fighter pilots, were waiting for directions that could not be given. Undisturbed, the RAF Pathfinders marked the target out accurately. Their immense line of followers began to ram in the bombs. As they turned away, they continued to sow Window. The effect of the raid on the city was catastrophic.

Hitler was wakened early that day and given details of the Hamburg disaster, including the use of Window. He at once ordered full priority for the production of his "revenge weapon," the V2 rocket, with which he planned to obliterate London. By doing so he unwittingly played the Allied game, since the V2 was an insatiable user of electronic components, and these were already in drastically short supply for German radar development. The rockets' demands were to hamper Plendl, Milch, and Martini in their search for the difficult answer to the clouds of tinfoil.

Three nights later, in a second RAF attack, Bomber Command turned Hamburg into an inferno. What the Germans described as "fire storms" raised winds of twice hurricane force that blew living people about like chaff, carrying them up into the smoke, sucking them into the hearts of shrieking furnaces or into the boiling waters of the lake. Half the city was destroyed and 50,000 were killed.

By contrast with such horror, Flight-Sergeant Cox of Wisbech in Cambridgeshire, standing on a cliff top in Brittany dismantling a Würzburg under fire, the snow around him, the moon above, seems a peaceful and peaceable figure.

22

On the morning of February 28, 1942, in the Bruneval area,
German patrols scoured the roads, fields, woods, and villages.
Farmyards were searched. Women were questioned as they
walked out to milk their cows in the fields, carrying their
stools and pails. The French police received orders to assist
in the capture of any "commandos" who might be at large
or of any suspicious persons. It was possible, the Germans
thought, that the British had used the raid to land agents
whose targets might be elsewhere. At eight in the morning
a general's Mercedes drew up in front of the Hôtel Beauminet, whose yard quickly filled with motorcyclists in steel
helmets and a squad of the Feldgendarmerie. In the hotel
office a British parachutist, wounded in one arm, was
brought before the general, who behaved courteously, it appeared, and spoke with the young prisoner in English. Paul
Vennier, the proprietor, watching through the partly open
door, saw the prisoner draw himself up and salute the general with his good arm, before he was taken out to the Feldgendarmerie escort. Three unwounded prisoners were then
questioned in the guard room on the ground floor of the
hotel. Mme. Vennier, who understood German and some
English—hence the faded ENGLISH SPOKEN notice that could
still be seen in the corner of the porch window—managed to
pick up scraps of the interrogation. She and the maid were
hidden in the partitioned serving area of the former dining
room. They admired the fresh, glowing skins of the prisoners
and their sturdy clothing and boots. When the Germans withdrew, the two women made signs of friendship and sym-

pathy. But the parachutists were laughing at something and paid little attention.[1]

Two dead German soldiers lay in what had been, in better times, a private dining room used for parties or for romantic assignations. They lay for forty-eight hours under the Ping-Pong table, each hidden by a blanket, only his feet showing and his hands in their gray-green gloves.

Several times that day the hotel was searched from cellar to attic. At midday the meal was ready as usual for the thirty German soldiers billeted there. Only seven or eight turned up.

Vennier and his wife had been awake all night, listening to the shooting, the rushing of boots, and the ringing telephone. They had thought, from the amount of firing as the landing craft foamed away from the beach and the heavy German vehicles came pouring down the La Poterie road almost nose to tail, that the Tommies were forcing a landing and that soon the war might be over. Dawn had brought more sober realizations. And the telephone never stopped shrilling. The sergeant who commanded at Bruneval was still unshaven in the late afternoon, his eyes wild. Usually he was an easy fellow to get on with. Very correct.

Three days later, Mme. Vennier was alone in front of the hotel when a black, well-polished front-wheel-drive Citroën drew up to a skidding stop beside her, and four men got out. Gestapo was written all over them.

"Where is the Englishman?" one of them demanded.

"Englishman! We have nothing as exotic as that around here." It looked as though somebody, some local enemy, had lodged a denunciation. It could be very serious.

"You are hiding an English soldier."

"How could we, when the hotel is packed like a box of dates with German soldiers?"

"You are of English origin."

"On the contrary, until my marriage I was Swiss, and now I am French, one hundred per cent."

"And why, in your opinion, did the English attack at Bruneval?"

"To prove to the German High Command that if they can get a footing in a place like this, they can get a footing anywhere," answered M. Vennier, who had hurried, breathless, round the corner of the yard.

"Please explain yourself."

"I am an officer of the Reserve," said Vennier. "It must be obvious that the English want to induce you Germans to weaken the Russian front by bringing more and yet more of your best troops back to France."

Mme. Vennier thought her husband's bold manner and the foolishness of his answers saved them from prison, because the Gestapo men deduced from them that the Venniers knew nothing of the radar station up above them near the cliffs.

"You possess a radio?" one of the Gestapo asked.

"Yes. In the office."

He switched it on, but only got static. To detune it after each listening to the BBC news in French had become second nature with the Venniers. "Can you certify that none of the people in Bruneval have English sympathies?"

"Certainly not! How should we be aware of their sympathies? We don't parade emotions round here. We're too busy trying to keep body and soul together on the rations."

A day or two later a German lieutenant requisitioned a bedroom and the maid had to sleep out in one of the farms. The lieutenant seldom slept there, but used his room, it appeared to the Venniers, as an excuse to arrive in the hotel at unusual hours of the day or the night.

One day towards the end of April the CND agent Charlemagne (Charles Chauveau) turned up with a couple of business friends from Le Havre. They ordered coffee and calvados, and Vennier, making up his mind not to ask for payment, even if they consumed the whole bottle, contrived to draw aside Charlemagne into the hall and from there into the office. He switched on the wireless, got some music, and turned the volume all the way up. Then he gripped the other by the arm and whispered fiercely right into his ear, "It was you! It was you, Monsieur Chauveau, you and that dark man, who went down to see if the beach was mined. . . . It was you or that other who planned the. . . ."

"Are you insane, my friend?" Charlemagne interrupted. He suddenly looked smaller, woebegone, tormented. "As for my friend. . . ."

"What's happened?"

On March 28—exactly a month after writing his message of congratulations to his colleague Pol in a private sitting room of the Waldorf Hotel in Aldwych—Rémy had returned to Paris and that first night he drank a glass with Pol and heard his news. The very next day Pol, as the result of a denunciation, was arrested by the Germans and imprisoned in Fresnes prison. The Confrérie Notre-Dame kept close watch and believed that Pol would be released, even if they held him for a considerable time. He had always been discreet in his clandestine work, and his alibis appeared to be sound.

But on Friday, May 19, Bob, Rémy's personal "radio," was taken by the Funkabwehr (Communications Intelligence). As he had always been audacity itself—Rémy had constantly tried to make him mend his ways—there was little hope for him or for his brother Pierre, who was also soon arrested. Bob was speedily put to the torture. (He was to die of his sufferings nearly a year later, in Fresnes.) Rare indeed was the man who could withstand that type of questioning. Those who risked such treatment were counseled to hold out for forty-eight hours to give their friends time to cover up, and then only to appear to give in, pitting such wits as they might still have left against those of the inquisitors. Bob, bravely, followed instructions. And seeking to give away secrets that were long out of date, he revealed the workings of Rémy's "Raymond-B" code. Bob knew that Rémy had abandoned that code. But he forgot, or never knew, that the extremely efficient monitoring service of the Funkabwehr filed and kept every message that it managed to intercept.

As soon as Bob told his interrogators that the key to Raymond-B was the *Petit Larousse Illustré*, the Funkabwehr went through their files. They knew that the real name of another prisoner being held was Roger Dumont and that his alias was "Pol." When they came to Rémy's congratulatory message, TO PACO FOR POL, Pol was doomed. The fatal message was one of the last to be sent in Raymond-B ("Raymond" was Rémy's radio pseudonym).

A year after his imprisonment at Fresnes, Pol was executed by a firing squad at Mont Valérien. An hour before his execution, he wrote to his family, "All that I have done I have done as a Frenchman. I regret nothing."

On a bitterly cold morning at the beginning of 1944 Field Marshal Erwin Rommel, commander in charge of the English Channel defenses, came to Bruneval as part of a major tour of inspection and reappraisement. A colonel asked the maid in the Hôtel Beauminet to bring out two bottles of brandy for the field marshal's staff. There were discussions in the roadway outside the hotel. The officers' breath "hung round their heads in clouds." None of them smoked, the maid noticed; Frenchmen seemed to smoke more than Germans these days. She was paid for the brandy and stood with the tray of empty glasses, watching the smart officers in their beautiful cars sliding down to the beach. It was one of those days when the air seemed a little warmer beside the sea. The officers spent some time under the cliffs standing on round pebbles that had been chilled by a below-zero night. To the north, in the direction of England, the Channel was a steely, relentless gray. A depressing day.

The following day an order came through to Bruneval for the evacuation of all civilians. On February 15, 1944, the Venniers left their Hôtel Beauminet, where they had known prosperity and much happiness, never to return.

There is no hotel in Bruneval today. There is no Lone

House up above. The Germans razed it before the D-Day invasion. Spotted cattle belonging to the Le Presbytère farms shelter from sun or rain in some of the ruined outhouses. They have to watch their footing because of crumbling airshafts in the grass, rising from underground bunkers dug by forced labor. And today there are many more eroding, grass-covered gun emplacements than there were on that night when Major John Frost and the men of "C" Company dropped from the sky.

Introduction

1. Most of the events covered in the early chapters of this book occurred before Lindemann's elevation, but to avoid confusion he will be referred to throughout as "Lord Cherwell."
2. Daphne du Maurier's husband.

Chapter 1

1. The captured parachutists were in Gavi POW Punishment Camp with the author. They were an unusually impressive batch of soldiers. Their mission, to blow up an aqueduct in southern Italy, had been hastily conceived. They had accomplished it with ingenuity and courage. The Bruneval project was in fact only the second parachute operation carried out by the British Army.
2. Frost's written account.
3. Air Ministry, *By Air to Battle*, p. 9.
4. John Frost's written account.

Chapter 2

1. In Britain the General Post Office has cognizance over all telegraphic communications.
2. Alfred Price, *Instruments of Darkness*, p. 56.
3. Ibid., p. 58.
4. Ronald W. Clark, *The Rise of the Boffins*, pp. 28 ff.
5. See Clark, *Tizard*, also *The Rise of the Boffins*, pp. 31, 32.
6. See Robert Watson-Watt, *Three Steps to Victory*, Clark, *The Rise of the Boffins*, pp. 34 ff.
7. Clark, *The Rise of the Boffins*, pp. 36, 37.

Chapter 3

1. C. W. H. Cox's written account.
2. John Ross, conversations and correspondence.
3. John Frost's written account.

Chapter 4

1. A. P. Rowe, *One Story of Radar*, p. 13.
2. *Hymns Ancient and Modern*, No. 254 by Stephen the Sahaite; trans. by J. M. Neale.

3. Graham Wallace, *R.A.F. Biggin Hill*, pp. 92–95; Ronald W. Clark, *The Rise of the Boffins*, pp. 49–54, etc.

Chapter 5

1. John Frost's written account, and conversations.
2. Conversations with Private Newman and Frost's written account.
3. Frost's written account.

Chapter 6

1. Description of Martini's radio searches with the *Graf* are based on the Prologue of *The Narrow Margin* by Derek Wood and Derek Dempster, pp. 17–20.
2. Paul Leverkuehn, *German Military Intelligence*, p. 195.
3. Wood and Dempster, op. cit., p. 101.
4. At this stage General Milch, who had probably done more than any other officer to make the Luftwaffe the great and successful service it was, flew his own Dornier to Göring's headquarters in Belgium to urge that the momentum of German victory must *immediately* be continued across the Channel. He wanted all the Stukas and all the parachutists to be flung into an all-out attack on two southern airfields, Manston and Hawkinge. With those in German hands and operational for Me 109s and Stukas, German army units, ferried in Ju 52s, would take Dover and Folkestone. These *points d'appui* would be supplied and supported from the air until a breakout could be made to take more of the English coastline. Milch's proposal was not accepted. Had it been, at that particular fulcrum in history . . . who knows?
5. It has been shown since the war that during the Battle of Britain whereas RAF claims of German aircraft shot down were twice too great, approximately, German claims were *five times* too great. These, on both sides, were "official" claims and were regarded as propaganda. But whereas the RAF, fighting over its own land, was hardly influenced by the claims, the Luftwaffe was. An important difference between the two fine services was to be found in the quality of their operational Intelligence. In this section the RAF was exceptionally strong, the Luftwaffe weak. British Intelligence officers were placed right through the service, down to squadrons, whereas their German equivalents were not seen in headquarters lowlier than those of Fliegerkorps until the end of the war was at hand. From 1940 on, RAF operational Intelligence was remarkably well informed about Luftwaffe strengths, plans, aircraft, and equipment. As to claims of aircraft shot down, Air Intelligence during

the Battle of Britain was unpopular with Fighter Command because it stated that the Command's claims were 50 per cent too high.

Chapter 7

1. Ronald W. Clark, *The Rise of the Boffins*, pp. 110–12.
2. R. V. Jones, letter to the author.
3. Jones, "Temptations and Risks of the Scientific Observer," *Minerva*, Vol. X, No. 3, p. 446.
4. Jones, ibid., p. 449.
5. Jones, ibid.
6. Winston S. Churchill, *The Second World War*, Vol. 2, p. 339.
7. The electron tube that defeated the U-boats, see Chapter 11.
8. Jones, letter to the author.

Chapter 8

1. Colonel Gilbert Renault (Rémy) is the authority for most of this and subsequent chapters concerning his end of the business. Much of the material here used can be found in his *Bruneval: Opération Coup de Croc*. That book and his others on the Resistance as he knew it (see Bibliography) give a direct and unforgettable picture of the Resistance with its agonies and its flashes of pleasure and wonder. Here the author feels himself at home. It is to people like those who worked with Rémy that he owes his life.
2. SOE, Special Operations Executive, was divided into two sections as far as operations in France were concerned. This writer served briefly in the British section, Rémy saw long service in the Gaullist one. See M. R. D. Foot, *SOE in France*.

Chapter 9

1. Ronald W. Clark, *The Rise of the Boffins*, p. 114.
2. Ibid., p. 117.
3. R. V. Jones, letter to the author.
4. Jones, letter to the author.
5. Alfred Price, *Instruments of Darkness*, p. 49.

Chapter 10

1. The author, who worked for SOE near the Franco-Swiss frontier, sometimes on, sometimes over it, constantly met this prejudice, which was never once justified. The French, like the British, mistrust "foreigners."

2. Source for these events is Rémy (Gilbert Renault), a close friend of Charlemagne, from his book *Bruneval: Operation Coup de Croc*, pp. 79–82.

3. For the work of the Tempsford squadrons, see M. R. D. Foot, *S.O.E. in France*, and Benjamin Cowburn, *No Cloak, No Dagger*. "Over a hundred successful pick-up sorties to France were made for S.O.E., delivering over 250 passengers and bringing nearly 450 out, for a total loss of two Lysanders, one pilot, and two agents." Foot, op. cit., p. 88.

Chapter 11

1. "I will never forget the invigorating atmosphere that prevailed at Bawdsey and, later, Worth Matravers. Here was brilliant individualism harnessed to make a great team without loss of individual freedom and initiative. This freedom of individual thought was given its full expression in those stimulating weekly conferences which, with the paradoxical humour which is so typical of our people, were called Sunday Soviets." Excerpt from the Foreword, by Lord Tedder, Marshal of the RAF, to A. P. Rowe, *One Story of Radar*.

2. Rowe, op. cit., p. 95.

3. On the development of the cavity magnetron, for an excellent non-technical description, see Ronald W. Clark, *Rise of the Boffins*, pp. 128–36.

4. Rowe, op. cit., p. 82.

5. Ibid., p. 64.

6. Alfred Price, *Instruments of Darkness*, p. 123.

7. R. V. Jones, letter to the author.

8. In August 1943 Hitler admitted a "temporary setback" (Allied shipping losses had fallen from 400,000 to 40,000 tons per month) caused by "a single technical invention of the enemy." This was H_2S/ASV.

9. Jones, "Temptations and Risks of the Scientific Observer," *Minerva*, Vol. X, No. 3, p. 450.

Chapter 12

1. For an excellent description of Kammhuber and his system of defense, see Alfred Price, *Instruments of Darkness*, pp. 63–70.

2. Sir Arthur Harris, *Bomber Offensive*, pp. 80, 81.

3. R. V. Jones, "Temptations and Risks of the Scientific Observer," *Minerva*, Vol. X, No. 3, p. 443.

4. Price, op. cit., p. 17.

Chapter 13

1. Ralph Barker, *Aviator Extraordinary*, p. 103. Soon after the end of World War II the author met Cotton and heard his story in some detail. But nearly all the material in this chapter and Chapter 14 is taken from Cotton's own account of his life as told to Ralph Barker.
2. Ibid., p. 104.
3. Ibid., p. 118.
4. Ibid., pp. 32, 33.
5. Ibid., p. 151.
6. Ibid., p. 153.
7. Ibid., p. 158.

Chapter 14

1. Ralph Barker, *Aviator Extraordinary*, p. 165.
2. Ibid., p. 169.
3. Ibid., p. 171.
4. Ibid., p. 175.
5. Ibid., p. 177.
6. Ibid., p. 180.
7. Ibid., p. 184.
8. Ibid., p. 189.
9. This secret classification no longer applies.

Chapter 15

1. Constance Babington Smith, *Evidence in Camera*, p. 68.
2. Ibid., p. 107.
3. Sidney Cotton in February 1940 had noted that Bomber Command had appointed "an imaginative and knowledgeable regular officer named Peter Riddell" to organize a photographic and interpretation center at High Wycombe.
4. Babington Smith, *op. cit.*, p. 167.
5. Ibid., p. 174.
6. R. V. Jones, letter to the author.

Chapter 16

1. Adolf Galland, *The First and the Last*, pp. 140–67. Summing up the operation, Galland, one of the great fighter pilots of World War II, who began his active Luftwaffe service in the Spanish Civil War and finally commanded the fighter defenses of the Reich,

attributes much of its success to "a clever trick" of Martini. He adds: "Unfortunately the German command did not draw the necessary conclusions from this victory in the radar war. . . . The British learned from their defeat and developed radar interference to a perfection which, in the later bombing war, became fatal for the Reich" (p. 165).

2. Alfred Price, *Instruments of Darkness*, p. 88.

Chapter 17

1. C. W. H. Cox's written account.
2. The raiding party totaled 120. On the night in question one man had been left behind in camp with a swollen jaw following dental treatment (the extraction of three teeth damaged in unarmed combat), and three had been left at the water's edge to guard the trolley and the weapons.
3. John Frost, discussions with the author.
4. Alfred Price, *Instruments of Darkness*, p. 82.

Chapter 18

1. Agents had to be trained as to the dimensions and surfaces required for clandestine landing grounds, setting out lights, flashing the code letter, security, and so on. See M. R. D. Foot, *S.O.E. in France*, and Benjamin Cowburn, *No Cloak, No Dagger*.
2. Gilbert Renault, *Bruneval*, p. 165.

Chapter 19

1. John Frost's written account.
2. C. W. H. Cox's written account.
3. Accounts of Dennis Vernon and Cox.
4. John Ross's account.
5. Euan Charteris was killed fighting with the 2nd Battalion, Parachute Regiment, between November 20 to December 10, 1942, under the command of John Frost. The battalion survived, but only just, one of the most desperate actions of the whole Tunisian campaign. Its losses were 16 officers and 250 other ranks.
6. Hilary St. George Saunders, *The Red Beret*, p. 67.
7. These are British names for the effective and wonderfully manned German light motor craft that fought in the Channel. Their opposite numbers were the British motor torpedo boats (MTBs) and motor gunboats (MGBs).

Chapter 20

1. From John Frost's personal account.
2. They nearly succeeded. Here is an exerpt from a letter from M. Maurice de la Joie published on February 3, 1946, in the newspaper *Havre Libre:* "We took in two English parachutists who had failed to get aboard their fast motor boats. After my sister, Mme. Delarue, had sheltered them for several days, we had them with us again. On March 9 [1942] we were arrested with them when about to cross the Line of Demarcation at Bléré, Indre-et-Loire. Condemned to death by a German Military Tribunal at Angers, we were taken to Paris, where we were imprisoned, my wife in La Santé, myself in the Cherche-Midi. In January 1943 we were deported to Breslau in Silesia. Then my wife was sent to Ravensbrück, and I to Buchenwald. We both survived the war, but as invalids." The two signalers, plus the four others missing from "C" Company, ended up prisoners of war and survived.
3. German Document TSD/FDS/X.378/51, Cabinet Office.
4. Two of "C" Company—the signalers—were still at large in France when this report was circulated.

Chapter 21

1. R. V. Jones, letter to the author.
2. A. P. Rowe, *One Story of Radar*, p. 130.
3. Jones, *Minerva*, Vol. X, No. 3, p. 243.
4. Rowe, op. cit., p. 134.
5. The object of the Bruneval Raid was not, of course, to knock out the Luftwaffe Communications Station at Cap d'Antifer, but simply to capture parts of the Würzburg. However, the Cap d'Antifer station acquitted itself extremely well that night and subsequently. Here is an excerpt from the war diary of the German admiral commanding the channel coast at the end of May 1944:

> "In the last ten days of May there has been a considerable increase in air attacks on radar stations, especially in the Seine-Somme and Normandy areas. In spite of the increased intensity of the attacks and a certain amount of damage to radar stations, a radar watch covering the entire coastal area of the command is guaranteed. . . ."

The diary notes further that an air attack on Cap d'Antifer on June 2, 1944, four days before D-Day, caused "slight" damage. "But the following day the station was again operational." On the other hand, had the Allies wanted to take out Cap d'Antifer radar station, they would have done so; they did not, because the station was one of the star targets of Dr. (now Sir Robert) Cockburn in his spoofing program, which was one of the main successes of the D-Day project. One of Cockburn's ghost fleets (the one called "Taxable") was indeed aimed directly at Cap d'Antifer so that that station's reports would suggest a powerful Allied assault fleet fronting it. For an excellent account of the D-Day spoofing, so ingenious, so versatile, so complete, see Alfred Price, *Instruments of Darkness*, Chapter 9, pp. 199–211.

6. Jones, letter to the author.

Chapter 22

1. Gilbert Renault (Rémy), *Bruneval*, pp. 227–37, and personal investigations in Bruneval and its neighborhood in 1970 are the sources of the material in this chapter.

Air Ministry, The. *By Air to Battle*. London: H.M.S.O., 1945.
——. *The Origins and Development of Operational Research in the Royal Air Force*. London: H.M.S.O., 1963.
——. *The Rise and Fall of the German Air Force*. London: H.M.S.O., 1946.
Babington Smith, Constance. *Evidence in Camera*. London: Chatto & Windus, 1958.
Barker, Ralph (as told to). *Aviator Extraordinary: The Sidney Cotton Story*. London: Chatto & Windus, 1969.
Blackett, P. M. S. *Studies of War*. Edinburgh: Oliver & Boyd, 1962.
Bryant, Sir Arthur. *The Turn of the Tide*. London: Collins, 1957.
Churchill, Winston S. *The Second World War*. London: 1948–54.
Clark, Ronald W. *The Rise of the Boffins*. London: Phoenix House, 1962.
——. *Tizard*. London: Methuen, 1965.
——. *Sir Edward Appleton*. Oxford: Pergamon Press, 1971.
Collier, Basil. *The Defense of the United Kingdom*. London: H.M.S.O., 1957.
Cowburn, Benjamin. *No Cloak, No Dagger*. London: Jarrolds, 1960.
Crowther, J. G., and Whiddington, R. *Science at War*. London: H.M.S.O., 1947.
Fergusson, Bernard. *The Watery Maze: The Story of Combined Operations*. London: Collins, 1961.
Foot, M. R. D. *SOE in France*. London: H.M.S.O., 1966.
Galland, Adolf. *The First and the Last*. London: Methuen, 1955.
Gaulle, Charles de. *Mémoires de Guerre*. Paris: Plon, 1954–59.
Goudsmit, Samuel A. *ALSOS: The Failure of German Science*. London: Sigma Books, 1948.
Harris, Sir Arthur. *Bomber Offensive*. London: Collins, 1947.
Hartcup, Guy. *The Challenge of War*. London: David & Charles, 1970.
Hill, A. V. *The Ethical Dilemma of Science*. London: Oxford, 1960.
——. *History of the Second Battalion, The Parachute Regiment*. London: Gale & Polden, 1946.
Horan, Rear-Admiral H. E. "Raid on Bruneval." From *The Navy* (Journal of the Navy League), Vol. LVI, No. 3, 1951.
Hutchinson, Walter, ed. *Raid on German Radio-Location Poste*. Hutchinson's Pictorial History of the War, No. 10, Series 15, 1942.
Information, Ministry of. Combined Operations 1940–1942. London: H.M.S.O., 1943.
——. *By Air to Battle*. London: H.M.S.O., 1945.
Jones, R. V. "Scientific Intelligence." *Journal of the Royal United Services Institution*, 1947.

——. *Winston Leonard Spencer Churchill 1874–1965*. Biographical Memoirs of Fellows of the Royal Society, Vol. 12, 1966.

——. "Temptations and Risks of the Scientific Observer." *Minerva*, Vol. X, No. 3, 1972.

Leverkuehn, P. *German Military Intelligence*. London: Weidenfeld & Nicolson, 1954.

Livry-Level, Philippe. *Missions dans la R.A.F.* Caen: Ozanne, 1951.

Longmate, Norman. *How We Lived Then*. London: Hutchinson, 1971.

Middleton, Drew. *The Sky Suspended*. London: Secker & Warburg, 1960.

Passy (André Dewawrin). *2e Bureau, Londres*. Monte Carlo: Solar, 1947.

——. *10 Duke Street, Londres*. Monte Carlo: Solar, 1947.

——. *Missions Secrètes*. Paris: Plon, 1951.

Price, Alfred. *Instruments of Darkness*. London: Kimber, 1967.

Reitlinger, Gerald. *The SS: Alibi of a Nation*. London: Heinemann, 1956.

Rémy (Gilbert Renault). *Comment meurt un réseau*. Monte Carlo: Solar, 1947.

——. *Une affaire de trahison*. Monte Carlo: Solar, 1947.

——. *Les mains jointes*. Monte Carlo: Solar, 1948.

——. *The Silent Company*. London: Barker, 1948.

——. *Courage and Fear*. London: Barker, 1950.

——. *Portrait of a Spy*. London: Barker, 1955.

——. *Ten Steps to Hope*. London: Barker, 1960.

——. *Bruneval: operation coup de croc*. Paris: France-Empire, 1968.

——, with Philippe Livry-Level. *The Gates Burst Open*. London: Arco, 1955.

Richards, Denis. *Royal Air Force 1939–1945*. Vol. 1: *The Fight at Odds*. London: H.M.S.O., 1935.

Rowe, A. P. *One Story of Radar*. London: Cambridge, 1948.

Saunders, Hilary St. George. *The Red Beret*. London: Michael Joseph, 1950.

Spears, Major-General Sir Edward. *Assignment to Catastrophe*. London: Heinemann, 1947.

Swinton, Lord. *I Remember*. London: Hutchinson, 1948.

Wallace, Graham. *R.A.F. Biggin Hill*. New York: Putnam, 1957.

Watson-Watt, Sir Robert. *Three Steps to Victory*. Odhams Press, 1958.

Webster, Sir Charles, and Noble Frankland. *The Strategic Air Offensive Against Germany*. London: H.M.S.O., 1961.

"Wing Commander, A." "The Bruneval Raid." *Royal Air Force Journal*, Vol. 2, No. 5, 1944.

Wood, Derek, and Derek Dempster. *The Narrow Margin*. London: Hutchinson, 1961.

INDEX

Waterloo was entitled "Three-Dimensional Dynamic Analysis of the Ice Hockey Stick During the Stationary Slap Shot." As a catchy title it may need work, but Murphy knows whereof he speaks.

In an office overlooking the old Blue Bonnets Race Track in Montreal, dressed in golf shirt and slacks on a hot July afternoon, Murphy seems a far cry from the mad hockey scientist. A native of Elliot Lake, Ontario, he was a rink rat who channelled his love of the game into the quest for a better stick. "There's no other Ph.D. doing what I do in hockey," he says from behind a desk heavy with research papers, printouts, and hockey tape. Murphy played on a couple of northern Ontario championship teams in the OHA and later played university hockey at Waterloo. He's a specialist in biomechanics, having done his master's degree at Ottawa University before adding the Ph.D. at Waterloo. In between, he started working for the forerunners of his current employer, Canstar. They encouraged him in the hopes of reaping the benefit of his research. Within months of this meeting, Murphy's findings will be incorporated into a new product: the Tri-Flex stick.

Murphy believes the usual design process for sticks puts the theoretical ahead of the intuitive. "People have been doing static tests – weigh the stick, do a three-point scan to see how much the stick deforms, come up with a flex number – but is that what actually happens in a slapshot? That's what we're investigating, different design approaches. What do players need to take a better shot?"

Murphy broke down video to 2,000 frames per second to study the minute changes that occur during shots, using players from pee-wee right up to varsity. From these break-downs he developed computer simulations to study what happens to the stick. He loads his computer to show a visitor a three-dimensional hockey hologram winding up, power-ing the cyber-stick, and then following through. "This enabled us to isolate events at the blade level, the shaft level, and the resulting velocity of the puck," he says, rotating the image from a side view to an overhead perspective.

Murphy attached strain gauges at key points on the shaft to measure the deformation of the material in the stick during a slapshot. "It's like a rubber band. If I take a really inflexible band and stretch it and let it go, it won't snap back a lot because it's too stiff. But if I have the right stiffness and the right stretch – wow! It really snaps.

"A player hits the ice about forty-five or fifty centimetres behind the puck, contacting the ice first. The first thirty cen-timetres are just bringing the blade tangentially to the ice – you're just skimming, you haven't lost any velocity yet, you're getting the biofeedback of being comfortable with where you are. It's happening quickly, in ten milliseconds. You're just ramping up, the load is two kilograms – five pounds – not a lot of weight down vertically yet.

"When you get close to the puck – about fifteen or twenty centimetres – you start leaning into the shaft, loading up the blade. Then you hit the puck with the blade. The puck is made of rubber, and the new blades are made from material that actually 'noodles' around the puck – the impact deforms the blade. That can make the puck move ahead of the blade, which isn't good because you're chasing it. But most of the time you're loading the puck onto the blade, and unloading it on the follow-through. The puck is on the blade 3.5 milliseconds, about seventy times longer than a golf ball is on the face of a club. By comparison, a golf ball stays on the club face about .5 milliseconds. Golf is pure impact."

Al MacInnis of St. Louis, the 1999 Norris Trophy winner, has long had the hardest shot in the NHL. Even nearing forty years old, he still fires lasers. MacInnis credits his big slapper to a boyhood of booming a thousand or more pucks a day against the barn of the family home in Inverness, Nova Scotia. Murphy says all that hard work is evident. "Where you contact the puck on the blade is very important, and MacInnis hits the puck in almost exactly the same spot every time. He's very consistent."

But the secret of MacInnis's shot goes beyond simple accuracy. "He has one of the longest sticks in the NHL," observes Murphy. "That means he can generate a higher blade velocity with a longer arc. To use a fancy term, there's a lot of strain energy involved. That means there's the right combination of flexible rigidity and the proper deformation of the materials in the stick. The longer the stick, the more strain energy you've got."

MacInnis's heel curve (a curve located closer to the heel of the blade than to the toe) is another key to his hard shot. Murphy props a blade on his desk to illustrate. "If I'm impacting the puck, it starts right here at the heel. When I deflect the blade back like this" – he shows a puck striking the blade at the heel – "it goes through there and then forward, because it's very stiff here. That's why a heel curve must be stiff. If I have a uniform curve in the middle, the puck tends to roll off to the end of the blade. You lose accuracy."

Blade science has come a long way since the days when Mikita and Hull used hot water and a door frame. One innovation has been to rocker – or curve – the underside of the blade. "If you look at the original curve that Hull had, it didn't have a rocker. When a rockered blade comes through, more of the blade contacts the surface on the ice. With Hull's flat, curved blade, it was supported at both ends, but you had a gap in the middle that was off the ice."

Murphy says MacInnis embodies another key to launching a puck 100 mph or more. "There's evidence to suggest that a young player doesn't know how to use his legs, how to bend his knees. He's more upright, giving it a sweeping blow without putting his weight behind the shot. But look at MacInnis – he's bent at the waist, transferring his weight from the back leg to the front leg, which allows him to generate energy, to deform the stick because he's loading it up while it's on the ice."

What about the wrist shot, for almost a century the weapon of choice for the game's great players? What has allowed players from Howie Morenz to Pavel Bure to score so many goals without a windup? "It's obviously a much slower motion," says Murphy. "You have to wrap your wrists over" – he grabs a stick and rotates his hands on the shaft – "so that they work against each other. I mean, if you watch some of the goals Bure scores, he's got his hands wrapped way around like this, so he can go up top with the shot.

"Looking at the wrist shot from a design perspective, that's where the curve in the blade is more important in your ability to 'load' the shaft. A stick designed for a slapshot – a stiff stick – isn't necessarily good for a wrist shot."

When a visitor asks why one stick can feel so different from another, Murphy grabs several models from a rack on the wall. "There's a lot you can do to change the feel of a stick. There's a way to make a stick feel lighter without changing its weight. You can make the blade lighter and put that weight in the middle of the shaft. You haven't changed the weight, but because you moved the centre of gravity up the shaft it feels lighter. It's analogous to a trip to the beer store. How is it easiest to carry a case of beer? It's easier to carry it at your belly button, the centre of your body, because that's where your centre of gravity is. You don't get rocked forward or back.

"One thing that's happened, we've made our composite shafts very light, but we haven't made the blades lighter. So the centre of gravity has moved down the stick. If you lighten the blade, you move the centre of gravity up the stick to where it's easier to manipulate. You can't move the centre too high, of course, or the stick will feel top-heavy."

After decades of shafts of uniform stiffness, Murphy has helped develop a stick technology explained by a bow and arrow analogy. "You look at a bow and both the tips can flex, but the centre is very stiff. In the Tri-Flex, we're looking at three zones. You have the flex in the top hand of the stick and flex down toward the blade. But in the middle, where the lower hand is, we're making that very stiff. We think this design is closer to the natural processes of the slapshot than taking a mechanical or manufacturing approach."

The idea is to achieve torsional stability in a lightweight construction. Murphy compares a Porsche and a big station wagon. The Porsche is light, with a tight suspension to allow for fast cornering. The station wagon is bigger and stronger, but because of its sloppier suspension, if it takes the same corner at the same speed, it rolls over.

Murphy is part of a new generation seeking to quantify hockey's unholy arts, to translate words such as "feel" and "balance" into numbers. Want to know how stiff a stick is? In the old days, when Bobby Hull went to McNabb's Sporting Goods in Belleville, he'd lean on each stick, trying to find one whose wood fibres offered just the right combination of stiffness and flex. "My dad would say, 'Go in and pick one out,'" Hull recalls. "I'd grab one and lean on it. My dad would say, 'Oh Robert, just grab any one.' I'd say, 'No, there's one in here that's got my name on it, and I'll know it when I feel it.' Finally, I'd hit the one that was balanced, had the right snap to it, the right weight. That's the way I picked them out."

When Hull was a kid, manufacturers gave sticks suggestive names like Tuff-Bilt and Roc-Hard. Nowadays, they use what they call a flex rating – that is, stiffness expressed in kilonewtons at five centimetres of deflection. A 15.0 is a medium flex; a 21.0 is labelled XX-Stiff, fit only for the likes of the mighty Eric Lindros, who adds a couple of blade wraps for extra stiffness just as a precaution. They'll also produce a lie (the angle of the blade to the shaft) of anywhere from four to seven. A number five lie is 45 degrees; each increment up or down corresponds to 1.5 degrees. Wayne Gretzky used an almost-unheard-of number four for much of his career, because his hunched-over style dictated a flat lie. By contrast, MacInnis employs a number seven, which suits his upright style.

In days past, almost every player would shave, file, rasp, and blow-torch his stick's handle to suit his particular grip. When Conn Smythe mandated twenty-two-ounce sticks for the Maple Leafs back in the '40s, Howie Meeker carved as much as five ounces off his stick to make it light enough to handle. More recently, tough guy Tim Hunter of Calgary was renowned for the hours of meticulous preparation he spent on his sticks under the stands of the Saddledome – this from a plugger who ended up with just 62 goals in his seventeen-year career.

Today, thanks to malleable materials such as graphite and aluminum, manufacturers offer ergonomic handles – concave, convex, square, oval. You can order virtually any shape to suit your grip, even on composite models. A finicky player might have a concave grip for his top (or power) hand and a convex grip for his lower (control) hand. Along the way, this evolution has produced a new vocabulary fit for a hockey Einstein: anisotropic, extrusion, isotropic, pultrusion, chem-fused, creel, fibre adhesion, filament winding, horizontal laminate, polymer composites, resin transfer moulding. Still, it all comes down to how the stick feels in a player's hands.

There are tales of almost preternatural sensitivity among players who agonize over their sticks. Sher-Wood executives were astonished when former NHL centre Ken Linseman told them he could tell whether the factory worker had cut the wood for his blade on the inside or the outside of the pencil mark. "I didn't believe it, not a bit," says Michel Drolet. "I did tests several times and Kenny was almost always right. He just had to hold the stick on the ground to tell if it conformed exactly to the pattern."

Claude Larose, a journeyman forward with Montreal in the 1960s and '70s, was forever changing sticks to get a more comfortable feel. One season, he changed his pattern four times before Christmas. After much fussing, he finally settled on a pattern he liked. His game picked up, and he told Michel Drolet how pleased he was with the new model. Drolet took him aside. "Claude, I'm your friend, so I want to let you in on something. The last model we worked on corresponds exactly to the first model we developed for you."

A nonplussed Larose replied, "Well, the problem must have been my skates."

Ironically, one of the most indiscriminate stick users was the best offensive player the game has seen. Grateful stick representatives called Gretzky the ultimate "zero-maintenance" guy. Gretzky tore apart NHL scoring records in his early days using a white Titan TPM 2020, which has been described as "a log," "a rock," and "a railway tie." "Did you ever see one of Gretz's sticks?" asks an NHL equipment man. "There's no one today who would use it."

That Titan may have been heavy and unresponsive, but in the hands of the master it was a magic wand. In Edmonton in 1981–82, he set the marks of 92 goals and 212 points in a season. In the late 1980s, he was lured to Easton's aluminum stick, another model about which stick experts are less than enthusiastic – particularly in the stick's early days. "Aluminum was very limited," says Stephen Murphy. "You couldn't get it as lightweight as you wanted. It was cold in your hands, it didn't have good dampening properties. It just